Woman's Day

Living Fiscally Fit

1,000 Ways to Get Out of Debt and
Build Financial Wealth

with a foreword by Mary Hunt

Contents

Foreword

It was a really bad day. Possibly the worst day of my life. So I did what I suppose any woman who believed she just ruined her husband's life and managed to throw her home into foreclosure would do: I had a meltdown.

It's not like I meant to do anything wrong. In fact, for 12 years I did what I was invited to do: I used credit cards to bridge the gap between my husband's salary and the lifestyle we deserved. I figured my husband should handle the money, and I would take care of the home and family. And when my house of cards crashed, I had to admit just how financially ignorant I was.

Hitting rock bottom was the jolt I needed that prompted me to make a U-turn on the financially destructive path I'd chosen. One step at a time I began to care about our money and to learn how to manage it. What I didn't realize was that with each new thing I learned and new money-saving tactic I tried, I became more financially fit.

Here's an example: My very first step was to make a vow that I would only buy groceries that I could pay for with cash (no checkbook, no plastic allowed). Wow. That was like throwing a bucket of cold water in my face. I had a new awareness of what things really cost. I had to keep track of what I was putting in my grocery cart. The next step came quickly: I had to find ways to spend less to buy what we needed so I could walk out with cash in my pocket. Finding ways to do that put a big smile on my face and gave me the confidence and the desire to take another step. And another and another.

In your hands you hold an excellent guide to financial fitness. I know what you're thinking: If it's about money and personal finances, it has to be boring. Well, don't believe it. I've read it and while I do admit to a tiny bit of prejudice, I believe you are in for a big surprise. Hint: Grab a highlighter because this is a book you will find yourself returning to again and again.

Here's my promise: If you are willing to read this book all the way through and are committed to making a few necessary changes in the ways you handle your money, you will get financially fit—not for just a few months or a couple of years, but for life!

I am excited for you because I know that becoming financially fit for life is going to bring you more joy than you could ever imagine.

—MARY HUNT

PART I

Assessing Your Financial Picture

1. Your Money Profile

What is Your Money Profile?

MONEY. You can't live without it, but it sure can be complicated to live with. How can you make the most of what you have? There are no easy answers, but here are seven key questions that can help you assess your money profile and set you on the road to a secure financial future.

- *Are you paying more than the minimum on your credit card bills each month?*

  Paying only the minimum is a good way to stay in debt forever. For example, making the minimum payments on a $2,000 debt—with no new charges added—means it could take as long as 11 years to retire the bill.

- *Will your emergency savings cover all your living expenses for at least three months?*

  If not, increase your savings. There are many ways to do this comfortably *(see "Get Out of Debt and Start Saving," page 38)* depending upon your specific situation. While you're raising the extra savings, just know what the potential sources of emergency funds are in the interim, so if an emergency does arise you'll be adequately prepared. For instance, borrowing against a cash-value life insurance policy may cost 5 to 9 percent interest. A home equity loan or a personal loan from a credit union or savings bank are other sources for money if you can't repay promptly. The last option, if you haven't already maxed out your credit cards, is a cash advance, but that's expensive. Even creditors who charge 8 to 10 percent interest on unpaid balances may charge 20 percent on cash advances. Use this option only in dire circumstances.

- *Is the interest on your home mortgage below 8 percent?*

  If not, consider refinancing. If you're able to lower your rate by at least 2 percent—and you don't move within three years—you could pay the closing costs and still save thousands of dollars.

- *Do you have—and follow—a budget that includes savings and investments?*

  You needn't be a budget slave or deprive yourself, but it is crucial to know where your income is going—and to put aside at least 5 percent of your income for the future. Remember, the sooner you start saving, the less it will take to meet your goals.

- *Are you making regular contributions to a tax-deferred retirement plan?*

  Both earnings and contributions are free of current taxes, so savings build up faster in these plans than anywhere else. Withdrawing money from a retirement plan before age 59 will cost you a 10 percent penalty, but you'll still come out ahead if your employer contributes to your plan. You can also borrow from many retirement plans in an emergency, but some require repayment within 60 days.

- *Are your long-term savings earning at least 6 percent a year?*

  You can probably earn twice that by investing in blue-chip stocks or good stock mutual funds. But even if you're unwilling to take any risks, you don't have to settle for the paltry 1 to 3 percent interest that banks pay on savings. At press time, treasury bills and notes paid a guaranteed return (if held until maturity) of around 5 percent. The yield on five-year certificates of deposit at some banks is now above 6 percent. Even government savings bonds and some money market mutual funds currently yield 4 to 6 percent.

- *Do you check your credit records regularly for errors?*

  A good credit rating is increasingly important now that some employers and insurers use credit checks to evaluate applicants.

  To maintain a top rating, pay bills and loans on time—and avoid opening more credit lines than you can handle or cancel those you don't use. Credit cards you never use can count against you when applying for a mortgage or other loan. You're allowed one free credit report a year from each of the three major credit bureaus. Log on to annualcreditreport.com.

AND DON'T FORGET TO:

- Participate in all decisions involving savings, investments and other family financial matters. It may be tempting to let your husband handle everything, but the world is full of poor widows and divorcées who regret having done exactly that. If you don't feel qualified to make wise decisions, it's time to learn.

- Keep a complete household inventory in a safe place. Put important papers and valuables in a fireproof safe or safe deposit box. Memorize the combination and/or location of the keys and give a key and relevant details to a trusted friend or relative, in case you become incapacitated.

- Store copies of all hard-to-replace documents apart from the originals. These include your house deed, driver's license, car title and registration, passport, birth certificate, marriage license, divorce decree and military discharge papers, among others. Some states seal safe deposit boxes at death, so copies of wills are best kept elsewhere.

- Make sure you and your spouse both have up-to-date wills; designate guardians for children who are under 18.

- Keep an "important people" list, with the names and phone numbers of all who should be contacted in an emergency. Include your lawyer, accountant, insurance agent, stockbroker and other professionals. Keep a copy in a prominent place in your home; give others to close friends and relatives.

- Grant power of attorney to someone you trust. If you and your spouse are both injured in the same accident, you'll need someone with power of attorney who can deposit checks, pay bills and handle other financial matters for you.

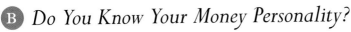 *Do You Know Your Money Personality?*

According to Julie Stav, author of *The Money in You!*, everyone fits into one of five financial profiles. An important first step in any move toward financial stability is to be clear and forthright with yourself about how you deal with money. The descriptions below can help you determine your basic style and advise you on how to bring a better balance to your financial life.

- ## THE DIVA
  Your fancy clothes and extravagant lifestyle give the impression that you're doing well financially. Problem is, you have a hard time keeping your spending in check.

  Force yourself to money manage. Set up a direct deposit so that your cash is funneled into two different accounts: one for savings, one for budgeted expenditures. Designate "splurge money" from where all of your major, nonessential purchases must be paid. Once that's gone, reign yourself in until the next month. Soon you'll develop a rhythm where your spending will not exceed your income.

- ## THE DIONYSIAN
  You enjoy spoiling yourself and your friends. Your car payment may be due, but so what? This night out is on your Visa!

  Start budgeting, using a simple, low-tech system. Designate one envelope for each expense in your life, including savings, without forgetting one for fun. Each time you get paid, divvy up your check—in cash. The fun envelope funds a night out. Since you tend to throw caution to the wind, be scrupulous about limiting credit cards to two and never—ever!— spend beyond what you can pay off in full each month.

- ## THE DILIGENT INVESTIGATOR
  You budget to the penny and are a victim of "paralysis by analysis." You research and research, only to get overwhelmed with information and end up doing nothing.

  Lighten up already! There are no perfect decisions in this world, only decisions to be made and lived with. Consider the worst-case scenario. If you can live with it, then take a chance. Once you've made your decisions about budgeting, saving and investing, act on them and let your money do the work for you. You'll feel liberated.

- ## THE DO-GOODER
  If you could, you'd donate every penny you make to Habitat for Humanity. But you neglect to manage your own finances.

  Consider socially responsible mutual funds (which include numerous companies, like Domini, all with a similar social mission) or individual "green" investments. These funds are popular and increasingly profitable. Plus, you'll be saving for the future while helping worthy causes.

- ## THE DEPENDABLE HOARDER
  You fear debt as if it were the plague, so you have sworn to pay bills immediately. A good hunk of your cash is channeled into savings.

  Many adults who fear debt and over-save had it tough growing up. Although the ability to save is an admirable trait, don't be so hard on yourself that you don't enjoy your money. While it is of utmost importance to save diligently, try giving yourself a treat once in a while to enjoy the fruits of your labor. You deserve it.

Ⓑ *Financial Styles of the Desperate Housewives: Who do You Resemble?*

Few of us addicted to the hit TV show *Desperate Housewives* watch it to become better budgeters or smarter savers. But maybe we should…

Each of the ladies of Wisteria Lane has a distinct personality, which translates into a distinct financial style—in terms of trust, risk tolerance, emotions and involvement. Thinking about how they relate to money can make it easier to recognize our own money habits and learn how to become more financially successful.

Read on to see which housewife you resemble the most financially and how you can improve your financial picture.

BREE VAN DE KAMP: SUPER SAVER

OK, so Bree (played by Marcia Cross) is probably the housewife we least want to emulate (she's such a priss), but we should when it comes to our finances. Given her attention to detail and meticulous planning, she's clearly a gal who's focused and analytical. From her perfectly pressed outfits to her spotless house, she does everything with precision (including, some thought, murder, after her husband Rex's suspicious death).

WHAT THIS MEANS FOR HER FINANCES: It's a pretty safe bet that Bree isn't impulsive with her money. If an investment dips, she doesn't rush to change it because she takes a long-term view of her financial picture, which is the best view to have. While she can afford expensive things, she'd rather get value for her dollar. Designer shoes at full price? No way. Designer shoes on sale? You bet! She's the kind who combs bank statements for errors and checks to see how her investments are doing. If she worked, she'd deposit part of every paycheck into a savings account. And we already know she has an emergency fund in place. (She dipped into it to give Gabrielle cash.) Bree's biggest problem: seeing a financial plan not as a means to an end, but as the goal itself.

IF YOU'RE LIKE BREE: You're doing everything right—technically. But money also has an emotional component. Ask yourself: "Am I spending more time managing my money than enjoying my life?" "Do my attitudes about money create friction between my family and me?" "Would I freak out if something unexpected messed up my financial plan?" If you answered yes, you could benefit from learning to let go. Allow your husband to manage some of the family finances (while consulting regularly with you, of course). Or use a financial planner—one you'll no doubt research extensively before hiring!

SUSAN MAYER: EMOTIONS RULE

Susan (played by Teri Hatcher) cares intensely about everyone in her world— her teenage daughter, Julie, her gal pals in the neighborhood, her flaky mom, her hunky neighbor, Mike. An adorable klutz who gets herself into trouble, Susan rarely sees the negative in any person or situation, but that Pollyanna attitude doesn't always serve her well. We smell trouble long before she does, and even

Julie seems to have a more sharply attuned radar than her mom. But Susan is driven by the need to please others and the belief that life happens to you—you don't control it.

WHAT THIS MEANS FOR HER FINANCES: Susan is the type who could easily be swayed by someone she really cares about, making financial decisions based on emotions rather than logic. Indeed, when her old friend and literary agent tells her he's starting his own agency because he's been dismissed from his firm for stealing (or, as he puts it, "borrowing") money from clients, Susan's initial impulse is to stick with him despite what he's done. Susan's also the type to throw unopened bank statements in a drawer and pay credit card bills without reviewing them. She would just assume the statements were fine.

IF YOU'RE LIKE SUSAN: Get more involved in your financial picture. Don't know where to begin? Consider taking an adult-education class on basic finance or reading books such as *Personal Finance for Dummies* and *The Complete Idiot's Guide To Managing Your Money.* Then start working on a savings and investment plan. Find help at bankrate.com or fool.com. And no more burying your head in the sand: Set aside an hour each month to review the past month's bank statement, bills and investment statements. Check for errors and track how much you've spent and saved in the last 30 days. To avoid impulsive actions, make no major financial decisions until review time. Once you know where your money's going and how it's growing, you'll be less likely to make financial decisions based solely on your emotions.

GABRIELLE SOLIS: LIVING ON THE EDGE

Ah, Gabrielle! Her husband, Carlos, tells her to put the brakes on buying, and she hits the accelerator. Even when times are tight, Gabrielle (played by Eva Longoria) dresses to the nines, drives a fancy car and drips jewels. But she's no dummy. She's gutsy enough to turn a bad situation into a bearable one. Some women would've crumbled if their husband were indicted for a felony (money laundering, in Carlos's case—surprise, surprise); Gabrielle got creative. She even, temporarily, got a job!

WHAT THIS MEANS FOR HER FINANCES: Gabrielle might spend money like there's no tomorrow, but she also clearly knows her financial situation. (She delights in telling Carlos she's aware of his offshore savings account.) She's also a risk-taker. She wants a big return and doesn't mind sticking her neck out to get it. The two big problems she undoubtedly has: spending without saving and taking risks that may be too risky.

IF YOU'RE LIKE GABRIELLE: Chances are you know what your financial picture looks like—you just don't have a solid plan in play. While covering your bills is great, you're tempting fate if you save nothing. Because the last thing you want to do is crunch numbers, create a budget that operates on autopilot. Set up automatic payments for monthly expenses, and give yourself a certain amount of "fun" money every week. You'll probably save only if it's not too much trouble, so consider having a portion of every paycheck automatically deposited into a savings or investment account. Or decide to save all your loose change—it can add up quickly. As far as your high tolerance for risk, it's all right if it's in moderation. A potentially good ratio for your investments is 70 percent in stock mutual funds and 30 percent in more conservative bond mutual funds, along with enough money in an emergency fund to cover at least three months of expenses.

LYNETTE SCAVO: IN ME I TRUST

Any woman who's ever juggled work and a family feels Lynette's (played by Felicity Huffman) stress. With a high-powered corporate job and four kids, she's frazzled and has her hands full. Still, she's likely to be on top of things. She brings a high level of involvement to every task, although as we've seen, she can overdo it. (Remember how she tried to help her husband, Tom, at work and messed up his chance for a promotion?) She seems to be convinced that no one can possibly take care of things as well as she can.

WHAT THIS MEANS FOR HER FINANCES: Lynette generally seems to have her priorities straight. When getting her unruly twin boys into a private school depended on a big contribution, she made Tom sell his boat in order to guarantee that the kids—who needed a structured environment—got in. She isn't a major shopper (she even planned to return that expensive suit she bought for her big presentation after wearing it), but with a family to support, she probably doesn't save a lot, either. Lynette's tendency to become overly involved could also wreak havoc on her financial plan, because it could lead to one of two extremes: constant changing strategies or "analysis paralysis." But her biggest problem is that she's on overload and doesn't trust anyone to help her with anything, including her finances.

IF YOU'RE LIKE LYNETTE: Money chores can take up a fair amount of time, so if you're stretched to the limit with other obligations but refuse to delegate the task to someone else, you've got a problem. Use your good research skills to find a financial adviser you can trust. It's never easy to squirrel away money, especially when you've got a family to raise, but there are ways to "find" money for savings. If your or your husband's company offers a matching 401(k) plan, put in at least enough to get the company match. Otherwise, it's like turning down free money. Figure out if you can lower your car or home insurance rates, or whether it makes sense to refinance your home, and save the difference. Do you get a sizable tax refund every spring? Consider changing the number of deductions you claim so the money shows up in every paycheck instead, and bank the increase.

Ⓓ *No More Money Excuses*

Excuses, excuses. We all use them—to avoid blame, to ease a guilty conscience, to get out of something unpleasant. Two of the most popular— "I don't have time" and "I can't afford it"—even have validity.

We all know people who could, with a little less rationalizing and a little more ingenuity and effort, reduce their money woes and increase their peace of mind. So, if you suffer from the large-debt, small-savings syndrome, take a hard look at your "explanations." If the following sound familiar, you may be guilty of excuse abuse.

"I JUST CAN'T STICK TO A BUDGET." You could if you had the right budget—one that's realistic and appropriate for your needs. A good budget is like a road map: It helps you get where you want to go. To plan the best route, though, you need to know exactly where you are now.

THE SECRET: Make a record of every dime you spend for a few weeks, then total each category. You'll quickly see places you can cut back to increase savings, but don't drop anything that gives you pleasure. Try to lower the cost of boring necessities—such as electricity, gasoline, cleaning supplies. And be flexible; every budget needs revision before it starts to work.

"IT'S ONLY A DOLLAR OR TWO." The cost of a lottery ticket, a lipstick or an ice cream cone seems too trivial to worry about—but that sort of dollar dribbling can wreck a budget in no time. If you're accustomed to letting two or three dollars slip through your fingers every day, you're wasting about $1,000 a year.

"I WORK HARD AND I DESERVE A TREAT." Of course you do. But the impulsive purchases made when you "deserve a treat" may not be worth what they cost.

"I CAN'T PAY MY CREDIT CARD BILL IN FULL, SO I MIGHT AS WELL PAY THE MINIMUM." Minimum payments barely cover the interest, which just puts you further behind. According to the Consumer Federation of America, the average American owes between $6,000 and $9,000 on credit cards. If you're typical, you could be spending $1,400 a year just on interest. Paying an extra $100 a month, however, could save you $132 in interest annually.

THE SECRET: Payments toward reducing debt are, in effect, earning the interest rate the bank or other creditor charges. And whether it's 8 percent, 22 percent or something in between, it's more than you'll earn anywhere else.

"I OWE TOO MUCH ON MY CREDIT CARD TO SWITCH CARDS." Some credit card companies will pay you a bonus if you transfer an unpaid balance of $1,000 or more to a new card. Others will waive the annual fee or lower your interest rate if you threaten to switch to another card that offers a better deal. Shop around. Paying more than 10 percent interest means it's time to negotiate.

"I'D RATHER SPEND MY MONEY NOW WHILE I'M HEALTHY ENOUGH TO ENJOY IT." It's true that some people are too obsessed with saving money to have any fun. But that doesn't mean we should spend everything today, depending on lottery winnings, Social Security or our children to take care of the future. Somewhere between those extremes is a prudent middle that allows us to enjoy the present and the future.

"I'M YOUNG AND HEALTHY SO I DON'T NEED HEALTH INSURANCE." Medical insurance is expensive, but almost everyone qualifies for a group plan these days. And a year's premiums usually cost less than one overnight stay in the hospital.

"I'M NO GOOD AT MATH, SO I CAN'T DO MY OWN TAX RETURN." Thanks to calculators and computer programs, you don't have to be good at math. Virtually anyone can fill out a simple tax form with the standard deduction. And you might still do as well as a paid tax preparer on a more complicated return, too. After all, no one cares more about your money than you do.

THE SECRET: If you've never done your own taxes before, you might ask a professional to check your return before you turn it in. That's not only cheaper than hiring an expert to do everything, it also teaches you a lot. Once you see the effect that various actions have on your tax bill, you'll find it easier to keep taxes to a minimum.

"INSURANCE POLICIES ARE SO CONFUSING I NEVER READ THEM." That's what insurance companies count on; why let them get away with it? Lisa E. from Montclair, New Jersey learned the importance of reading the fine print after her house caught on fire and she discovered that her full-replacement-cost coverage didn't apply to furniture and clothing. As a result, she collected as little as 30 percent of the cost of replacing my possessions.

THE SECRET: You don't have to experience a disaster to benefit from studying your policies, though. A friend who'd been reluctant to repair a cracked windshield because she had a $500 deductible on her auto insurance discovered a "full-glass" provision that covered her windshield in full.

"I'M TOO YOUNG TO TIE UP MONEY UNTIL I'M 59½." Although you do pay a penalty for early withdrawal from a retirement account, most plans allow borrowing in an emergency. And even if you take the money and run in a few years, you'll still be way ahead.

THE SECRET: Stashing $72 in a piggy bank every month would give you $4,320 after five years. But contributing $72 of your monthly take-home pay to a 401(k) plan with an employer match should give you nearly $11,000. You could pay the 10 percent penalty, plus 28 percent tax, and still have $6,820 left.

"I DON'T WANT TO RISK LOSING MY SAVINGS." Nobody does, but it's impossible to avoid all risks. An insured bank account exposes your savings to another risk: loss of buying power to inflation. Other investments carry a high-tax risk.

THE SECRET: Mary's widowed mother couldn't afford to take risks, but she had faith in the stock market. "I don't care whether my stocks go up or down," she said, "as long as they keep paying dividends." She invested in blue-chip companies like AT&T and lived comfortably on her dividends for 41 years after her husband died.

"I DON'T EARN ENOUGH TO PUT MONEY INTO A RETIREMENT PLAN." Do you earn enough to turn down a raise and a tax deduction? That's what you're doing if your employer offers a tax-deferred retirement plan and you don't participate.

THE SECRET: The money put into 401(k) and other plans is free of current taxes—and many employers match at least part of your contribution. That's like receiving a tax-free raise—one that lets you sock away $200 a month, for example, by giving up only $72 of take-home pay (in the 28 percent tax bracket). Taxes are deferred on dividends and interest, too.

"I DON'T UNDERSTAND THE STOCK MARKET." You probably don't understand the internal combustion engine, either, but you still drive a car. You can be a successful investor without knowing much about the stock market. The no-brainer method: Buy shares in a stock index mutual fund, one that owns a broad range of stocks. Index funds have gained 63.33 percent over the last few years—and their fees are low, too.

"MY INSURANCE AGENT, FINANCIAL PLANNER AND/OR STOCK BROKER WOULD NEVER CHEAT ME." Not intentionally, perhaps, but most receive commissions on everything they persuade you to buy. And few can resist recommending the insurance policies, mutual funds and other investments that produce the highest commissions, whether appropriate for you or not.

A SAFER ALTERNATIVE: Consult a CPA or a fee-only financial planner who charges an hourly rate. Those who don't sell any products have no incentive to cheat you. Better yet, become well-informed so you don't have to rely on others for advice.

"I PAY ALL MY BILLS ON TIME SO I'M NOT WORRIED ABOUT MY CREDIT RATING." A good credit record is more important than ever because credit checks are now used to screen applicants for some jobs and insurance. And it takes more than prompt payment to maintain a good credit rating, as Laura learned. Enticed by discounts of 10 to 20 percent for opening new accounts, she acquired more than 20 credit cards that she never used again. She didn't bother to cancel those accounts, so her bank totaled the open credit lines, decided she was overextended and refused to give her a car loan.

THE SECRET: You could be denied a loan for another reason: an overdraft protection account. Although you never use it, the bank may consider it an outstanding loan because you could tap it at any time.

DO YOU THINK YOU CAN'T SAVE?

It's easy to find excuses that let you off the hook. But if you really want all the advantages of a healthy nest egg, try changing your attitude.

Don't think of saving as giving up the pleasures that money can buy. The cash you put away today is not lost; it's just "planted" temporarily so that it will grow and provide even more money for you to spend in the future. Patience pays.

2. Money and Marriage

A *Is Money Hurting Your Marriage?*

There is probably no one single factor that influences a marriage more than money. As important as money is to our lives and relationships, it doesn't have to cause problems. Money can actually strengthen a relationship and bring couples together. By recognizing potential problems, or the money issues already affecting a relationship, you can significantly reduce the risks and pitfalls that occur around finances. While there may be no single answer for any couple, there are many techniques that can significantly reduce the likelihood of unnecessarily damaging your marriage over money and help lead you to financial and marital health. Following are four major hot spots to identify and easy-to-follow steps to help solve your couple's money issues once and for all.

Leza R. and her husband, Mark, are money opposites: She's a spender, he's a saver. Even before tying the knot, they realized that when it came to money they were hopelessly at odds. So they decided to keep their money separate by dividing their expenses—she pays the mortgage and he saves for their retirement. Like Mark, Leza has her own bank account and credit cards. "Neither of us has any concept of what each other's bills are," she notes. It may sound bizarre, but this system of money management is what has kept the couple from fighting over who's spending what—and how.

Trina and Jack H. of Omaha almost ended up in divorce court over their money differences. Trina quit her job to relocate when Jack got a new job and soon the couple was arguing daily. "I couldn't stand asking my husband for money because he questioned every penny I spent. He thought he had the right since he was bringing home the paycheck, and I resented it." It took a therapist to help the couple to figure out their problem. Indeed, arguing over money is one of the reasons why as many as 67 percent of divorces occur today. Couples fight over too much, not enough, how to save it, how to spend it. There's no household left untarnished when it comes to money.

Why? Times have changed radically since husbands brought home the bacon and balanced the bank account. So the values we associate with money—how secure and powerful it makes us feel as individuals—play a bigger role in our marital happiness than ever before.

The dynamics of communication about money are different today because women are working outside the home, families are living beyond their means, thanks to credit cards, and few are saving for the future. This puts us at great risk when it comes to emergencies, educating kids and retiring.

Here are four financial hot spots that may be undermining your marriage, and how to resolve them.

When One Partner Is a Spender, the Other a Saver

The truth is, almost all couples are opposites when it comes to dealing with money. And lack of communication only makes matters worse. Couples rarely talk about how they're going to handle their finances. So when one partner goes merrily on his way, that's when problems result.

A variety of different money personality combinations can occur in marriages, the most common of which is when "spenders" marry "hoarders" or "avoiders" marry "worriers." Even if you both start out as hoarders, one partner will become the one who spends more, otherwise you'd never own anything. *(To determine your money personalities, take the "Are You Two Money Opposites?" quiz, page 31.)*

And battles over money tend to escalate. Over time, these differences become more conflict-ridden, as each partner attacks the other for his or her failings. You may have once admired your mate's skill at financial planning, for instance, but eventually you come to think of him as stingy and petty.

Money problems are really behavior problems. Some partners may even use money as a weapon against each other. Learning to live with the differences takes patience and compromise. Each household has to develop its own conflict-management system.

These strategies can help:

- Practice doing one thing each month that's more like your partner's style. You might buy a new dress if you're a hoarder, or balance your checkbook if you're an avoider. But be careful not to undermine your own financial goals: For a hoarder, the stress of charging such a splurge can take all of the enjoyment out of it. So pay in cash. Small steps like these will make it easier to understand each other's thinking.

- Accept the fact that money differences in marriage can be a good thing. A spouse who is a saver can counterbalance your spending, or make investment decisions for the future that you'd never get around to.

- Consider the notion that you might be secretly jealous of your partner's style. Perhaps you'd like to splurge once in a while, but can't bring yourself to do it.

- Get the spender in your marriage to agree that purchases over a set amount must be discussed in advance.

- Know when it's time to stop trying to compromise and simply agree to disagree. For some very loving couples, an extreme solution like Leza and Mark's can work well.

WHEN SHE GIVES UP HER PAYCHECK TO RAISE THE KIDS

More and more working couples are discovering that paying for childcare eats up one of their two incomes. But deciding to forgo your job and babysitter can mean double trouble: less income but many of the same household expenses. And suddenly having to ask your partner for grocery money after years of financial independence can put a real strain on a marriage.

"Nobody's telling me I can't spend money. But I'm just not as apt to buy things that aren't a priority," says Mary O., a stay-at-home mother in Blauvelt, New York, who gave up her job as a police officer after nine years. "There's something about a paycheck that gave me an identity apart from my family and a sense of accomplishment because I was doing a good job. At home, nobody says 'Hey, Mom, we're not going to fight today because you made such a great lunch.'"

Still, the important thing to focus on is not who earns the paycheck, but how you decide what to do with it. The ideal is when the final decisions on spending and saving are mutual.

The couple worked out a compromise: Mary's husband takes care of the bill paying, but Mary keeps close tabs on the bank account so she always knows how much she can withdraw. "Even though Peter does the paperwork, we feel jointly in control of our finances," says Mary.

Try these tips for sharing the money and the power in your marriage:

- Give the partner who stays home a weekly paycheck for performing the household and child-care duties.

    All couples should set aside a quiet time each week to discuss their budget. But it's particularly important in this case that whoever is handling the money keep the other spouse up-to-date. Discuss how that one paycheck gets spent: Do you need to replace the old dishwasher this month, or have the car tuned up instead?

- Consider splitting money-management duties evenly between you so that no one feels the other partner has the upper hand.

- Make sure both spouses have easy access to all financial records—whether they're kept on the computer or in a shoebox in your dresser drawer.

    Part of feeling in control is simply knowing the information is available anytime you want it.

WHEN ONE PARTNER LOSES A JOB

In this era of layoffs and downsizing, many couples are finding their income halved in their prime earning years, an especially tough hurdle for men. Sole supporter or not, when a husband can no longer perform the role of breadwinner, many a marriage crumbles under the strain.

Just ask Jennifer M. of Houston, whose husband has not earned a steady paycheck for over a year. "I married my husband because I wanted to share my life with him, not support him," she says. "Now, I'm beginning to think he's taking me and my income for granted. The rent still gets paid, and the groceries are bought, but I want to spend some money on me for once."

It's natural for the spouse footing the bills to begin to feel resentful. But, in fact, you may need to be more supportive than ever of your spouse during his unemployment.

When one partner loses a job, he also loses status and power within the relationship. The other partner needs to understand that her spouse is going through the same stages of denial and grieving that occurs with the death of a loved one. Reassure him that you still love him, and help him find constructive ways to refocus his goals. By recognizing that there is going to be stress and disagreement, you begin to work out a process for conflict management.

Use these strategies to take stock of both your feelings and your savings:

- Take steps immediately to reduce your living expenses. The longer you wait, the bigger the crisis will become. If you don't already have a household budget, create one.

- Include children in this decision-making process so they understand what's going on.

  Make a chart of your family's goals and how to reach them. Discuss how each member of the family can contribute. Decide together if purchasing big-ticket items, such as a new car, can be put off.

- Try to manage money conflicts sensitively. For instance, use "I" statements, rather than "you" statements: "I feel anxious about the bills being this high," not "You spent too much money." And recognize that no matter how carefully you word things, some statements can't help but sound hurtful.

- Find positive ways for both of you to release your anger about the situation—write your feelings in a journal, talk to a marriage counselor, participate in physical activity. Before you can help your partner through this difficult time, you need to come to terms with your own distress.

- Make an effort to communicate. If it's too hard to talk about, write letters to each other. In order to work through this together, you each need to know what the other is thinking.

WHEN BOTH PARTNERS WORK AND ARE STILL STRUGGLING

Two paychecks do not make a big bank account. The fact is, almost half of all working women are bringing home 50 percent of their families' income, and have to work just to pay the bills.

But ironically, single-earner families tend to save more than those households living on two incomes. How is this possible? With two incomes, stress interferes with financial decision-making. Couples make short-term decisions with long-term consequences because they are in a rush. They also have a false sense of security with two paychecks and tend to live on the entire income, rather than saving one salary. Add in the cost of take-out or restaurant food because you have no time to cook, childcare, even someone to help clean, and there really isn't any money left. So what's the answer? Reassessing your lifestyle. There's no income level that can't result in savings if you school yourself to do so. By prioritizing your goals together, it will diminish your resentment toward your jobs and each other.

Some strategies:

- Reduce debt as quickly as possible by making extra payments on credit cards and mortgage.

- Put aside some "mad" money (as little as $15 or $20 will do) for each member to indulge with once a month; and teach the kids money awareness—such as switching off lights when leaving a room or lowering the thermostat (and putting on a sweater) to keep utility bills down.

- Develop a monthly spending plan with three categories for each expense: the amount you plan to spend, the actual cost, and the variance between the two. You'll see clearly where the money is going and what you can cut back on.

- Even though you earn two paychecks, don't succumb to the trend of overconsumption. You need to live by your own values, not the expectations set by the media. Follow the "just enough" rule: use "enough" shampoo, not too much; put "enough" cheese in the lasagna, but don't overdo it.

- Make a habit of paying yourselves, before your bill collectors. Since you both earn salaries, put a little money into savings from each paycheck, then live on what's left over. Aim to amass an emergency fund equivalent to three to six months' worth of living expenses. The payoff? You won't be so stressed, and you'll probably find you can get by on what remains.

- If one of you hates your job, consider the possibility of reducing your living expenses so you can quit. After all, when one or both of you isn't happy and feels trapped in a job, marital strain escalates. You may be much happier driving a used car and not commuting an hour each way to work, for example.

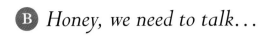

Ⓑ *Honey, we need to talk...*

—MARY HUNT

LOOK UP MONEY IN THE DICTIONARY and it's defined as a commodity of exchange. But don't kid yourself. Money is a lot more than that.

Money is the currency of life and that makes our relationship to it very emotional. It determines where you live, what you drive and where your children grow up and go to school.

Financial issues are challenging for everyone, but especially difficult for couples. Money habits expose the differences in our personalities and the ways we were brought up. To complicate matters, your spouse may also be hanging on to a lifetime of money attitudes, secrets, habits and goals. Once it's our income, our mortgage, our pension, our future, money can cause tension and even has the power to ruin a relationship.

Why does financial stress and strain destroy some marriages but strengthen others? After years of observing marriages, including my own, I've concluded that strong couples enjoy what I call "financial intimacy."

When I was first married, I discovered that my husband and I were on opposite ends of the spectrum when it came to money and credit. But instead of allowing myself to know and be known so we could move toward compromise, I pretended to be the financial partner he wanted me to be. The spender I really was operated in secret. And that was a recipe for marital disaster.

Allowing your spouse access to that deep emotional place in your heart is the key to financial intimacy. It's the freedom and confidence two people enjoy when there's an emotional safety zone that says, "No matter what, we will get through this."

Whatever your current financial situation, you can start building this foundation of trust right now. Plus, once you agree on shared goals— whether it's college for the kids, a bigger house or early retirement—you both become invested in building a future together. Couples who are financially healthy know the secrets of how to make that happen.

THEY ARE COMMITTED TO HONESTY

Couples who are completely open and honest about money don't go shopping or make financial decisions without the other knowing.

STRATEGY: A call to integrity means no money secrets, no lies—big or small. Most of us would agree that hiding a five-figure credit card debt is lying—and damaging to a relationship. But so is telling your spouse you got something on sale when you didn't, or other sneaky little ways we hide our financial activity. Track your spending in writing to keep everything visible.

THEY KNOW HOW THEY'RE SPENDING

Couples who are financially in sync actively figure out how to spend their paychecks instead of winging it, then wondering where the money went.

STRATEGY: Write down how much income you'll have in the next full calendar month. Then subtract your obligations. If you like what you see, great. If not, decide where you can cut to balance your budget.

If you have a lot of credit card debt or can't pay the bills on time, the only way to get out of that hole is to dig out together. Is it necessary to downsize to a less expensive house? Cut back on eating out? When you make tough decisions and follow through together, it brings you closer.

THEY FUND THEIR OWN EMERGENCIES

Financially intimate couples never spend it all, but opt to save part of everything they earn. They have an amount stashed away that could cover all of their bills for an extended period of time. They do not depend on credit to bail them out of financial jams.

STRATEGY: Money in the bank promotes intimacy. It breaks your dependence on credit, and the more you have in the bank, the more self-reliant you become. You need at least three months' living expenses (six is better). You will be most successful if you set up an automatic savings deposit with either your employer or your bank. Arrange to have the same amount (it can be a lot or a little to start) automatically moved from your paycheck to your savings account.

The more it grows, the more content you will be with finding ways to spend less so you can save more. Just for fun, use a calculator to estimate how much you can save over time.

They know the state of their finances

In good times and in bad, financially intimate couples know their bottom line—their net worth. They know where their retirement accounts are and the balance in their checking account. They stay current with their investments.

Strategy: To figure out your net worth, write down what you own and estimate the current value of each asset—your house, cars, etc. Next list all you owe—credit card debt, mortgage, etc. Subtract what you owe from what you own. This is your net worth. It should be a positive number, but if it's negative, it's still your net worth. Repeat in six months to see how you've progressed.

Keep in mind that every dollar of debt you repay and every dollar you save increases your net worth. Once you see where you are, you'll be more inclined to begin pulling together to improve your financial situation.

They share the responsibility

Not everyone is well suited to looking after investments or running the day-to-day household spending. Couples who work together determine who's good at what, and then they share the tasks. Both are fully engaged in their finances, acting as co-CEOs—each has a job and area of responsibility.

Strategy: If you're like most couples, only one of you balances accounts, tracks investments and meets with planning and tax professionals. If that's you and you are comfortable, don't change. Just make sure your spouse is always up to speed on the decisions you make.

They have money to call their own

Financially intimate couples give themselves an allowance—money they can save or spend as they like.

Strategy: Decide together how much money each of you should take from your total monthly income. Whether it's $5 or $500, it's important that you both understand this is yours—what you do with it is totally up to you.

My husband and I struggled for 12 long years, living anything but a financially intimate life. But things changed. And slowly over the years as we learned to trust one another, we got out of debt, and have gone on to enjoy the safety and satisfaction of financial intimacy.

Five Warning Signs You Can't Ignore

1. You're afraid to bring up the issue of money because it can result in a fight.

2. You feel the need to hide your purchases or lie about the amount you spent.

3. You buy competitively—your spouse bought a new watch, so you get yourself some earrings.

4. You have no idea how much money you really have—or don't have—because your partner handles all the finances.

5. You use money to put your partner in his place—for example, refusing to give in to his desire for a new car because you think he should have gotten a bigger raise.

Ready to come clean?

Financial infidelity—consciously, deliberately lying to one's spouse about money, credit and/or debt—can be devastating to a relationship. But it doesn't have to destroy it. When the offending party is sincerely ready to come clean, follow these steps.

- **Confess fully.** Tell it like it is and don't argue or justify.

- **Show remorse.** You probably can't say this too often: "I was wrong and I am sorry."

- **Accept reality.** Remorse will not take away the pain, but it will put recovery in motion.

- **Promise change.** Accept accountability to begin rebuilding trust.

- **Share details.** Offer a plan for how you will address the financial mess.

- **Consider counseling.** This process may reveal underlying issues in your marriage.

Are You Two Money Opposites?

To tell, you and your spouse should each take this quiz created by Olivia Mellan in her book *Money Harmony*, then compare your results.

1. *If $20,000 unexpectedly came to you, your first impulse would be to:*

   A) Spend it on things I really want
   B) Pay off outstanding bills and put the rest into my savings account
   C) Feel so overwhelmed that I'd put off thinking about it for a while
   D) Invest it to turn it into even more
   E) Give most of it away to charity

2. *When it comes to following a budget:*

   A) I hate the word budget! I prefer "spending plan"
   B) I enjoy following mine closely
   C) I don't have one and don't want one
   D) I tinker with my budget often to try to maximize my saving and spending ability
   E) I take pride in living conservatively, so I've really never needed to budget myself

3. *When it comes to saving money:*

   A) I have trouble saving and I worry about it now and then
   B) I do it regularly
   C) I know I ought to be, but I never quite get around to it
   D) I enjoy saving money and plan often for it
   E) I save only for total necessities

4. *As far as credit cards are concerned:*

   A) I use them often and just make the minimum payments
   B) I prefer paying in cash
   C) I don't take much notice of what I owe; in fact, I often forget to pay the bills until I get late notices

D) I don't mind using credit cards frequently as long as I can pay them off each month

E) I have only one and use it as little as possible

5. *When I'm feeling mad or depressed, spending money:*

A) Always cheers me up

B) Is just about the last thing I'd do

C) Is not what I think about to cheer myself up

D) Is OK, but thinking about how to make more certainly makes me feel better

E) Just makes me feel worse; money can't buy happiness

RESULTS:

- If you chose mostly (**A**) answers, you are a **SPENDER**. You love using money to bring you pleasure, and as a result, you have a hard time saving and delaying gratification for long-term goals.

- If you chose mostly (**B**) responses, you are a **HOARDER**. You enjoy holding on to your money and find it difficult to spend on luxury items or for immediate pleasure.

- Mostly (**C**) responses are the sign of an **AVOIDER**. You probably feel anxious or incompetent about dealing with money and therefore neglect everyday tasks like bill paying and balancing your checking account.

- (**D**) responses are most common of **AMASSERS**. Having large amounts of money at your disposal to save, spend and invest makes you feel secure and happy. Amassers equate money with self-worth, so a lack of it can lead to depression.

- (**E**) answers indicate that you are a **MONEY MONK**. You think money corrupts and feel guilty about having more than you need. A large raise or inheritance would make you anxious.

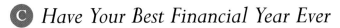

Ⓒ *Have Your Best Financial Year Ever*

—MARY HUNT

LADIES, WE NEED TO TALK. I just read the shocking results of a new study on women and money. According to this Harris Interactive survey, nearly 90 percent of women in this country—in other words, virtually all of us—admit they are financially insecure and worry about becoming destitute.

For much of my life, I lived under a dark cloud of worry that I would become a bag lady, so I can relate. But enough!

We don't have to accept financial insecurity as some kind of life sentence. Financial confidence is a choice. It's a matter of learning simple principles, then consciously applying them over and over again until they become automatic responses—financial habits.

Are you ready to say, "I'm not going to remain financially insecure any longer"? Are you ready to make this year your best money year ever? Start doing these three simple things today and you'll make that happen in the new year.

BECOME A SAVER

Saving money is like magic because it changes our attitudes and calms our fears. I can honestly say that I saved my way out of a six-figure pile of debt. As long as I knew I had some money to call my own, I was willing to go to great lengths to repay the debt. And in the process I gained financial confidence and security.

The simple act of choosing not to spend money so you can save it is a soul soother, a nerve calmer. You must start doing it now, today—no matter what your situation. Even if you're in debt, even if you're struggling to catch up and even if you're already contributing to a 401(k) or other kind of retirement plan at work. This is different. Every woman needs money in a secure place that she can get her hands on.

Start with a dollar and stuff it in a coffee mug, if that's all you can manage. Then make it $5. Soon you'll be saving $10, $20, even $50 a week. And make it automatic. Set up a plan where you have money automatically transferred to your savings. Check out online savings banks like ING Bank (ingdirect.com), or fill out an automatic deposit authorization form at your job or at the bank or credit union where you have your household account. Here's the principle: If you don't see it, you don't miss it.

Saving money will affect your life in ways you never dreamed possible. You will find yourself choosing not to spend just so you can save more.

That dark cloud of financial fear will begin to melt away. Soon you'll start to enjoy the wonder of compounding interest. That's interest calculated not only on the initial principal but also the accumulated interest of prior periods. Albert Einstein called compounding interest "the eighth wonder of the world."

Set a Financial goal

Check the calendar. Twelve beautiful, unspoiled months are right ahead. Decide on one specific financial goal you want to accomplish in the coming year.

For any plan to succeed, it needs to be specific, reasonable and measurable. Example: Let's say you want to save $2,500—about $52 a week. That may be reasonable provided you are willing to really stretch and make adjustments in other areas. You can measure your progress by checking the balance in your savings account.

Perhaps your financial goal is to repay your credit card debt. Excellent! Now you need a plan. One idea is to target your smallest balance. Divide it by 12 to determine the amount you need to pay on that balance in addition to its minimum required payment each month. Start thinking about all the ways you can spend less in other areas so you can reach this goal. You'll be amazed at how much you can accomplish in a single year when you're committed to reaching your goal.

If the thought of creating a budget this year gives you a rash, relax. A budget is just a way to "pre-spend" your money while it is still in your possession and while you can still change your mind. If you have access to a computer, consider using a simple money-management program to help plan your spending and keep track of where your every dollar goes. Life is so much more enjoyable when you are in control of your money.

Venture out of your Financial comfort zone

Many of us are so paranoid about anything having to do with money or finance that we avoid books and the financial pages of the newspaper like the plague. It's time for you to venture into those waters.

There are many excellent books on money written by women for women. Stop by the library or browse an online bookstore. Start a reading club with friends with the specific goal of reading a certain number of personal finance books. Here's a good one to start: *Money, A Memoir: Women, Emotions and Cash,* by Liz Perle.

You may find an online personal finance discussion group helpful. You'll find active forums at sites such as The Motley Fool (fool.com), womansday. com and my website, debtproofliving.com. (Don't worry—you can learn from the collective minds of others in your situation without ever posting.)

Read personal financial columns in newspapers and blogs on the Internet. A couple of my favorites are mdmproofing.com/iym/weblog/ and sharonhr.blogspot.com.

If you discipline yourself to step out of your financial comfort zone for a specific period of time each day or even once a week, I guarantee that before long it will cease to be uncomfortable. As you begin to understand that money and personal finance are not frightening, you will allow yourself to take control of your finances and make progress. Single steps made consistently add up to miles.

This really can be your best money year ever. I'm going to be right here to cheer you on. Let's go!

EVEN THE ODDS

Women still earn about three-quarters of what men make. In a divorce, we get less of the assets and more of the children. Becoming a habitual saver (no matter what your life situation) is the way to even the odds.

EXTRA PAYCHECKS

If you're paid twice a month, you receive 26 paychecks a year. In most months you receive two checks, or 24 paychecks. That leaves two "extra" paychecks every year. Look at a calendar to see when you'll get those two. Rather than absorbing them into your regular household account, put them into savings.

PART II

Save More, Spend Less

1. Get Out of Debt and Start Saving

How to Start Saving

—MARY HUNT

Years ago, when I had some major problems with credit card debt, I made a startling discovery: Saving money allowed a tiny ray of sunshine to poke through the darkness. It gave me hope.

Stashing away even a small amount gave me a feeling of satisfaction similar to spending, but with this exception: It lasted much longer. A spending high vanishes quickly, but the satisfaction of saving money goes on and on. That was the catalyst that started me back on the road to financial health.

There are other reasons to save money. Saving quiets your insatiable desires, and that allows you to be content with what you have. Putting aside money regularly lets you fund your own emergencies, instead of turning every little thing that happens into new debt. But more than anything, saving money lets you decide where you want to be financially.

If you're not a saver, start today. And if you are a saver, increase your commitment. Stretch yourself to find new ways to avoid spending so you'll have more to put away. You can start with a quarter or a dollar—the amount you save doesn't matter. But don't stop. Save again tomorrow, and the next day and the next.

SET AN AMOUNT

Write down how much money you spend each month and on what. Compare that to your income to see what you have to work with. You don't want to save so much you end up creating new debt. But you don't want to save too little either by wasting money.

Find a parking spot

Stashing cash in your underwear drawer is one way to get started, but soon you'll want to move it to a regular account. Credit unions are a great place to start saving because most don't charge monthly fees for low balances. Many supermarkets now have bank branches that make saving money convenient. Or go online to ingdirect.com or hsbcdirect.com to open a no-fee, high-interest savings account.

Let it multiply

Few people get rich from their wages alone. But if you put your savings to work for you by placing your money in mutual funds or other investments, you'll enjoy the "miracle" of compound interest—earning interest on interest. That means almost anyone can reach long-term financial goals.

Save the difference

Every time you save some money, whether it be with grocery coupons or by eating at home instead of going out, calculate the savings and put the cash aside. Didn't buy those shoes you wanted? Save the amount you would have spent. Have you reduced your phone bill or hot water usage this year? Great! Calculate your savings and put that amount into your savings account.

Stop the waste

That spoiled lettuce you just threw out was really hard-earned cash in the trash. Finding ways to stop wasting food (one hint: stop buying more veggies and fruits than your family will use within a week) and energy around the house will help plug the leaks, and that means more money in your savings account.

Stash the windfalls

All of us get unexpected money from time to time. It might be a $5 rebate check or a fee that got waived. Big or small, make it a new practice to save all windfalls.

Make it routine

Once you've determined how much you will save each month, treat that amount like a regular bill—and pay it first. One idea is to make payment coupons and put them in the front of your "bills-to-be-paid" file. That way, you'll get into the routine of saving, so it becomes second nature.

Go automatic

A universal principle that we don't miss what we don't see. At work, send a set portion of your paycheck to your savings by creating an automatic deposit authorization. Before you know it, saving money will become painless, and you'll have some serious money in the bank.

No matter what the amount you sock away, if you save regularly and consistently, it will relieve your stress, boost your joy and give you renewed hope for the future.

No more excuses

"It's too late for me to start saving." Nonsense! It's only too late if you don't start now and keep going.

"I don't have enough money to save." There is no magic amount you'll need to get started, but you need to start somewhere. You can open a savings account with $1.

"I'm too busy paying off debt." You still need to be wise about saving or you'll never get out of debt. Without savings you'll find yourself running back to the credit cards for a bailout whenever anything unexpected happens. You'll be better prepared when you have money in the bank.

A little goes far

By saving as little as $50 a month you can build considerable wealth. With 5 percent interest, in one year you will save almost $614; in five years, $3,400. And in 40 years, you will have $76,301—the $24,000 principal you saved, plus $52,301 interest!

SNEAKY WAYS TO SAVE	MONTHLY SAVING	YEARLY SAVING
Save 50¢ a day in loose change	$15	$180
Cut soda consumption by 1 liter a week	$6	$72
Comparison-shop for gas (saving an estimated 25¢/gallon)	$4	$48
Bring lunch to work (saving an estimated $3/day)	$60	$720
Eat out two fewer times a month	$30	$360
Pay off $1,000 of credit card debt, reducing interest	$15	$180
At work, trade your daily cappuccino for a regular coffee	$40	$480
Maintain checking account minimum to avoid fees	$7	$84
Pay credit card bill on time to avoid late fee	$25	$300
Borrow, rather than buy, 1 book a month	$15	$180

Ⓑ *A Five-Step Plan to Take Charge of Your Money*

There are two kinds of people in the world: the haves and the have-nots. Luckily, the category we belong to isn't written in stone. Every one of us can get what we want by doing a few simple exercises.

The key to accomplishing our dreams is focusing them. Forget wasting your energy and substance fretting over every little thing that someone else owns and you want. Don't drown in envy. Instead of losing steam trying to explain why life is so hard for you, vow that this is the year you'll take charge of your financial life. Decide what you want to do and get to work on it. We'll show you how in five easy steps.

Step 1: Set Goals

Many of us fail to accomplish what we'd like with our lives simply because we don't think it through and set realistic goals. Most people have no idea how much it will cost to send their kids to college, to retire, to buy a house. On the other hand, some of us become so overwhelmed by our immediate financial obligations that breaking even becomes our sole focus. Preparing for anything beyond tomorrow seems impossible.

Just as it is in the rest of life, though, the trick to getting what we want is breaking the process down into manageable parts. Setting long-term goals becomes the means for getting where you want to be.

Sit down now and make a list of your long-term goals. Be honest with yourself about what you want, but be practical as well. In other words, give yourself room to dream, but don't set yourself up for failure. Here are some things to think about:

- Are you really happy in your home or apartment, or do you want more space, a nicer neighborhood?

- How about your job? Would you like to switch careers? Train for something better? Work at home? Start your own business?

- How about your children? Will you pay for college? Will you pay half? Have you named a guardian to care for your children in your absence? Have you discussed it with your kids? What would you like to do to get them started in life? What would you like to leave them when you're gone?

- How old do you want to be when you retire? What will you do in retirement? How will you pay for it? Will you work?
- Don't forget to factor in fun. What is your passion? What do you dream of doing in your free time? Traveling? Buying a boat?

Now, break some of these broad, lifetime goals down to a workable size. How? By establishing one short-term goal in each category to get you started.

For example, you might do research on what kind of skills you will need to get a good part-time job or to open your own business, and then sign up for a course this spring. Or you could open a savings account earmarked for your child's college education.

STEP 2: FIGURE OUT WHERE YOU STAND

You need to know how much you own, how much you owe and how much you spend. Start by listing your liquid assets, or those you could readily cash in, with a value attached to each one. Include here such things as cash, and checking and savings accounts.

Add your investment assets, which include stocks, bonds, mutual funds and retirement accounts.

Finally, add your personal assets. Go lightly on clothes, jewelry and most home furnishings. These items cost a great deal of money but they are wasting assets because they are declining rather than increasing in value, and you won't retrieve the money you spent for them. Do include your car, your home and other equipment here.

Now list your liabilities—or debts. Include credit card balances, personal, auto and student loans and your home mortgage balance.

Now subtract your liabilities from your assets to find your net worth. One of your long-term goals should be to increase your net worth each year by adding to your investment assets and decreasing your liabilities.

Next, look at what you earn and what you spend. Start with your monthly income from employment or from a business. Add investment income and child support or alimony to arrive at your total income. Now take a look at your expenses. Don't forget the cash you take from the ATM machine.

Divide your expenses into fixed expenses—those you can't change, such as taxes, groceries, insurance, utilities and the monthly mortgage payment—and discretionary expenses, those where you have some leeway. Be sure to split clothing into two parts: Some of what you buy is essential; the rest is clearly discretionary. Don't forget to put meals out, vacations and video rentals on your discretionary list.

If your expenses exceed your income, do something about it now. Even if your income covers your expenses, take a look at your discretionary expenses to see if you can cut back somewhere to help accomplish your long-term goals. You can spend it all now, or spend some money now and some money later. The money you spend later is called saving.

STEP 3: GET OUT OF DEBT

Americans carry too much debt. Take a look at how much interest you pay each month on your home, your car and your credit card purchases. Anything you can do this year to whittle that down is an important investment in yourself.

Paying off debt is your best first investment. That's because paying down debt earns a much better guaranteed return than any investment you can find. If you are carrying credit card balances at 16 percent interest, paying off that balance earns you a 16 percent return.

Make a list of all the things you owe, starting with the one that carries the highest interest rate. List them in order of interest rates. Your home will probably be at the bottom of the list. Resolve to pay as much as you can each month on the most expensive debt and minimal amounts on the others until you get the first one paid off. Then move to the next most expensive item.

If you have no credit card debt, make extra payments—or just add extra dollars—to your car or home payment. If you need help, Bankcard Holders of America, a consumer group in Salem, Virginia, is an excellent resource (540-389-5445).

STEP 4: INVEST

After you pay off debt, pay yourself first. Start with an automatic savings or investment program. Start small so you won't get discouraged. For instance, arrange to have $25 a month deducted from your paycheck or bank account to go into a savings account. Aim to raise that to $50 a month by mid-year.

With $50 a month, you can start an automatic investment program with a mutual fund company. A good choice for beginners is the T. Rowe Price Spectrum Growth Fund. This fund invests in a variety of T. Rowe mutual funds, providing you with a diversified portfolio in just one fund. T. Rowe waives an initial minimum deposit provided you sign up for regular contributions.

An investing program is suitable only for long-term money. Money that goes into stock mutual funds must be left to grow for a minimum of five years. Ten years is a better target.

STEP 5: REMEMBER ESTATE PLANNING AND LIFE INSURANCE

If you have dependents, you need life insurance whether you work at home or for an employer. Get a low-cost term insurance policy. Insurance Information, Inc., in South Dennis, Massachusetts, shops around for the least expensive policies for consumers. For $50, you receive five illustrations or cost estimates from different companies to choose from.

Estate planning sounds like something for rich people. But it's important for anyone with children to have a will and to name a guardian. It's also critical to write a health care proxy that allows someone to make health care decisions for you if you are incapacitated.

This may sound like a tall order for one year, but you really can make good progress toward these goals if you start now. Remember, that even those people who have their financial lives under tight control use the first month of the year to make resolutions and to set goals for themselves.

Get started on your resolution now. Review your progress on February 1 and then again at mid-year. Don't get discouraged. You can accomplish all your goals if you set your mind to it and take them one step at a time.

Pay Down Your Bills and Start to Save

Let's face it, we all like to spend money. We get immense pleasure from buying the perfect gift or leaving the mall with a new outfit—not to mention buying big-ticket items like a car or a home.

In fact, Americans like to spend so much that we've currently racked up $1.7 trillion in debt (not including mortgages), of which $745 billion is credit card debt. According to cardweb.com, a firm that tracks the credit card industry, the average household has 6.2 bank cards with a total average balance approaching $8,000. Scary? You better believe it. Yet for many of us, getting into debt isn't the result of a wild shopping spree or a trip to Disneyland. It often starts with the unexpected, such as an emergency medical expense, a temporary layoff, or a home repair that can't wait.

To determine if you're seriously in debt or just temporarily overextended ask yourself the following five questions, if you can answer "yes" to two or more chances are you are in debt.

- Will it take you longer than three months to get caught up?
- Are you using credit cards to pay for routine expenses, like groceries?
- Are you postponing visits to the doctor or dentist because you feel you can't afford them?
- Are you using one credit card to pay the balance of another?
- Is debt (not counting your mortgage) eating up more than 25 percent of your monthly paycheck?

When you are only temporarily overextended, you can see yourself paying off that emergency medical bill or home repair within 90 days. With serious debt, the balance carries over from month to month and doesn't seem to go down because you're only making minimum monthly payments.

If you are one of the millions who feel the financial pinch, read on to find out the ten most common debt questions—and their answers.

What's the first step to getting out of debt?

Stop spending! Make paying off bills your number-one priority. Next, draw up a spending plan. What are your expenses, including your debts? Don't forget to include "periodic" expenses, such as car insurance, property taxes and holiday gifts. On average, 10 percent of a person's income goes toward periodic expenses. Yet for many, these expenses are treated as unplanned.

Next, track your spending for a month, and compare your spending habits with your spending plan. Most people are shocked to see where their money goes, but once you track your spending, chances are you can save 20 percent of your discretionary income, which can be applied toward debt.

How do I stick to a plan?

Look for fixed budget items where you can cut back. Two of the biggest areas where people overspend are telephone and cable. People tend to have top-of-the-line packages, but by switching to basic service, they could save a nice chunk of money each month. Not surprisingly, food and entertainment are the other areas where people can cut back.

The whole point of the plan is to find the hidden extra money to put toward debt.

Which debts should I pay first?

Most experts suggest putting the greatest amount of money toward bills with the highest interest rate.

When you think about how much you're paying in interest over time, logically, it makes sense to pay these bills first. Some experts say that paying off small debts in the first few months has a great psychological benefit. Paying off a couple of smaller debts allows you to see immediate progress, and it frees up money to use toward bigger bills.

The most important thing: don't miss payments. Late fees average $29, so not only are you adding to your debt, but you risk slipping into the "slow pay" category.

Should I borrow from savings, get a home equity loan or declare bankruptcy?

While it may be tempting to clean out your savings, most experts don't recommend it.

Borrowing from savings may make sense in terms of interest rate returns, but savings brings peace of mind. So while it's OK to borrow a small amount (and pay it back), it's not good to wipe out the account.

Consolidating your debts into a home equity loan at a lower interest rate can be a good idea if, and only if, you don't start using the paid-off cards again. If you run up more debt and then can't make the home equity loan payments, you could lose your house. Bankruptcy is the last option. When there's nothing left after you pay the necessities, and you can't cut back any more, then bankruptcy is probably your only choice.

But before it comes to that, consider getting a second job that can provide extra income during the tight period. (And before you choose any of these options, consider calling a nonprofit credit counseling service.)

What should I know about ads that promise to get me out of debt?

If a company promises to get you out of debt quickly, run in the opposite direction, especially if the company charges hundreds of dollars up front for its services.

Instead, look for a nonprofit agency that examines how you spend money and teaches you how to avoid future debt.

Most nonprofit agencies offer an array of services from budget counseling (they help you help yourself) to debt management (they negotiate directly with your creditors). Two-thirds of the people who come for counseling are able to help themselves.

Funded by creditors, most nonprofits only ask for a nominal "contribution" for their services ($20 to $35 for counseling—although in some states counseling is free—and $5 to $20 a month for debt management).

With so many finance charges, how can I get ahead?

Contact your creditors and try to negotiate a lower interest rate. If you explain your circumstances, they may be willing to work with you. And if the first person you speak to says no, ask to speak to his or her supervisor.

If that's unsuccessful, try to move high-interest balances to lower-interest credit cards. But read the fine print. That card promising 6 percent interest may switch to 18 percent after three months.

And once you've paid off a credit card, either get rid of it or reduce the credit line, so you can't get into trouble again.

How long will it take to get out of debt?

Paying only the minimum could mean you're not only in debt for years, but also paying much more for your purchase than it originally cost.

If, for example, you have a $2,000 balance with an 18 percent annual percentage rate (APR), and you pay $40 a month, the debt will take almost eight years to pay off; plus, you'll have paid almost $2,000 in interest. If you add $25 to that $40 payment, the debt will be paid in three and a half years, with total interest of $722. (Find that extra $25 by bringing your own coffee or lunch to work.)

How can I build up savings?

Difficult as it sounds, try to save while you get out of debt, even if it's only a small amount at first. As you write up your spending plan, factor in savings. Then have your bank automatically withdraw the money out of your paycheck. The goal is to make saving a habit, so you can weather future temporary setbacks.

If I have bad credit once, will I be labeled a credit risk forever?

No. If you miss payments or are a "slow pay," it'll be on your credit record for seven years. But that doesn't necessarily mean that you're not eligible for credit during that time. If you've been diligent about making payments and explain the circumstances under which you fell behind, you may be able to get credit.

Ⓓ *Are You a Conscious Spender?*

Are you always short of cash? Do you buy things you never use and spend more than you need to? If so, you may be an unconscious spender. Most people spend unconsciously and wonder where the money went. Conscious spending means aligning what you spend with what you value in life. It's focusing on spending habits that allow for everyday costs and future expenses while still spending money on things you really enjoy.

These tips will help you rethink how you save and spend, so you have more room for the occasional splurge (or two).

YOU SPEND MORE THAN YOU SHOULD

What to do:

- **ONLY BUY WHAT YOU CAN CARRY.** In order to generate savings at discount stores you have to eliminate the impulse buy. Walk right past the shopping carts. When you see something you want, carry it in your arms. Eventually, you can juggle only so many items and you have to put some stuff back.

- **FIND A SHOPPING BUDDY.** To avoid waste and overspending, make a relative or friend your warehouse shopping club buddy, providing she has similar tastes. Make out a list, go once every two weeks and divide it up. You save and the quality is great.

- **GO ON A TREASURE HUNT IN A DOLLAR STORE.** Basic stores, like 99¢ stores, have become much more sophisticated. They know that in order to build up foot traffic they have to offer treasure-hunt items, which are really good deals—say a $10 item for $1—either a result of a manufacturer mistake or goods from a bankrupt retail chain.

- **SATISFY THAT SHOPPING URGE FOR LESS.** Instead of a mall, hit thrift shops, a flea market or yard sales. It's a much more economical option and satisfies the need to take time for yourself and self-nurture by buying something. It's not the amount that is spent but the time and attention spent that makes the difference.

YOUR MONTHLY CREDIT CARD TAB SQUEEZES YOUR FINANCES

What to do:

- **USE CREDIT CARDS THE RIGHT WAY.** Instead of using them to build debt, use them to help send your kids to college. Fidelity Investments will put 2 percent of the money you've spent on your Fidelity Investments 529 College Rewards Card into an account for your child's college education. Learn more at fidelity.com.

- **CLEAR UP CREDIT CARD DEBT FASTER.** Prepay every two weeks online. Unlike mortgage companies, credit card companies are required to credit your payments immediately, so you save on interest and finance charges. Use the Smart Payment method (it comes out of your checking account) and your account is credited that day. It makes a huge difference in terms of the interest you pay on the card.

- **TRACK WHAT YOU CHARGE.** Charging is like a false paycheck; you have to be able to back it up. If you know that you can only afford to spend (and pay off) $300, make sure that when the bill comes due you have the cash in your account. Otherwise, it becomes a rolling balance and can lead to excessive debt. It can make or break a person financially.

- **Climb down the debt ladder.** With "laddering" you pay extra on the credit card with the lowest balance to wipe it out, and minimums on the others. Going from five to four cards can give you a sense of progress. Or you may decide to pay extra on the card with the highest interest rate and the minimum on the others. Once you've paid it off, move that money to the card with the next highest interest rate and so on, until you're debt free.

You don't have enough cash to meet daily expenses each month, let alone save for a rainy day

What to do:

- **Make your sock drawer an ATM.** Instead of paying ATM fees every week, figure out your monthly expenses and put that much cash in a drawer or shoebox on the first of every month. Whenever you need more cash, take out $20 at a time. By having only $20 in your wallet, you'll tend to be more careful with your money so that it lasts all month long.

- **Get the best tax advice.** Many people overpay on their taxes every year (on average, $1,000) because they try to do it themselves. This means billions of dollars more for the IRS. It may be worth it to pay a tax professional to make sure that you're getting all the proper deductions you're allowed. Or, if you want to save money by doing it yourself, have a tax professional look over your finished return. It will cost less.

- **Refinance your car loan.** It's common to refinance a mortgage, but you can do it with your car, too. Dropping your rate by just four percent on a $15,000, 60-month loan will save you $1,723 in interest over the life of the loan, and your monthly payment will drop from $319 a month to $290, or $29 less. If you keep paying the extra $29 as usual, you'll pay off your car six months sooner.

- **Don't spend money on biweekly mortgage programs.** Mortgage companies can hold your payments until the end of the month, so it's a waste. Instead, pay one-twelfth extra of the principal on your mortgage every month, which equals a thirteenth mortgage payment every year. With a $150,000 mortgage at 6 percent, you can save over $30,000 in interest and cut a 30-year mortgage by almost six years.

- **INSURE THE COST OF REBUILDING YOUR HOME.** Ask your insurance company to send an appraiser to estimate how much it would cost to rebuild your home in its current condition, allowing for increased construction costs. Add in coverage for your possessions. That's the number you go with. This way, if the worst-case scenario does happen, you'll have the money to replace your home.

WHAT YOU BUY DOESN'T REFLECT WHAT YOU VALUE IN LIFE

What to do:

- **TAKE A LOOK AT YOUR BIG MONEY MAGNETS.** "This is where values don't match up with what you spend," explains Lewis. Think about the changes you might make to free up money for what really matters to you. Some possible money busters are:
  - a large house you can't afford
  - hefty car payments
  - too much personal debt with no plan to get out
  - large cell phone bills
  - clothes you don't need
  - dining out
  - overspending on Christmas and birthday presents
- **PUT A PHOTO OF YOUR DREAM IN YOUR WALLET.** The toughest part of spending less is staying on track day to day. To become a conscious spender, start with a compelling goal, such as putting your kids through college or taking a six-month sailing trip when you're 55. Use that goal to help you cut the unexpected splurges by keeping a reminder in your wallet, such as a photo of your kids with this year's college fund goal written on it or that sailboat you've been dreaming about. It's much harder to splurge on a cute pair of shoes or a new pair of earrings when you're looking at a picture of your dream. Live within your means.

  If you spend 10 percent above what you earn at $25,000, you'll probably spend 10 percent above what you earn at $50,000. All that buys you is a lifetime of catching up. Living within your means is about living in the present, not mortgaging your future.

- **HAVE FUN WITH YOUR MONEY AS MUCH AS YOU CAN AFFORD.** First, be clear about what makes you happy and what you value. For example, list five values you feel you do not fully honor in your life today, e.g., not taking time for yourself. Next to each one, list three ways you could use your money to honor each value, such as hiring a cleaning service every two weeks, for example. Then, direct your resources to those things and activities.

ARE YOU A CONSCIOUS SPENDER?

Choose the word that best describes your behavior: never, sometimes or always.

1. I don't know how much I have spent in a month until my credit card bill arrives.
2. I often buy things spontaneously.
3. I often say no to things I really want because I don't think I have the money.
4. I have purchased things that I have never used.
5. I never seem to have money for what I really want even though I earn a reasonable amount.
6. If I have money in my account, I spend it.
7. I do not know the cost each year of my regular habits, such as buying lunch or getting regular manicures.
8. I automatically upgrade my lifestyle when I earn more money.
9. I don't save for retirement because the future seems so far away.
10. I cannot clearly list what I value in life.

Conscious spenders are likely to answer "never" to most of these statements. "Sometimes" is OK, too. But if there are any questions that you answered "always," ask yourself if that habit is keeping you from getting what you really want with your money.

The Money Diet: Simple Ways to Cut the Fat Out of Your Budget and Gain Savings

- **Choose the right program for you.** No eating or spending plan works for everyone. Customize. First, determine where all of your money goes now, then set lower limits in the flexible categories (food, cosmetics, clothing, entertainment) so you can put more into savings and debt reduction.

  If you prefer a looser arrangement, try to cut overall spending by 10 percent. Financial planners recommend taking savings off the top of each paycheck, depositing the money in an interest-bearing account, then making do with what's left. Or, here is a different approach: add 10 percent to the checks you write to creditors every month.

  Do you suffer anxiety attacks when bills arrive? Are your debts growing faster than your income, or are you worried about having enough money for a new car, a home of your own, college tuition or some other important goal? Put yourself on a "money diet." The techniques are similar to a weight-loss plan; the difference is, the sooner you start, the more you'll gain.

- **Start small.** It's less daunting to begin with a series of short-term goals. If you've ever tried to lose weight, you know that each small achievement helps to strengthen your resolve.

  A good initial objective: save $1 a day. Once you've achieved that, aim for savings of $15 a week, $75 a month or more. Don't worry about how long it will take to reach important goals; once you start earning interest instead of paying it to creditors, your nest egg will grow with surprising speed.

- **Satisfy your needs in new ways.** Psychologists say that certain kinds of emotional states (such as loneliness or boredom) can lead to overspending as well as overeating. If you head to the mall when what you really crave is a break from your routine, it's time to broaden your horizons. Almost any activity—including enrolling in a class, joining a garden club, or meeting friends for lunch—can serve the same purpose.

- **Change your thinking.** Do you ever feel that you deserve to splurge because you've had a hard day? Do you feel entitled to something new because you pinched pennies elsewhere? Well, you may be right, but that kind of thinking won't reduce your waistline—or your debts. Instead of calculating how much you can spend without increasing your debts, determine how little you can spend and still enjoy life.

- **BREAK THE "IT'S ONLY" HABIT.** We all do it. "It's only a hundred calories," we say. "That won't make me fat." Or, "It's only a dollar—I can afford that." But try asking yourself whether you'd still buy it at triple the price. If not, you probably won't miss anything by skipping it.

- **AVOID TEMPTATION.** You don't wander through the candy store when you're trying to lose weight, so why tempt yourself with mail-order catalogs or visits to favorite stores? When you must shop for necessities, reduce temptation by taking a limited amount of money and sticking to a list. Leave credit cards and checkbooks at home, and carry only as much cash as you need each day. Also, be wary of saboteurs—well-meaning people who undermine your best efforts.

- **ADOPT THE 30-MINUTE RULE.** Some weight-loss experts recommend that dieters wait half an hour before giving in to any craving. The same technique works when you covet something that would break your budget. In many cases, waiting causes the urge to pass, sparing you from making an impulse purchase you'll regret later.

- **FIND PAINLESS WAYS TO TRIM THE FAT.** Keeping track of every dime you spend for a week is certainly a nuisance, but it's very revealing. The most expendable "fat" in many money diets, for example, is weekly lottery tickets. Other people can save a bundle by giving up afternoon snacks, or drinking water instead of costly beverages with meals. For example, save $1 every morning by passing up the gourmet coffee shop for a less trendy place nearby. Or save $50 a month by avoiding costly trips to convenience stores. Instead, plan your supermarket trips more carefully and do without anything that gets used up before market day.

- **ADD TO INCOME.** The best way to drop pounds is to add exercise while subtracting calories. The financial equivalent is to increase income while decreasing spending. Among the possibilities: Sell that heirloom jewelry or china you never use. Clean out your attic and have a yard sale. Rent a spare room to a student. Teach others how to knit, play bridge, refinish antiques, or do anything else that you do skillfully. At your job, you might volunteer to work overtime or to take on extra assignments that could lead to a pay raise. Consider returning to school or seeking other ways to upgrade your skills so you can qualify for a promotion—or for a better-paying position elsewhere.

ACCENT THE POSITIVE

- **DON'T FOCUS ON WHAT YOU'RE GIVING UP.** Concentrate on what you're gaining from your diet, whether it's financial security or the home of your dreams. It's far more fun to spend money than to save it, of course, but money you put aside today will give you a lot more to spend in the future. Keeping that thought in mind should help you weather the rough patches.

- **REWARD YOUR SUCCESSES.** Each time you reach a milestone—whether it's paying off a credit card bill or adding another $100 to your savings account—give yourself a small treat. Planning the next treat in advance gives you something to look forward to and helps insure that each splurge is really worth the cost.

How to Start a Budget

Unless you know how much you really earn and spend, you can't budget. To find out, follow these five simple steps:

1. Total your monthly fixed expenses: mortgage or rent, auto payments, insurance premiums, loan payments and other sums that stay the same month to month. They may include health club fees or children's allowances.

2. Calculate your household's monthly net income—what paychecks add up to after taxes and deductions. If income varies, use a typical month or the amount earned last month.

3. Subtract fixed expenses from your income. This is the amount left for variable expenses.

4. For the next month, record every item you buy in a small notepad. Record purchases like gas and groceries, but also the bills for electricity, gas and phone service. Be ruthless. If you buy a candy bar or lottery ticket, write it down. Don't forget to jot down video rentals, kids' music lessons, newspaper or magazine subscriptions and lunch money.

5. At the end of the month, total your variable expenses.
   How do they compare with what was left after you subtracted fixed expenses from your income? Since you wrote everything down, you'll be able to see where you need to cut back.
   At last...a budget.

2. What You Should Know About Credit Cards

Credit Cards: What You Probably Don't Know

—MARY HUNT

We're buried in debt:

- U.S. consumers hold more than 691 million credit cards and use them to charge $1.8 trillion each year.
- About 58 percent of consumers carry a balance on their credit cards.
- 11 percent of cardholders pay interest rates of more than 25 percent.
- 35 percent of active cardholders were charged a late fee in 2005.

I find it ironic that what nearly ruined my life—a credit card…no wait, make that 36 credit cards!—has now become the focus of my life, but in a different way. My experience with the dark side of credit cards fuels my passion to help others find their way back into the light.

A credit card will work for you or against you, depending on how you handle it. As long as you consistently use a card in ways that improve and simplify your life, it's a helpful tool. Learning all you can about how credit cards work will help you avoid the potential pitfalls.

What the big print giveth, the small print taketh away. The small print to which I refer is on the application you signed to get the card, along with the even smaller print on your monthly statement. If you've long since parted company with that paperwork, call the customer service number on the back of the card and ask for a copy of the Terms and Conditions.

I get a lot of mail and much of it contains the same questions about credit cards. This leads me to believe you might want some of those answers, too. You may be surprised by what you don't know.

Q *Which credit card bill should I pay off first, the one with the smallest balance or the one with the highest interest rate?*

A My opinion is that you should target the smallest debt first. Here's why: We are emotional creatures who crave instant gratification. Yes, we are. If it takes you five years to pay off that high-interest card because it's also your largest debt, you'll get discouraged. But if you pay off the smallest debt in a few months, seeing that $0 balance will give you a huge emotional payoff and you'll be energized to tackle the next largest debt, then the next.

Q *How are "default rate" and "universal default" different?*

A The default rate is the penalty interest rate you'll be socked with if you violate your card's Terms and Conditions. If you're late with a payment or go over your credit line, the default rate is always high and could be 18 percent, 30 percent or more. "Universal default" is a disturbing practice in which the lender changes your current interest rate to the higher default rate if the bank learns that you've been late or missed a payment with another lender—even if your account with them is up-to-date. Translation: Being late with your student loan payment could cause your credit card to jump to the default rate—even though you have never been late or missed a credit card payment.

Q *What happens if I pay less than the minimum payment?*

A The credit card issuer, by law, must accept any amount you send at any time during the billing cycle. However, if you send less than the minimum amount, you'll be charged a late fee that could be as high as $39 in some cases. And if that bumps you past your credit limit, you could get socked with another $39 over-limit fee. Add that $78 to your current balance and you can see that a credit card account, when abused, can simply grow all by itself—without adding new purchases.

But wait, there's more! Being late will likely send your interest rate to the moon. And then that universal default clause kicks in and other creditors may raise your rates with them as well. Believe me, you do not want to be late. That's like pushing over the first domino and watching helplessly as all the others follow.

Q *Does it make any difference when I send in my credit card payment as long as it's not late?*

A It does! There are two reasons you should get into the habit of paying credit card bills as soon as they arrive. First, you avoid incurring horrendous penalties for being late if there are mail delays. Second, you'll pay less interest. This is especially important if you don't pay off the whole balance each month. If you make your monthly payment early in the billing cycle, you reduce the daily balance for more days in that cycle. This also reduces the total balance used by the credit card company to figure out the average daily balance for that month.

Let's say your balance was $200 for the first 23 days of the month, and you charged a $1,200 computer on the 24th day. Your average daily balance would be figured like this: (23 x 200) + (7 x 1,400) divided by 30 for an average daily balance of $480.

Q *Should I transfer my higher-interest credit card debt to a zero percent credit card?*

A It's tricky. It depends on your situation, and the terms of the new 0 percent card. If you're transferring a balance you are fairly certain you'll be able to pay off in a year or less, perhaps you should consider the switch. But first make sure you read every word of that fine print and that you fully understand it.

Is there a transfer fee? A 4 percent fee on a $5,000 balance is $200 right up front. Ouch! And be sure to determine how long the 0 percent "teaser rate" lasts. If it's only 60 or 90 days, when it expires you could wind up in a worse situation than you have now. More seriously, what is the default rate, and could you handle it if something unforeseen happens and you fall behind? If you are determined to pay the balance in full within, say, the next six months and there is no transfer fee, you just might come out ahead. Bottom line: With credit card accounts, it's always a gamble.

Q *Should I take out a home equity loan to pay off my credit cards?*

A No, and here's why: If you fall behind on your credit card payments, the bank or credit company will charge you fees and penalties and trash your credit report. And that's about it. But if you transfer that unsecured debt to your home by means of a home equity loan and then run into a rough patch, you could find yourself on the street.

Defaulting on a home equity loan is serious and can lead to foreclosure. Also, you need to remember that your home's equity is an appreciating asset. The goal of home ownership is to eventually achieve 100 percent equity—that's when you can burn the mortgage and throw a party. You'll never reach that goal if you keep treating your equity like a big ATM or secret savings account.

Q *Should I really put money into savings even though I have a lot of credit card debt?*

A Absolutely. You need an emergency fund—a stash to cover at least three (ideally six) months' worth of expenses—that will be there when you find yourself in a financial pickle. If you don't have enough money to cover stuff that happens (trust me, stuff always happens), you'll keep running to credit cards for a bail-out. You'll never get out of debt if you keep adding new purchases.

Start saving immediately—a little bit all the time—and soon you'll kiss your credit card debt goodbye for good.

Credit cards appear to be so easy and convenient. But it takes discipline, knowledge and personal restraint to use a credit card well. It's like walking a tightrope—one false move and you crash. Cash sounds so much easier, doesn't it?

Ⓑ *Attack of the Killer Banking Fees: Stop Draining Away Your Precious Earnings*

—MARY HUNT

One of the best ways to make money is to hang on to the money you've already earned. Sounds simple enough, but money does have a way of leaking out of our wallets undetected. A little bit here, a little more there, and before you know it you're strapped for cash.

Take banking fees. A conservative estimate is that the typical family pays between $600 and $1,000 a year in service charges on checking, savings and credit card accounts, and ATM and debit cards. That doesn't even include interest or punitive fees for paying late or going over-limit. For many of us, this drain goes undetected because it's buried in the fine print.

Follow these simple strategies to keep more money in your pocket, where it belongs.

CHECKING ACCOUNTS

Typical service fees on checking accounts can include a flat monthly fee, per-check fees, fees for speaking to an account representative ($3 per conversation at one of the nation's largest banks), fees for checking your account balance by phone, fees for failing to meet the minimum balance, fees for receiving copies of your paid checks and fees for using telephone banking. Even if you have a "free" account, there are plenty of fees banks can charge—for balance inquiries, check printing, dormancy and closing the account early, for example.

KEEP YOUR CASH: Find a completely fee-free checking account. They're out there, you just have to know where to look. Your best bet is a local, independent bank or credit union. Ask to see a schedule of fees before you make the switch. To find a credit union, go to creditunion.coop and click on "Locate a Credit Union."

DEBIT CARD ACCOUNTS

Debit cards are all the rage in plastic these days, but hidden fees can outweigh their convenience. To avoid paying annoying service fees, you need to understand the difference between PIN-based and signature-based debit card transactions.

A PIN-based debit card, sometimes called an ATM card, requires a personal identification number to complete a transaction. The money is deducted from your checking account immediately. A signature-based debit card with a MasterCard or Visa brand is similar to a credit card, but without the credit. You sign for your purchases and the money is debited from your checking account within two to three business days.

Some banks now charge a fee for each PIN-based transaction, often without warning the consumer. And the trend is spreading.

KEEP YOUR CASH: Always opt for a signature-based transaction, rather than a PIN-based one. Press the "credit" key, sign your name on the receipt and, in most cases, no fee will be charged.

CREDIT CARD ACCOUNTS

Many credit card issuers charge an annual fee ranging from $35 to $300. More companies than ever before are also tacking on monthly maintenance fees of $6 to $9. These fees are charged simply for the privilege of spending with plastic.

KEEP YOUR CASH: Limit yourself to one good, all-purpose credit card. It should have no annual fee, a grace period of at least 25 days and a reasonably low interest rate. For example, Town North bank has a Platinum MasterCard (tnbonline.com) that has no balance-transfer fee and no annual fee. And Cardtrak (cardtrak.com) maintains a current list of other no-annual-fee, low-rate credit cards. Log on to the website, then click on "Find a Card." Another site to check out card rates and current offers is indexcreditcards.com.

ATMs

Americans waste nearly $4 billion each year making withdrawals at the "wrong" bank's ATM. If you withdraw money from an ATM not associated with your bank, there are often two fees charged: one from that ATM, the other from your bank—which could result in fees up to $2.75 for each withdrawal.

KEEP YOUR CASH: Learn the exact nature of your bank's ATM network so you know which ATMs you can use fee-free. Look for this information on your bank's website. Banks usually don't levy fees on their own customers using the bank's ATMs.

BREAK THE RULES, PAY DEARLY

Think service fees are bad? Credit card companies charged $14.8 billion in penalty fees (for things like late payments and spending above the credit limit) in 2004. With that kind of potential for profit, companies are making it easier for customers to unwittingly break the rules.

Never pay late!

Many credit card companies rely on "universal default" clauses built into the fine print of the agreement you signed to get the card. This lets them make routine checks of your account and raise the interest rate if you're late making a payment—even to another credit card or bank, say, for a car loan.

Ⓒ *Conquering Credit Cards: We've Done Our Homework, Here's What We Learned*

—Mary Hunt

Credit cards can protect you and your money. But it's soooo easy to get burned! Are you feeling more controlled by your credit cards than in control? You have legal rights that protect you, but loopholes give credit card companies an advantage. Consumer confusion can mean big profits for them. Here's the insider info you need to take charge once and for all.

The freebies may not add up

Many credit cards offer enticements such as frequent-flier mileage, cash rebates and purchase discounts, but may charge higher interest rates and big annual fees.

> **Insider tip:** If you don't pay your balance every month, chances are the heavy interest plus the annual fee will be greater than the value of any freebies you'll get. You may be better off switching to a no-fee, low-interest rate card.

Oh, That Fine Print

Is a "fixed rate" set in stone? Unlike a mortgage, "fixed rate" credit card interest rates aren't fixed at all. The law allows credit card companies to change their rates at any time, with only 15 days' notice to the cardholder.

INSIDER TIP: Read everything you receive from the card company. When you see a notice of a rate change, which may be buried in tiny print on the statement or on a scrap of paper, call customer service. If they will not reinstate your old rate, consider switching cards. By law, you have the option of not accepting the new rate, and paying off the balance at your current interest level. But if you make any new charges, the rate will automatically go to the higher one.

WATCH THOSE INTEREST RATES

Remember the application you signed and the disclosure statement that came with your new card? That's where the company probably said it would always apply your payments to the portion of your balance with the lowest interest rate first. This is bad news if you have different interest rates for balance transfers, purchases and cash advances.

INSIDER TIP: Do not take cash advances. Factor in the outrageous cash advance fee (many charge 3 percent of the advance and fees of up to $50) and the fact that you may not be allowed to repay the advance until all lower-interest balances are paid in full. In the end, you could end up with triple-digit interest on your cash advance. You are better off getting cash from your bank account, if possible.

FIND THE BEST CARD

Every household should have one good, all-purpose credit card with these features:

- No annual fee
- 25-day grace period
- Accepted in many places
- Low interest rate

GO TO: Bankrate.com at bankrate.com; RAM Research Group at cardweb. com.

THE GOOD SIDE OF SAYING "CHARGE IT!"

You get built-in protection with every purchase. When you pay for something with cash, check or debit card, you do not have the protection granted by the FCBA. This can be bad news if the seller does not deliver goods or services as agreed.

INSIDER TIP: Always use a credit card to pay for something you order by mail, phone or the Internet, or when you put down a deposit on an item. This way, if the company fails to deliver goods or services as agreed, you have the law on your side.

YOU'RE NOT LIABLE FOR THEIR MISTAKES

The FCBA requires the credit card company—not you—to absorb the loss from fraudulent charges and in cases where the cardholder has made a valid billing-error dispute. Absolutely anything you do not like about your credit card bill can be a "billing error" if you say it is. This means charges for things you didn't buy or can't figure out, goods and services you did not receive or items you did not accept. In the law, "acceptance" does not mean you took the merchandise from the seller. It means that you found no hidden problems later on when you took the goods home.

INSIDER TIP: Scrutinize your bill. If you see anything that is questionable or unacceptable, write (do not phone) the card company so they receive your letter within 60 days of the date they mailed the statement.

Date your letter and include your account number, name and address. Identify the "billing error" (being careful to use that term), the problem, and a request that the amount be credited to your account. Use the address listed on your statement for "Disputes and Billing Errors," and keep a copy of the letter for yourself. Send it "certified mail, return receipt requested." This way, you'll get a receipt signed by a company employee. The credit card company must, within 30 days, reverse the charge, fix the problem or tell you it will investigate. While the matter is unresolved, you do not have to pay the disputed amount (if you do pay the bill, you will not lose your rights). But they cannot charge you interest on that amount or report you delinquent. If there was no error, the company can charge you interest for the weeks or months the charge was under investigation.

AND HOW ABOUT THOSE EXTRA FEES?

Can't seem to avoid late charges? No wonder you keep getting socked with those extra $25 or $30 fees. The Fair Credit Billing Act (FCBA) allows a card company to hold your statement until two weeks before payment is due. When it arrives, you might only have a few days to send your check. Companies can also set an early morning cutoff time on the due date, effectively lopping off another day.

> **INSIDER TIP:** Don't assume you will have sufficient turn-around time once you receive the bill. Call the toll-free number on the back of your card to find out when your next payment is due. Even if you haven't received the statement, mail your payment two weeks before the due date. Write your account number on the check and send it to the address printed on a previous statement.

KNOW YOUR (SPENDING) LIMIT

Most companies allow you to go over the limit, but beware: You will probably get hit with an over-the-limit fee of $25 or more.

> **INSIDER TIP:** Make sure your balance is always well below your limit. If you've been hit with this fee recently, request it be waived. You'll be paying interest on the entire balance anyway.

HOW TO GET OUT OF DEBT

When used intelligently, a credit card can simplify and protect your financial life. The best way to get that protection and convenience while avoiding the danger of getting burned is to pay the balance every month. If you need help paying off those credit cards fast, try this advice:

- Stop using the cards. Don't take on any new debt!
- Arrange your debts on a simple chart with the one that has the highest interest rate at the top, the rest in order below.
- As one debt reaches a zero balance, take its payment and add it to the payment of the next debt in line to help pay it off very quickly. When the second debt is paid, add the first and second to the third, and so on until all are paid.

- "Fix" your payments. Whatever your monthly payment is now, make a commitment to pay that same amount (or more) every month. Ignore the "falling" payment schedule the card companies prefer.

Need help? The free Credit Card Cost Calculator at debtproofliving.com will help you create your own debt repayment plan.

Customer Satisfaction Not Guaranteed

But persistence often works. When you write a credit card company about a billing error, its initial response may be, "Sorry, you still must pay," even if your claim is legitimate.

Insider tip: Send a second request. If the company responds by asking for more information, provide it if the request is reasonable. But make copies of all correspondence for your files. If they make another request, respond by certified mail to the president of the company. Include a letter explaining the situation and describing your disappointment in the handling of the matter.

And your last resort is...

The Federal Reserve Board and the Federal Trade Commission enforce credit card laws, along with more than 50 state agencies. That means enforcement is complicated, confusing and often lax.

Insider tip: Don't be hasty to move to that level of big government bureaucracy. The threat of filing a complaint may be more powerful than actually making one, so exhaust your best efforts with the card company first.

Cut Your Credit Card Costs

For 12 years I charged through life assuming I'd find the money to pay for all the things I was buying, stuff I couldn't afford. If I'd known then what I know now, I could have saved myself a lot of grief. And a ton of money.

When it comes to convenience, it's hard to beat a good credit card. And that's the problem. The more convenient they are, the more apt we are to get in over our heads. When that happens, carrying expensive credit card debt is like trying to navigate a minefield. Just one wrong move and you could really mess up your life.

Look, credit cards themselves are not the problem. You need a credit card to rent a car or make hotel reservations. Using a credit card is the safest way to buy online. The problem is the mounting debt, interest and fees that result when we use credit cards to live beyond our means. Learn to live below your means, sock away the difference, and know the ins and outs of credit cards to escape the debt cycle.

Universal default

Buried in the fine print of the credit card agreement you signed is permission for the company to check your credit report routinely. If they see anything they don't like (late payments to another credit card or your mortgage bank, for instance) you've given them permission to increase your interest rate, even if you've always paid their account on time.

Your credit score

Everything on your credit report is reflected in this three-digit number. Insurance companies look at your credit score to determine how much you'll pay in premiums, and many landlords and potential employers consider credit scores a kind of character reference. So a negative credit history may mean higher car insurance rates or missing out on that dream job.

Pare down

You only need one major credit card, or possibly two to keep things separate if you cover work-related, reimbursable expenses. Any more than two and you're just asking for trouble in these days of rampant identity theft and increased fees. Keep the card you've had the longest to enhance your credit score. Once you've paid off the other card balances, consider closing them. But pace yourself. Closing too many accounts at once can hurt your credit score.

REDUCE YOUR INTEREST RATE

If you're in too deep to pay your balance in full every month and have at least six months of on-time payments, call customer service and ask for a rate reduction. If you don't succeed at first, keep trying. Getting a lower interest rate can save you lots of money.

PAY EARLY

Thirty percent of credit card companies' profits come from late and over-limit fees. Foil their plans by paying your bills early and not going over your credit limit.

GET OUT OF DEBT

You need a realistic plan to pay off your credit cards. I want to help by inviting you to visit Debt-Proof Living Online. Go to debtproofliving.com and head for the Rapid Debt-Repayment (RDRP) Calculator. Give yourself time to get a plan in place. You'll be out of debt sooner than you ever dreamed possible.

ASK MARY

We pay $99.99 a year to a company that monitors all three credit bureaus for us. This seems like it might be a waste of money. What's your take?

YVONNE, MINNESOTA

Credit monitoring companies offer a viable service, but I bet you could put that $100 to better use and monitor your own credit. You can get one free credit report a year from each of the three nationwide reporting companies at annualcreditreport.com (or 877-322-8228). It's best to get all three reports at once to compare. You may want to do this a few times a year so if your identity is compromised, you'll catch it early. As for losses, you may already be covered. Check your homeowner's or renter's insurance policy. If not, depending on what state you live in, you may be able to add identity fraud expense coverage for only a few dollars per year.

Establish a Credit Rating

- **Reliability.** Creditors want to see timely payments made over the course of at least a year. Keep records of every bill and payment you make. If you're applying for a first mortgage, hold onto canceled rent and utility checks.

- **Stability.** Moving every year or switching jobs frequently might notch up your income, but it may hurt your credit rating.

- **Restraint.** If you already have a lot of credit available, you may be considered a risk. Say no to more credit cards and higher lines of credit. Use one credit card, pay on time and try not to max out the credit. Most importantly, never borrow money from one credit card to pay off another. That means your credit is really out of control.

- **Preparation.** Before applying for a major loan, check your credit report with each of the three credit bureaus. And do so at least a couple of months before you plan to borrow, so you'll have time to address any errors or other problems.

Credit Bureaus:
Trans Union LLC 800-888-4213; transunion.com
Equifax 800-685-1111; equifax.com
Experian 888-397-3742; experian.com

Mary's wipe-out-debt rules

- **Stop.** If you carry a balance on a card, stop using it. Period. This is crucial.

- **Pay the same.** Adopt your current minimum payments as your fixed monthly obligation from now on. Even if creditors accept less, don't change it.

- **Create order.** Line up your credit card debts with the smallest balance you owe at the top. Try to pay more than the minimum on that card.

- **Gang Up.** Once you pay off that first debt, take its payment and add it to the fixed payment of the next debt in line. Repeat until you are debt-free.

3. Saving Strategies

Ⓐ *Avoid Money Blunders*

1. Are You Throwing Away Your Money?

Here are ten common money mistakes that many of us make:

RELYING ON CREDIT

There are clear advantages to paying cash, or writing a check. You'll save money and get more control over your cash flow. Discounts are available from car dealers for cash purchases, too. Whenever you plan to make a big purchase, call and ask about cash discounts. Even for smaller purchases— like groceries—consider using a debit card rather than a credit card. A debit card, which can also serve as your bank ATM card, deducts the money directly from your bank. It is a pay-as-you-go kind of purchasing that puts you in control.

CAVEAT: If you lose the card, a thief can clean out your bank account. Report the loss within two business days and your liability is limited to $50. Nor will you earn mileage or bonus incentives on most debit cards.

CARRYING TOO MUCH DEBT

Many who use credit cards pay them off every month. But most don't. The average credit card holder carries debt of between $2,000 and $8,000. That doesn't include car loans and home mortgages either.

If you are part of this group, do what you can to get out of debt. Make a list of what you owe on your credit cards and the interest rates on each. Set aside the two cards with the lowest interest rate; use only these cards for purchases and cut up all the others.

Pay extra on the highest-rate card until it's paid off. Continue with the second-highest rate and keep going. Once you've paid off all your credit cards, charge only what you can pay in one month. Put any extra money into your savings account.

FAILING TO BUDGET

OK, budgeting is boring. It also forces us to confront exactly how much or how little we have. But budgeting is essential if you are to have control of your money. Laying out your income and your outlay helps you see what you're spending. And it can help you get the most bang for your buck. Part of your budget process should be planning long-term purchases like furniture, a car, a house, a special vacation. It can also spur you to save more because you have a goal in mind.

WITHDRAWING TOO LITTLE

People sometimes reason that if they take just enough cash from the ATM to cover their current needs they will save money because they won't have extra cash on hand.

Many banks charge a fee for each withdrawal. That means paying five times as much to withdraw $20 on five occasions than withdrawing $100 once. Better to make a weekly trip to the ATM and make it part of your budgeting. Decide what you need for groceries, gas, gifts and other expenses that week. Then withdraw it and parcel it out, sticking to your budget.

IGNORING RETIREMENT PLANS

Nearly 12 million eligible American workers either don't participate in their company's plans or don't invest enough to take full advantage of free matching contributions from their employers. But the money you put into the plan is not locked up forever. About three out of four plans permit loans, usually for any reason whatsoever. So contribute. You will save on taxes. And you will collect money from your employer that would otherwise be lost to you.

BUYING WARRANTIES

Before you sign up for a warranty on an appliance, camera or VCR, remember, electronic equipment rarely needs repair. By the time it's on the fritz, it's usually simply worn out.

You might want to consider one if you buy a computer for your home business, for example; computers do sometimes have bugs and are often expensive to fix. Instead of automatically electing the extended warranty, do some research before you buy. *Consumer Reports*, which is available in most libraries, is a good place to start.

PAYING IN ADVANCE

Often you are offered a discount if you pay for two years of a service or a subscription, rather than pay one year at a time. Is $16.95 for two years a better deal than $9.95 for one year? In most cases, no. Giving up a dollar today is more costly than giving up a dollar a year from now because of what investors call the "time value of money."

AVOIDING INVESTMENT RISK

Statistics show that more than 90 percent of American women will be minding their own money at one time or another because they are either single, divorced or widowed. The average age of widowhood is 55. Nearly half of all marriages end in divorce. The outlook for Social Security for the baby boomers is not bright. All of this adds up to a need for investing.

If you don't invest for your future, you risk running out of money. Start slowly. Many good mutual fund companies waive their steep initial minimum deposits if you will agree to regular investments of as little as $50 a month. Here are some places to start your research: Fidelity Investments (fidelity.com), Vanguard (vanguard.com), or for increasingly popular socially responsible mutual funds, try Domini (domini.com).

TAKING BAD ADVICE

Don't take investment advice from your insurance agent, your brother-in-law, coworker or next-door neighbor. None of these people know any more about investing than you do.

Where should you go? Many employers now have software programs that help employees see how much they need to save for various goals in life. They also help you with asset allocation, which simply means splitting up your money among different types of assets such as stocks, bonds and cash. Check with your human resources department.

Banks also offer basic financial plans that help with a financial checkup. Visit your local bank and take a look at the financial plans. Remember that the bank will try to sell you its own products, but you don't have to buy.

Playing favorites

When you look at your monthly expenditures, everything should be reconsidered. Sure, we have to eat, but it doesn't have to be lobster at the Ritz.

Each of us sees certain budget items as sacrosanct: a membership at the gym, long-distance calls to grandchildren, dinners out. This is not to say that we should deny ourselves all pleasures. But we should look carefully at each choice we make about spending money and make certain it is a sound one.

2. Are You Paying More Than You Should?

You may be paying more than you need to for all sorts of things—insurance, utilities, food, clothes, travel, even your bank account. Maybe you're buying frills or extras you'll never use. Maybe there's a better deal elsewhere. You might even be paying more in the long run by paying too little now. Take a look at these common and not-so-common traps that hide in monthly bills and learn how to put money back in your pocket.

Cost-Cutting Myths

- **Bigger is cheaper.** Buying things in large quantities usually lowers the cost per unit—but not always. For example, a 10-pack of fluorescent tubes in one home center sells for $19.98 ($2 per tube), while a 2-pack in the same store sells for $1.98 ($1 apiece).

- **No-haggle auto superstores will give you the best deal on a used car.** Probably not, so shop around. *Money* magazine finds that these car supermarkets hardly ever offer the lowest price.

- **Setting the clothes dryer to "air-dry" cuts energy bills.** Not so. The machine has to run longer and use heated or cooled air pulled from the house, so you may end up paying even more.

- **Insulating your water heater saves on electricity.** Yes, if your heater is older than ten years. No, if it's younger. These newer heaters are so well insulated it's redundant to wrap them in an insulation blanket.

Ask and Ye Shall Receive

- Ask your insurance company if it offers any discounts on your homeowner premiums.

- Ask if you can reduce your auto premiums by enrolling in a defensive-driving class. With some companies, completing the class will earn a 10 percent discount.

- Always ask your doctor (or have your pharmacist ask) if you can substitute a generic drug for a brand-name prescription.

- Talk to your bank manager about waiving the fee for a bounced check. Maybe you can make a convincing argument that the mistake wasn't your fault (e.g., one of your creditors cashed your check sooner than usual, which threw off your records). Or you can threaten to take your business elsewhere. Such tactics sometimes work.

- Ask your bank about a no-fee checking account. Some offer them as part of a homeowner or senior-citizen package. Some waive the fee if you have your paycheck deposited directly in your account. Others will cut a deal if you don't require them to return canceled checks with your monthly statements. You could save as much as $10 to $15 a month.

- Arrange for regular monthly bills like insurance premiums and mortgage payments to be paid automatically from your bank account. It usually costs nothing. You save yourself a check and a stamp for every bill.

- Negotiate a lower interest rate on your credit card balance. Call your credit card company's 800 number and say, "I've had a lot of offers to transfer my balance to other credit cards. Can you do something for me?" You may have to speak to the supervisor, but it's worth a try.

Money Savers That Backfire

- Don't order from a catalog just to save sales tax. Shipping charges may far exceed what you'd pay in state and local sales taxes. For example, eight catalogs we surveyed charge an average of $7.71 (or 15 percent) for shipping and handling of a $50 purchase; $13.18 (or 13 percent) for a $100 purchase; $17.80 (or 9 percent) for a $200 purchase. How many sales-tax rates run that high?

- Don't use an unfamiliar mechanic for major car repair problems. If you don't have a trusted mechanic, take the car to a dealership's repair shop. It will cost more, but at least you'll have the full faith of the dealership to stand behind the work. In the end you may pay less.

- Don't make too many small claims on your homeowner's policy (or even call the company to find out if you can file a minor claim). If you do so often, you're bound to be labeled a bad risk. Some companies now pool such information, so eventually you could be dumped into an assigned-risk plan that provides only bare-bones coverage and, in some states, costs up to 20 percent more.

- Don't use a NOW account (a checking account that earns interest) if it requires a stiff minimum deposit. Such accounts pay a paltry 1.5 to 2.25 percent a year on average. If you park a $1,500 minimum in one, it will earn only $22.50 a year. That's $77.50 less than you'd get if you opened a no-interest account that requires a minimum balance of $500, then put $1,000 in a mutual fund that returns 10 percent a year.

- Don't put rainy-day savings in a bank money market deposit account or passbook savings account. The average interest they pay (2.5 to 4 percent and 2.2 percent respectively) can be beaten almost anywhere. You'll also be charged a sales commission on the fund. A no-load money market mutual fund is a much better place to put money you're saving for emergencies and special things. For example, T. Rowe Price's Prime Reserve Fund charges no commission, pays 4.84 percent interest and lets you write checks on your money ($500 minimum).

- Don't shop for bargains only to carry them on your credit card balance for months. In the end, they could cost you $25 to $150 extra.

Save on the Internet

- For heavy-use families who surf the Net for hours, a flat monthly fee for unlimited use can save money.

- But for people who use the Internet only for sending a few e-mail messages a month and looking up airline fares or stock prices now and then, an hourly rate may be best.

- Be sure your online service provider has a toll-free telephone number for technical support so you don't pay long-distance charges when you need help.
- Send e-mail messages rather than talking long distance on the phone. Or use a computer-to-computer system such as Skype that allows you to make international long distance calls for free.
- Find a scholarship for your college-bound kid on the Internet. Financial aid information page fastweb.com has data on 180,000 private scholarships.
- Surf the Net for travel savings on everything from airfares to hotels and vacation sites. There are numerous bargain travel sites and individual testimonials. Check out BudgetTravel at budgettravel.com and Travelocity at travelocity.com.

It's Better to Give and Receive

- Many charitable organizations, such as the Jaycees, sell city books filled with coupons good for savings on everything from restaurants to dry cleaning and oil changes. A typical book costs $30 and offers over $1,500 worth of useful coupons.
- Public television stations often offer excellent premiums in exchange for fundraising pledges. For example, a $65 pledge to PBS in Tallahassee, Florida, is rewarded with a membership card good for "buy one, get one free" dinners throughout the state.
- Charity auctions can yield great finds. At a recent art museum silent auction, for example, a local gym had donated three free months. One woman who regularly exercises at that gym bid on it and got those three months for half what she'd normally pay.

Bill Padders: Overinsuring

Prune these options from your auto insurance policy and you'll see the following savings:

- Car rental in case of a breakdown, $15 to $25 a year.
- Glass breakage, 10 to 20 percent of your comprehensive premium.

- Towing, $5 to $10 a year. (Joining an auto club costs more, but it offers more service when you need it.)

- If you have good health, life and disability insurance, you might consider dropping the personal injury protection option from your car insurance.

- Cut out collision coverage if your car is five or more years old and worth less than $1,000.

- Be sure you're not insuring your home for the full value of both the house and land. You're just paying extra for coverage you'll never use. Pay only to cover the value of the house—about 80 percent of the property's total value.

LOW DEDUCTIBLES

- Save 15 to 30 percent of your car insurance premium by raising your deductible (the amount of a claim that you pay before insurance kicks in) from $200 to $500 on your collision and comprehensive coverage.

- Raise the deductible and cut your on your homeowner's policy premium by this much:
  - From $250 to $500   10 percent
  - From $250 to $1,000   15 percent
  - From $250 to $2,500   20 percent
  - From $250 to $5,000   30 percent

INADEQUATE INSULATION

- On average, properly insulating various parts of your home can save...
  - $61 a year: water heater (one that's more than 10 years old)
  - $45 a year: attic (to an insulation value of R-38)
  - $45 a year: windows (adding weatherstripping and storm covering)

WRONG THERMOSTAT SETTINGS

- For every 10°F lower you set your hot-water heater, you'll save an average of $1.68 a month. (But don't set it lower than 120°F or your dishwasher won't operate properly.)

- In winter, for every degree above 68°F that you raise your thermostat, you'll add roughly 3 percent to your heating bill.
- In summer, for every degree below 78°F that you lower your thermostat, you'll add about 6 percent to your air-conditioning bill.

WHEN SECONDHAND SAVES

- Buy a used car. A new car typically undergoes almost 42.8 percent of its five-year depreciation in the first two years of ownership.
- Look for a used car that has just come off a one-year lease. Program cars, as they're called, usually have quite a bit of their warranties left and have been well maintained.
- Even if you don't go for secondhand clothes, you can pick up standard items in nearly new condition at Goodwill or the Salvation Army for awfully good prices. Examples: belts for 50¢, knit polo shirts for $3.50, jeans and permanent-press men's dress shirts for $4.

THE BEST DEAL

- Shop for the best gas price—it can vary as much as 15¢ a gallon.
- Search high and low for a bank that doesn't charge a fee of $1 or $2 to use its automated teller machine. Try to find one that doesn't charge a fee if you use other banks' ATMs, too.
- Make sure that low interest on your credit card will last at least one year. (After that, transfer to another low-fee card.) Ask if the rate applies to all transactions, even cash advances.
- Buy checks through a mail-order house (Sunday newspaper supplements usually advertise them) for as little as $4.99 plus $1.29 shipping for 200 checks. The checks you purchase through a bank can cost as much as $15 for 200.
- For people who pay off their credit card balances every month, the best card is one that charges no annual fee and offers some kind of bonus— frequent-flyer miles, rebates, points for a new car, whatever.
- Slash eyeglass costs by buying them at discount-store optical departments.

For example, the cheapest pair of glasses at one Target store is $56, compared to $110 at a national optical chain store in the same town. Contact lenses are $29 a pair, compared to $49 a pair. A box of six disposable lenses is $18 versus $24. (Exams for glasses or contacts cost roughly the same at both stores.)

ALMOST-FREE FUN

- Borrow videos and CD-ROMS from the library.
- Share a newspaper subscription with a neighbor.
- Go to movie matinees and second-run theaters.
- Swap babysitting with neighbors.
- Make your own birthday cakes from scratch or a mix and canned frosting and beat the bakery's cost by 70 to 80 percent.
- Decorate with fresh flowers from your garden.

RENT RATHER THAN BUY...

- Anything you'll use only once or twice, such as power tools, special party decorations and formal gowns.
- Musical instruments, if you or your child are just starting to take piano lessons, for example, rent the piano for a few months until you're sure lessons will continue.
- Cottages or boats, if you can't use them much more than twice a year.

MONEY WASTERS

- Buying things you don't need and can't use just because they're on sale.
- Buying discounted clothes that require expensive alterations and dry cleaning.
- Overbuying fresh produce that you may have to throw out before you can use it.
- Driving more than ten miles to save $1 or less.
- Not selling your buying mistakes or good castoffs to a resale shop.

- Not carefully inspecting items at resale shops for stains and tears. There are usually no refunds.

Expert Advice

- Check *Consumer Reports* or your insurance agent for the profile of any car you're thinking of buying to see if that model is expensive to repair or has a high theft rate. If so, it's going to be more expensive to insure.

3. Cash-Flow Control: How to Keep Your Money Where It Belongs...in Your Wallet

We call it Empty Wallet Syndrome. You could swear that you hit the ATM just yesterday, but when you swing by the supermarket to get a few things for dinner, you open your wallet and...nothing! Or maybe your bank account is running on empty and you still have bills to pay.

Lay down your credit cards and step away from the sales rack. It's time to get your cash flow under control. You can do this. Just change a few bad habits and reassess some of your bigger monthly expenses and, bingo, no more unpleasant surprises at the ATM.

Money Pit #1: Shopping the Sales

We've all been seduced by the lure of a sale. After all, if prices are discounted, you'll save big, right? Not always. Sale tags are a great marketing strategy because they make consumers think that merchandise is marked down, but that's not always the case.

- Remember that buying a sale item you don't need is still an expense that requires cold, hard cash. People buy things just because they're on sale: clothes that don't fit well, home furnishings that don't match.

- Beware of splurging at outlet stores. Years ago outlets existed to farm out the remaining items in a product line. But now, some retailers make items exclusively for outlets that may be of lesser quality but sold at a similar price. Check the quality, pricing and return policy at the retail store before going to the company's outlet.

- To stop overspending, arm yourself with a list, and hit the store with a thrifty friend. She'll make you stick to what you need. Or tape a picture of something you're saving for on top of your wallet. You'll be reminded of it every time you take out money.

MONEY PIT #2: OVERSHOPPING AT THE SUPERMARKET

In our time-starved world, it's very easy to shop meal to meal, which can be just as expensive as going to a restaurant.

- To purchase only what you need, shop with a list that includes a week's worth of meals, taking into account a night or two of leftovers.

- Clip coupons solely for items you currently use, not ones you want to try. Always look for stores that double or triple your coupon savings.

- Before you hit bulk stores, check prices at your local shops. Some paper goods might be less expensive on sale at the drugstore. And forget about super-size perishables. They often go bad before you finish them.

MONEY PIT #3: SPOILING YOUR FURRY FRIENDS

We love our pets. In fact, Americans spend billions caring for them. There are many ways to save money on your pets, and they'll be none the wiser.

- Medical care for a pet can be a real financial drain. The SPCA or local Humane Society has very good low-cost vet care.

- Nutro offers a frequent-buyer program, and Purina will send you coupons for two free cans of food. Just log on to their websites for information.

- Resist buying too many products for Spot. Skip the special pads when you're house-training. Newspaper works just as well. And a dog or cat needs only a few toys; if you rotate them, he won't get bored.

MONEY PIT #4: PAYING LATE FEES

Each time you miss a credit card company's payment deadline, you risk much more than a one-time late fee. Soon, you may find your low interest rate has shot up to as high as 29.9 percent. But it gets worse. If other credit card companies that you do business with see you've been late with another creditor, they may bump up your rate on their card as well.

- Try to pay off your balance each month and send your payments early. The postal service is under no obligation to get your payment to the bank on time, you are. Check what bills have arrived each week and plan accordingly. Use electronic bill payment—it's faster.

- Review your credit report annually to ensure there's no misinformation on it, such as incorrectly reported late payments. With the passage of the Fair and Accurate Credit Transactions Act, you're allowed one free credit report a year from each of the three major credit bureaus. Log on to annualcreditreport.com.

- When all else fails, call the credit card company. If you've had a good relationship, they may waive the fee or lower the rate.

MONEY PIT #5: OVERPAYING TAXES

Many people unknowingly have too much in taxes withheld from their paychecks, and are overpaying throughout the year. People get so excited when they get a refund in April, but this isn't found money, and it's not a windfall.

- The average refund in 2005 was $2,436. That's an extra $175 a month you could keep for yourself. To determine how much you owe per paycheck, look at last year's tax return for a line that notes your tax liability to the government (the total taxes you owe). Divide this amount by the number of times you get paid each year. If your tax liability reads $5,000, and you're paid 25 times a year, you should be paying $200 in taxes each paycheck. Go to your human resources department and change the number of deductions on your W-2 to keep your hard-earned money.

MONEY PIT #6: NOT UPDATING YOUR PHONE AND CABLE PLANS

In 2001, American households spent an average of $225 a month on their combined phone, cable, Internet and cellular bills. Chances are that since you've signed up with your carrier, it's introduced lower rates, though it might not advertise them to current customers.

- Call the carriers of your present cell phone, long-distance and cable plans (or go online) and ask about current promotions. If you've seen a cheaper plan with a competitor, let your current carrier know you'll make the switch if it can't beat it.

- When possible, consolidate your service, such as cable and Internet, or local, long-distance and cell phone, with one company. You'll often get a discount for doing so.

LOOSE CHANGE

It's easy to think that a dollar here, a dollar there doesn't make a difference. But people are being nickeled-and-dimed to death. Avoid these classic money-wasters:

- Don't take children with you when you shop. They often persuade you to buy unnecessary items.

- Shop for cleaning supplies, beauty items and toiletries once every three months and stick to a detailed list.

- Ask your employer about flexible-spending health benefits. These plans let you pay for OTC medications, prescription drugs and physician co-pays with pre-tax dollars.

- Switch to a bank with a large network of ATM outlets to avoid fees each time you withdraw cash. Or take out more money at one time, then tuck it away until you need it.

- Americans are increasingly ordering in or taking out, and it's setting us back to the tune of more than $2,000 a year. So start cooking a few meals a week. Fast-food restaurants aren't cheap solutions either. An American Dietetic Association study notes that forgoing fast food in favor of home-cooked meals boosts your health as well.

4. How to Avoid the Biggest Financial Mistakes Women Make

For Omaha, Nebraska, mom Linda F., raising four kids was her job. Her husband's job was taking care of the family finances.

"Big mistake," says Linda, now divorced and working full-time to pay off debts incurred while she was married. "I should have been more involved in knowing where our money was going." Instead, she has had to learn money management under dire circumstances.

Financial planners agree that Linda's "money mistake" is one of the more common ones women make. Too many women tend to assume that men just understand financial stuff better than they do, so they turn things over to them. The solution? Taking a course in money management or investing can be a quick path for getting up to speed. So can reading books or attending seminars on money.

Not all money mistakes have straightforward solutions. Still, all financial faux pas are solvable. But first you have to know what they are.

Money Mistake #1: Thinking it's too late to start saving

It doesn't matter if you're 40, 50 or 60. The only time it's too late to start saving is when you're dead.

What to do: If you save now, you'll have money when that emergency car repair or root canal comes up, which means you'll be better equipped to keep debt at bay.

Money Mistake #2: Having a financial goal, but no plan for implementing it

If you want to lose ten pounds, you don't just wish it away, you follow a diet plan. In the same vein, if you want to have a certain amount saved by age 65, you've got to follow a plan to make it happen.

What to do: If creating a plan seems too complicated, get some outside help. Talk to a friend or relative whose financial acumen you respect. Or you can ask your accountant or a financial planner. Log on to fpanet.org/plannersearch, the website for the Financial Planning Association, to find a planner that is specific to your needs.

Money Mistake #3: Thinking you don't make enough to save anything

Unless you're living at poverty level, every one of us has something to save.

What to do: Keep track of your daily expenses for one month to see where the money goes. Then look for a way to spend $3 less each day. Once you have $100 (in a short five weeks, since $3 a day adds up to $21 a week), consider investing in a mutual fund at TIAA-CREF, which allows small, regular investments. At 8 percent interest, in 20 years your $3 a day will grow to approximately $49,477.

MONEY MISTAKE #4: LOANING MONEY TO OR COSIGNING A LOAN FOR A RELATIVE OR A FRIEND

It's not uncommon for a person to borrow from a relative or friend and not be able to pay back the loan.

WHAT TO DO: Loan money only if you're prepared to write it off as a gift. You can draw up rules for repayment, but the bottom line is that most loans to family and friends are never repaid. As for cosigning a loan, remember, it doesn't matter whose name is on top. If your cosigner misses one payment, it will affect your credit rating. Don't cosign unless you can afford to pay off the loan yourself.

MONEY MISTAKE #5: PAYING ONLY THE MINIMUM ON A CREDIT CARD

If you make the $50 minimum payment on a $2,500 credit card bill (at 18 percent interest), it'll take you 34 years to get out of debt and you'll have paid $6,430 in interest, much more than twice your original charge.

WHAT TO DO: After three years of paying the minimum on her credit card bills, Brenda G. realized that most of her payments went to interest, while the principal went down by only $3 to $5 a month. As soon as she began to pay a little more than the minimum balance, the principal started to go down steadily. The lesson: Pay as much as you can and always more than the minimum. And don't charge another thing until that debt is paid off. It's also wise to look into transferring your balance to a credit card with a lower rate.

MONEY MISTAKE #6: PUTTING THE KIDS' COLLEGE FUND BEFORE YOUR RETIREMENT FUND

Good intentions, bad move. There are no student loans for retirement. While you can find many creative ways to fund a college education, no such option exists for retirement, except saving, saving, saving.

What to do: Ask yourself: "Do I want my kids to have to support me when I'm old?" Because that may be the result of not having your financial priorities in the right order. Loans, grants, scholarships, work-study programs, Community College—those are options for getting an education even if you haven't saved four full years of tuition. Start putting money for your retirement away first—and don't feel one ounce of guilt.

Money Mistake #7: Thinking you aren't entitled to negotiate with your creditors

The roof springs a leak and you're hit with a $4,000 bill. Many women assume all bills must be paid in full as soon as they arrive, which can mean putting a big charge on the credit card or wiping out savings.

What to do: After Linda F. got divorced, she found herself facing bills she could not always pay all at once. "I called the orthodontist and asked if I could make smaller payments," she says. The office manager agreed. She also called her utilities provider and asked to switch to a plan where the monthly payments were always the same. She even told them what she could afford as her monthly payment, agreeing to pay the balance— if there was one—at the end of the year. The utilities provider agreed. Businesses and doctors' offices want to get paid. They are generally eager to negotiate rather than fight for money.

Money Mistake #8: Using credit to get into debt

According to cardweb.com, the average credit card balance carried by a typical American household is about $7,000. Many people are living way beyond their means.

What to do: The next time you're tempted to buy something on credit that might be beyond your comfort level, try this experiment. For a few months, set aside what your monthly payment would be. If, for example, you want a new car that would cost $350 a month, take that amount out of your paycheck first, put it in savings and see if you can get along without it. If you find yourself dipping into it out of necessity each month, you've got proof you'll be borrowing beyond your means.

Money Mistake #9: Paying by automatic withdrawal for regular services you no longer use

When you keep paying for a health club you no longer go to or subscribing to a movie-by-mail club long after the excitement has worn off, you're throwing money away.

What to do: For almost two years, 37-year-old Catherine B. paid for a health club membership that she had used a total of five months. "I kept thinking I'd use it more," she says, "but I really didn't." Finally, she canceled her membership, but she still wanted some type of workout option. "I found a month-long yoga class for a flat fee of $150," she says. "I went all month and now I can do the exercises I learned at home—for free."

Money Mistake #10: Not having a debt-reduction plan

It's easy to get overwhelmed when what you owe is more than what you earn. But you make the problem worse by not determining how to get out from under.

What to do: Write down all your debts, ranking them by interest rate, with the highest at the top. Make only the minimum monthly payments on all of your debts on the bottom part of the list, and use any extra cash to pay down those at the top of the list. If your debt is really out of control, do as Brenda G. did. She went to a reputable credit counseling service, which consolidated all her high-interest credit card debt into one lower-interest loan. Then she made monthly payments to the credit counseling service, which for a small fee made payments to her creditors for her. She's recently gone from drowning in bills to seeing herself debt-free a year from now.

Money Mistake #11: Spending money to make yourself feel better

According to a survey conducted by myvesta.org, 17 percent of the respondents use money to improve self-esteem, 16 percent spend money to relieve stress and 40 percent feel a mood shift just before or after spending money.

What to do: Jane L., 47, shopped a lot during the last few years of her rocky marriage just to make herself feel better. Eventually she was so severely in debt, she couldn't afford to keep shopping. "I had to find new ways to relieve stress," she says. She found that taking her dog for a walk made her feel great, and spending time with her 12-year-old son was also wonderful. "I don't have to spend money to perk myself up," she says.

5. The Tag Says $50: What Will it Really Cost You?

—MARY HUNT

If I could get back all the money I've spent in my life on financial mistakes, I'd be a wealthy woman. Believe me, I've made some real doozies. Some had big price tags—that 7,500-gallon, above-ground, inflatable swimming pool, complete with heater and filter, comes to mind. But mostly it was the constant accumulation of one stupid purchase after another, ever expanding into a huge pile of debt.

While it would be easy to wallow in regret, I'd much rather concentrate on the lessons I've learned from those years of impulsive spending. That's what keeps me out of debt and headed in the right direction.

I've devised two simple tools that I keep handy and use nearly every day. I have to because I am so impulsive. These tools aren't complicated. Keep them in the back of your mind and use them to get a handle on everyday spending. That way, you'll think twice each time you pull out the old credit card or your hard-earned cash.

JUST ANNUALIZE IT

We often fail to see small purchases in light of our annual income, and that's a big problem. Let's say you earn $60,000 a year. Not bad! And you enjoy a $4 coffee drink each morning on your way to work. What's the big deal? You work hard, make a decent living and deserve great coffee. It's only $4.

LET ME SHOW YOU THE BIG DEAL

First, you don't really make $60,000. Chop it by one-third because your net income is more like $40,000. Next, let's annualize that daily coffee habit— no calculator required. Four times five (workdays) is easy: Twenty bucks a week. Per month that's $80, right? Now add a zero—$800 for ten months.

So you know for a year it's going to be closer to $900. And the truth is, $900 compared to $40,000 is a lot different from $4 out of $60,000.

What if you also spend $4 a day on sodas, $6 a day on lunch and $40 a week on dinner out with the family? Pretty soon, small expenditures pile up, and before you know it you've sucked off a huge chunk of your annual income on stuff you don't even remember.

What about cable TV, your gym membership, high-speed Internet connection and cell phone? Annualize quickly by simply adding a zero to the monthly rate (that takes you to ten months) plus a little. My quick estimate puts an $85-a-month cable TV bill at over $1,000 a year and a $45-a-month gym membership at $540. At this rate, $40,000 isn't going to last long— and we're not even talking about rent, groceries, transportation and other necessities.

Once you've estimated an annual figure for these ongoing expenditures, ask yourself: "Is this the way I really want to spend [fill in the blank] of my annual income?"

Do you actually want to commit $1,000 of your annual net income to cable TV? Cutting back to basic cable or canceling it altogether might give you the jump start you need to repay your debts or boost your savings. This exercise is not about deprivation. Managing your money is about making choices and understanding that saying yes to one thing may require saying no to another.

POP THIS QUIZ

Want to stop making foolish purchases? Take this test before you get to the checkout or sign any contract.

- **DO I NEED IT?** If the answer is no and you don't have lots of discretionary income, case closed. You've just avoided an unnecessary purchase.

- **CAN I AFFORD IT?** If you have to go into debt to make the purchase, you cannot afford it. Forget it.

- **DO I ALREADY HAVE SOMETHING THAT WILL DO JUST AS WELL?** An honest assessment of the stuff you already have could produce a yes to this question. End of discussion.

- **CAN I WAIT UNTIL I FIND A CHEAPER, MORE REASONABLE SUBSTITUTE?** A false sense of urgency brought on by overwhelming desire—or a sale—can skew otherwise good sense. If the purchase is right for you today, it will still be right a few days from now. The bonus? As you wait, the need often disappears.

- **HAVE I FOUND THE BEST DEAL?** It takes time and effort to comparison shop, and that gives you breathing room. Time is a valuable ingredient when it comes to making wise decisions.

- **WHAT IF I DON'T BUY THIS NOW?** Make a list of what will happen if you don't make the purchase. If it's paying the rent you're questioning, that's simple—the consequence is eviction. But if it's buying another pair of shoes, a faster computer or season tickets to the symphony, the consequences of not making the purchase will be quite different. You may need to give up a bit of lifestyle today to have a lifestyle tomorrow.

- **WHAT IF I DO?** What will be the exact consequences if you go ahead with this transaction? Don't accept "I don't know" as an answer. If you don't know the true costs, you're not ready to decide. My impulsive pool purchase was an expensive mistake. But truth be told, that purchase was relatively mild compared to some things I've considered since then. Thankfully, by stepping back long enough to consider the consequences and take my little quiz, I've saved myself from untold financial disasters.

MARY'S PET PEEVE: *Why are products shrinking?*

Remember when a pound can of coffee meant 16 oz? Or a dozen tortillas promised 12 tacos? Have you checked the fine print on diaper boxes lately? Products are shrinking on the inside while the outside packaging appears the same. It makes me crazy!

A pound of coffee is now 10.5 oz. Four-dozen diapers are really 42. A dozen tortillas? You'll only find eight.

It's a sly way manufacturers boost prices while keeping consumers unaware. So forget package prices. Instead, zero in on the unit pricing (per ounce, per serving) to make more intelligent comparisons.

MARY'S POCKET QUIZ

START HERE

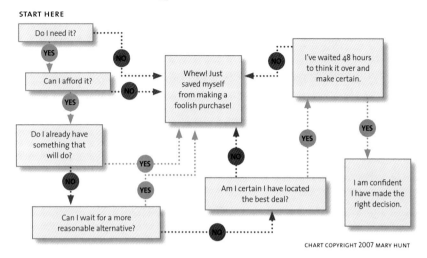

Do I need it?

YES → Can I afford it?

NO → Whew! Just saved myself from making a foolish purchase!

Can I afford it? NO → Whew! Just saved myself from making a foolish purchase!

YES → Do I already have something that will do?

Do I already have something that will do? YES → Whew! Just saved myself from making a foolish purchase!

NO → Can I wait for a more reasonable alternative?

Can I wait for a more reasonable alternative? YES → Whew! Just saved myself from making a foolish purchase!

NO → Am I certain I have located the best deal?

Am I certain I have located the best deal? NO → Can I wait for a more reasonable alternative?

YES → I am confident I have made the right decision.

I am confident I have made the right decision. YES → I've waited 48 hours to think it over and make certain.

I've waited 48 hours to think it over and make certain. NO → Whew! Just saved myself from making a foolish purchase!

CHART COPYRIGHT 2007 MARY HUNT

READER'S TIP

All my loose change goes into my daughter's piggy bank. Each month, it's rolled and put into her savings account. At the end of the year, it's transferred into her mutual fund.

—KRYSTIN C., TAYLOR MILL, KY

---

6. How to Avoid the Latest Scams and Protect Your Wallet from Con Artists

Can you spot someone who's trying to rip you off? Con artists can be amazingly creative and, unfortunately, they keep coming up with new scams. Although the national "do not call" list has cut down on annoying sales calls and telephone scams, crooks are turning to junk mail and the Internet in greater numbers than ever.

Even if you are savvy, your aging parents may not be. And what about your teenagers? Look out for these suspect come-ons.

Congratulations! You've Won!

GIFTING SCHEMES. An acquaintance calls and says that if you give a cash "gift" of between $100 and $2,000 to a particular group (some that already have been prosecuted include the Mentor Network, Dinner Party or Trek Alliance), you'll get $8,000 to $16,000 back when enough new members join. You're also asked to recruit eight new members. These are illegal pyramid schemes, which collapse when not enough new members can be recruited. Most people never get the promised payback. What's really sad is that innocent consumers who are lured into these programs become not only victims, but perpetrators when they sign others up.

AUTOMATIC DEBIT SCAMS. A telemarketer says that you've qualified for a sweepstakes that pays $100,000. "For verification purposes," she needs your bank account number. She then puts this information on a "demand draft," which is processed just like a check and sent to your bank—for any amount the thief desires. You don't know you've been scammed until you get your bank statement. If you give a telemarketer your checking account number and verbal authorization, you've given her permission to access your bank account.

BOGUS SWEEPSTAKES AND PRIZE OFFERS. You get a phone call saying you've been "specially selected" to receive a fabulous vacation, a new car, a luxury condo or a large cash prize. But first you must send a specific amount of money, sometimes as much as $3,500, to cover taxes and "processing fees." In most cases it's just a scam. Being called and told you've won something is a red flag for fraud, especially if you have to pay any processing fees to obtain your prize. Whether you've "won" a dream vacation or a magazine subscription, it should be free, although you may still have to pay taxes on the prize.

Can You Spare a Dime?

PHONY CHARITIES. These scam artists often spring up after disasters such as fires or floods. They invent names that sound similar to real organizations: Cancer Society of America, for instance, rather than the legitimate American Cancer Society. They then request "donations" by appealing to your sympathy. Some offer to send a courier to pick up the money, which is against the law in some states. Ask them who they work for and how much of the money you give to them goes to the charity. Get a name, address and phone number, and request they send information in the mail. Then call the FTC's Consumer Response Center (877-FTC-HELP), and they can advise you. Or check out the FTC's websites at consumer.gov and ftc.gov. Then make your decision.

FICTITIOUS APPEALS. These groups often mix fiction and fact to make people anxious. Some recent scams implore you to "Save Social Security!" or claim that Red China is taking over the Panama Canal and the U.S. is in danger of being invaded. That money will go right into somebody's pocket. Basing claims on deliberately erroneous information is mail fraud. Older people are especially vulnerable to these tactics.

LET US HELP

CREDIT RATING REPAIR. These companies claim that for several hundred dollars, they can reverse a poor credit rating by advising you on how to get a new Social Security number, which is illegal, or challenging items on your credit record, which you can do for free. Credit repair is almost always a fraud. Everybody has a legal right to challenge inaccurate information. You don't have to pay somebody to do this. If you've been denied credit or employment because of bad credit, you may be entitled to a free copy of your credit report. Because each agency records somewhat different information, you may want to get a copy from each: TransUnion, 800-888-4213/transunion.com; Equifax, 800-685-1111/equifax.com; Experian, 888-397-3742/experian.com. Everyone is entitled to a free credit report from all three agencies once every 12 months at annualcreditreport.com. Remember, no one can remove a bad report if it's accurate; only time (seven years in most cases) and good credit habits can do that.

CREDIT CARD LOSS PROTECTION. You're told that, for a fee, you'll be protected from paying the charges if someone steals your card and runs up a debt. These are often fraudulent or just unnecessary. People have rights under federal law that limit their liability to $50 per card in case of lost or stolen cards. They do not need to buy credit card protection.

Debt-consolidation companies. Be careful or you could lose money to a bogus "debt consolidation" company and still be left with the same delinquent bills. The FTC urges consumers to check its website, ftc.gov, to be sure the company hasn't been sued or shut down by the federal government for deceptive practices.

Coming Soon to a Computer Near You!

Internet business opportunities. E-mail is one of the most efficient ways to tempt you with get-rich-quick and work-at-home offers. With gas prices soaring, expect to see gas and oil investment schemes popping up. But the oldies are still around, such as how to make huge profits in the world currency market, buy real estate for nothing down or earn $4,000 in a day. If there's a claim that you'll earn a certain amount of money, that's a big red flag. Legitimate offers of business opportunities and investments do not make these claims. Check each offer thoroughly. Ask the person making the offer who has worked for them and if they have made any money. Then check with your regional Better Business Bureau or the state attorney general's office to see whether there have been any complaints against the company.

Bulk e-mail. Internet companies offer to sell you a list of e-mail addresses or software that automatically sends thousands of solicitations out, so that you can send bulk e-mail, otherwise known as spam. Women who want to work at home are targets for these Internet scams.

But there are risks of violating various state laws if you use a false return address in your header or become involved in an illegal pyramid scheme. Also, your Internet service provider can shut you down if you're sending spam. What's more, you could face a substantial fine or jail time for sending spam.

Diploma mills. You'll be seeing more "Internet universities" as computer con artists look for new ways to bilk the unwary. Before you pay for classes at DotCom U., call the branch of your state government that licenses and accredits schools (check the government listings in your phone book) and ask whether a degree from that particular school will qualify you for work—or a raise—in that field. Even if the school isn't located in your state, it will be subject to some sort of overview by the authorities to make sure it meets the required standards. If you skip this step, you may end up with some credential that's completely worthless.

KEEPING SENIORS SAFE

Dorothy B. knew her mother, Mabel, was having financial problems, but she was shocked when she discovered how deeply in debt she was. "In eight months my mother lost between $50,000 and $75,000 to telemarketers," Dorothy says. "She was vulnerable to scams because they promised her that if she sent a check, she would win money." Mabel called some telemarketers by their first names, Dorothy says. "She thought they were her friends." In the end, she declared her mother's estate bankrupt and sold an inherited piece of land at a $40,000 loss to pay off Mabel's debts.

Be calm, not judgmental, when talking to a parent about her finances. Say something like, "Mom, could I help you balance your checkbook?" or "Could I sit here while you go through the mail?" If she's very private, it may help to have someone from the sheriff's office or police department talk to her. Also:

- Urge your senior to sign up for the national "do not call" registry at 888-382-1222 or online at donotcall.gov.

- Consider having her switch to a cell phone exclusively, and share the number only with family members. Federal law prohibits telemarketing calls to cell phones when an automatic telephone dialing system is used.

- For the latest on consumer scams, visit the Federal Trade Commission's websites at ftc.gov and consumer.gov. Ask for the series of articles called A/PACT, Aging Parents and Adult Children Together, which offers advice on protecting seniors. Call 877-FTC-HELP or write Consumer Response Center, Federal Trade Commission, Washington, DC 20580.

STATISTICS SAY
- In 2002, federal law-enforcement agencies received 102,500 complaints about Internet scams. *Source: The FTC*
- In 2004, 26 percent of Internet fraud victims were between ages 30 and 39. *Source: The National Fraud Information Center*

Ⓑ *Hidden Cash*

1. Small Ways to Save Big

Getting a bargain is often a simple matter of knowing where to look for one. Sometimes a good deal is just waiting to be plucked from a pile of junk mail or a new website. We've asked consumer advocates and industry insiders across the country for their favorite tips on saving money on everything from TV repairs to household goods to airline fares.

Save Around The House

- **Buy new at deep discounts.** Find a local flea market that sells discounted new items. Household supplies and packaged goods may be sold cheaply due to overstocks, dented boxes or misprinted labels. At a recent market in southern New Jersey, for instance, you could buy a box of cereal for $1 (regularly about $3), face cream for $10 (regularly $32), and a jug of laundry detergent for $2 (regularly $4). Other common sale items at these "new item" flea markets include school supplies, snack foods, extension cords, perfumes, tools and gift wrap. Insider tip: Check expiration dates on all products.

- **Hire a fledgling Mr. Fix-it.** Is your television, VCR or other appliance broken? Call your local vocational or tech school about fix-it services. Many offer to repair or refurbish such items at very low cost in exchange for projects that give students hands-on experience. Some might also offer automotive repair and maintenance. Insider tip: just don't expect overnight service.

- **Exercise on the cheap.** Check local pawnshops for great deals on home-exercise equipment. Best bets include cross-country ski machines, stationary bikes and treadmills. Scan newspaper classified ads as well.

- **Go to the source.** Check the classified advertising pages in the back of specialty magazines for discounted niche items you can buy direct. For carpeting and flooring bargains, for instance, check magazines such as *The Family Handyman* and *Country Living*. For low-cost car parts and tires, check *Car and Driver* and *Road & Track*.

- **SHUT OUT WASTED ENERGY.** Keep closet doors closed. Heating or cooling them wastes energy.

- **CONSERVE UTILITY DOLLARS.** If you're 65 or older or have limited income (the guidelines vary), inquire about discounts on your water, gas and other utility bills. Many municipalities offer as much as 25 percent off to such customers as long as they live at the property being serviced and are responsible for paying their own bills.

WHEN OLD IS NEW

- **NAIL A TOOL TRADE-IN.** Replace broken hand tools for free. Many major toolmakers—including Husky (by Home Depot) and Snap-on—offer lifetime guarantees on their hand tools. (Craftsman hand tools by Sears are guaranteed forever.) Regardless of where you find the tool (a garage sale, curbside), these companies will either repair the item or replace it with a new one—no questions asked. Insider tip: Home Depot now offers to replace any Craftsman hand tool with a brand-new Husky, a generous way to get customers to give their tools a try.

- **DRESS TO IMPRESS FOR LESS.** Women's formal wear rental shops are opening around the nation, offering designer cocktail dresses, business suits, even bridal gowns for rent—at a fraction of their retail prices. Check your Yellow Pages under "Consignments" or "Formal Wear."

- **SALVAGE THAT SWEATER.** Make shrunken wool sweaters as good as new with this tip from the Woolmark Company: Mix 1 gallon lukewarm water with 2 tablespoons baby shampoo. Soak the sweater for ten minutes. Then, without rinsing out the soap, blot away excess water. Reshape and carefully stretch the sweater to its original size, then dry flat on towels away from direct heat.

- **ADOPT A PRICEY POOCH.** Each year, thousands of people buy pure-bred puppies and later change their minds, relinquishing the animals to volunteer breed-rescue groups. These organizations then try to place the dogs with suitable new owners. Often, the only required fee is a donation to cover veterinary costs such as vaccinations, spaying and neutering.

  To find a pup: Animal shelters can usually refer you to local breed-rescue programs. Contact the American Kennel Club and ask for the list of rescue-referral contacts at the national club sponsoring the breed you prefer. Call the AKC's customer service center at 919-233-9767. Or visit their website (akc.org); remember to type the word "rescue" or "bredclub.htm" into its search program. Another excellent resource is petfinder.com.

- **BUY DISCOUNT VIDEO GAMES BY MAIL.** Video Game Liquidators in North Hollywood, California, offers 50 percent discounts on games that have been discontinued. Systems include Sega, Sony Playstation and others. Call 818-765-0093. For monthly e-mail lists of new stock, check their website (vglq.com).

- **TONE DOWN PRINTER COSTS.** Recycle used laser or ink-jet toner cartridges. Thousands of companies now offer this service, providing refurbished cartridges for about half the price of new ones. Check out *Recharger* magazine's website (rechargermagazine.com) to locate such a company in your area. To ensure you get a high-quality product, choose companies that offer money-back guarantees.

SPEND NOW, SAVE BIG LATER

- **AVOID ROOT CANAL.** Visit the dentist at least twice per year. Preventive maintenance is the best way to keep your dental costs low. A minor problem, such as a small cavity, that isn't addressed early can quickly become one that costs you an arm and a leg.

- **SUIT UP FOR THE LONG RUN.** If your husband wears business suits to work, purchase two pairs of the pants when you buy a new suit. Because men tend to wear out pants more quickly than suit jackets, having an extra pair on hand will eliminate the need to discard a perfectly good jacket that has lost its mate. Insider tip: You may need to special-order the extra pair at some stores.

- **START CHRISTMAS SHOPPING NOW.** Jot down names and budgeted amounts and stow the list in your purse for quick reference. By spreading the cost of holiday shopping over several months, you can easily avoid using credit cards this holiday season.

SAVE MORE, SPEND LESS

- **GET A CHECKUP FOR YOUR APPLIANCES.** Have your furnace or boiler tuned up. Most oil or gas companies offer to test, clean and make adjustments annually for peak efficiency. The cost may range from $50 to $100, and you can expect a tuneup to reduce your heating bill by up to 10 percent, reports the American Council for an Energy-Efficient Economy. Insider tip: If you spend $200 per month on heating during the cold months, a tuneup can save you up to $120 each year.

- **TEACH THE VALUE OF A DOLLAR.** Offer your kids a weekly allowance to cover lunches, scouting dues and other weekly necessities as well as a little extra for spending money. Explain that they can use the spending money as they wish. If they want something special, they can use their allowance to save for it. Insider tip: This is a great way to eliminate the "gimmes" when shopping with kids. It also teaches them valuable lessons about budgeting and making spending choices.

TAP INTO TRAVEL BARGAINS

For big savings on airfare, hotels and other travel expenses, many websites now offer substantial savings.

- For budget-minded travelers willing to be a little flexible, Priceline airlines ticketing service (priceline.com) allows you to get a cheap flight, hotel or car rental. You punch in where you want to depart from and travel to, on what dates, and how much you're willing to pay. The service then runs your offer by all major airlines and within 24 hours notifies you of any takers. If Priceline finds a flight for you at the price you've bid, you're obligated to take it, and you only get one chance to bid on a particular flight. The downside: You don't get to pick which airline or flight times— only the days.

- To access to get insider information about vacation spots, airfare sales, or to compare flights and prices try smartertravel.com or travelocity.com.

- Other good sites are cheaptickets.com or kayak.com

2. Hide-and-Seek Savings: Find Hidden Cash in Common Places

Discover the world of discount shopping. With the $120 you would plunk down for a blouse at a department store, you can end up buying two blouses, a pair of jeans and a pair of very cool sunglasses at an outlet!

Find hidden savings everywhere: Whether it's a coupon tucked away on page C32 of the newspaper, a special offer from a membership group or a promotional code lurking on some obscure website. Look in these everyday hiding places for simple ways to save big.

Hiding Place: Your local government

Find It: It took only a phone call and an application for Theresa A. to receive more than $14,000 in grants to make repairs on her home. Many local governments at the municipal and county levels offer a wide range of discounts and services to their residents. People seldom think of these as a place to go for free or low-cost services.

Some areas offer incentives in the form of grants, low-interest loans or tax credits to rehab your home. Theresa's eligibility was based on her household income. "As long as I had been living in the house for seven years, the repairs were free to me," she says.

Find More: The wide array of services and benefits your local government offers may include free health care and immunization services, subsidized child care, free or discounted access to golf courses, swimming pools and other sports facilities, discounts to local attractions, even free classes and events. Check the government's website, sign up for program newsletters, or contact the county or municipal clerk to request information about benefits for area residents. Ask for specific departments related to your needs (health, housing, recreation), and contact them directly.

Hiding Place: Your neighborhood

Find It: Team up with friends and neighbors who need the same services you do and negotiate deep discounts.

Many service providers will reduce their prices if you bring them several jobs that can be done at roughly the same time. Piggybacking jobs is more profitable for the service provider, who is then more willing to negotiate on price.

Find More: Whether you're taking turns babysitting or organizing a book exchange, trading with friends, neighbors or even coworkers can be a great way to save. You can also save big—up to 30 percent—by teaming up with a few neighbors to buy groceries in bulk and divvying up your purchases.

Hiding Place: Your supermarket

Find It: Don't scour your local supermarket circular. For the best savings, plan your meals around what's on the front and back pages. Those are loss leaders, the really deep prices that they use to get people in the store. If you make those two pages, which are often meat and produce, the base of what you're going to eat all week, you'll save about 30 percent.

Although coupons can be great, they may not always offer the best savings. Because they're often issued for pricey brand names and convenience foods, you may be better off buying store brands or whatever's on sale.

Find More: If you take grocery store prices at face value, you may be missing out on savings. You can wheel and deal in the grocery store with the department managers. Ask the produce manager for a discount on the slightly bruised bananas. Tell the deli guy you'll take the ends of the salami if he slices the price. Ask the dairy manager for half-price on the yogurt that's near its sell-by date.

Hiding Place: Your pharmacy

Find It: You might think assistance programs are just for older or low-income patients, but that's not always the case. Those who have chronic illnesses or require very expensive medication may qualify regardless of their finances. Go to the drug company's website for more information.

Find More: Shopping around for your prescriptions is another way to reap significant savings. Different pharmacies often have different prices on various drugs. Making a few phone calls before you fill your prescription can save you money.

Hiding Place: Your gas station

Find It: Many gas stations engage in zone pricing, increasing prices near highways or other major traffic arteries. Stray off the beaten path, and gas may be as much as 20 percent cheaper. Using a major oil company's gas card could get you a rebate or discount.

Find More: Keeping your car in good condition can also save you money. By keeping your tires properly inflated, you can get up to 15 percent more gas mileage. Clogged air filters and other maintenance problems can also decrease a car's fuel economy.

Hiding Place: Your closet

Find It: The next time you're heading out to Banana Republic, stop by your computer first. By typing the name of your favorite store and the word "coupon" or "discount" in a search engine, you can often find special offers on the items you're planning to buy. Nancy D., who lives in Ludlow, Massachusetts, scours the Web for coupon codes before she shops online. "I'll also forward them to family and friends when I think they can use them." Sites such as jumpondeals.com have codes that offer additional discounts.

Find More: Remember that January and July are buying seasons for many stores, and a time when old merchandise needs to be cleared out to make room for new. Look for the store's private label. Many stores will discount their own brands as much as 70 percent, even going below cost, during end-of-season sales.

Hiding Place: Your vacation

Find It: Find savings by choosing lodging on the outskirts of tourist attractions. Hotels a town or two away are often much less expensive than those close to major attractions. So if you're heading to Washington, DC, you might look for hotels in nearby towns in Virginia or Maryland.

And if the area has a good mass transit system, you may not need to rent a car. You can get into the swing of things within 10 or 15 minutes, but you're not paying the premium prices of hotels in the hot spot.

FIND MORE: Membership organizations, credit card companies, your employer and even the products you buy may entitle you to discounts on hotels, rental cars or airfares. Iona College alumni, for example, get 20 percent off lodging costs at participating Choice Hotels, including Comfort Inn and Clarion Hotels.

Shop by the Calendar

January Holiday decorations, appliances, furniture. White sales offer significant discounts on linens and towels.

February Air conditioners, electronics, computers, exercise equipment, mattresses, used cars. Many catalog companies have closeouts this month.

March Winter clothes, camping and gardening equipment, laundry appliances.

April Spring clothing.

May Gardening supplies, luggage, mattresses, late spring clothes, jewelry, outdoor furniture, televisions.

June Electronics, summer sporting goods, mattresses.

July Furniture, bicycles, mattresses, refrigerators, tires, air conditioners, electronics.

August Back-to-school items, furniture.

September Cookware, dishes, fans, pool and patio supplies, recreation items, tires. This is a great time to save on new cars from the current model year.

October Early sales on fall and winter clothing, fishing gear, school supplies, women's coats, appliances, new cars after the introduction of next year's model.

November Shoes, boys' clothing, blankets.

December Candles. Beware of shopping around Christmastime, when prices may be inflated. If possible, wait for post-holiday sales, when prices are cut across many sectors, and reap the savings.

Ⓒ *Painless Saving*

1. Cut Your Bills By 10 Percent or More

—MARY HUNT

Is your money a little tight? The secret to getting the cash coming in to exceed the cash going out is to reduce your spending. It's as simple—and as tough—as that.

But once you understand that cutting expenses is really like giving yourself a tax-free raise, the job gets much easier. The challenge is to find realistic yet painless ways to trim spending without taking all the fun out of your life.

GO ON A CASH DIET

It's best to spend only cash in order to curb mindless spending. Surveys indicate that cash customers are more mindful of what they're doing, and therefore spend 17 to 23 percent less than those who pay with plastic.

Also, limit ATM trips to once a week. Develop an envelope system for areas that can get out of control, such as office lunches and entertainment. Take your ATM cash and distribute it among your marked envelopes. When you go to lunch or a movie, take the money from the corresponding envelope. When the money is gone, that means no more spending until the next fill-up.

$$ SAVER A $100 traveler's check stashed in your wallet will give you an uncanny sense of security and willingness to leave the plastic and checkbook at home.

SLASH THE COST OF HOT WATER

Twenty percent of your utility bills may be attributed to the water heater, which does nothing but keep about 40 gallons of water very hot, day in and day out. Keep the water temperature on low or 120°F (the highest temperature recommended for a household with children or the elderly, and the lowest temperature recommended for washing clothes), or to a temperature that is comfortable for your needs. Check the instructions for exactly how to do so.

For every 10°F you lower the temperature, you will save about 10 percent of your water-heating costs—a considerable savings over the course of a year. Save even more by buying a $35 electric water-heater timer, available at most home improvement centers. The timer—which you can install in less than an hour—lets you set specific on and off times that suit your lifestyle, so the water is hot when you need it.

STOP SHOPPING

Unless you have a specific need for something in particular and the money to pay for it, don't wander aimlessly through the mall or surf the Internet to see what looks good. Instead, plan purchases, then find the best value for what you need. Remember, you rarely discover a true need while in a store.

$$ SAVER As you identify a need, write it on your "To Buy" list for your next planned purchasing trip.

INCREASE GAS MILEAGE

The average American car travels 13,000 miles a year and gets 25 miles to a gallon of gasoline. That works out to about $675 per car annually. Adopt new driving habits and you can easily lop off 10 percent, or $67, from that bill:

- Empty your car trunk of everything but emergency equipment. Weight is the enemy of gas mileage.

- Opt for radial tires. They last longer and save fuel.

- Keep your tires inflated. Driving a car on semi-flat tires uses more gas, so check your tires whenever you fill up on gas.

- Do not use high-octane gasoline unless the owner's manual specifies it. Mileage efficiency does not increase with more expensive gasoline. Your car will run fine on the cheaper stuff.

CANCEL LONG-DISTANCE SERVICE

Have you scrutinized your long-distance telephone bill lately? Even a reasonable calling plan can become unreasonably expensive when you factor in that list of mysterious fees and charges. Switch from a calling plan to a high-quality, reliable prepaid telephone card issued by a big-name service provider such as AT&T or MCI. You can get them for as little as 8.5¢ per minute (all fees included) at warehouse discount clubs.

$$ SAVER A prepaid phone card is the equivalent of spending cash, so you'll become more judicious with your calling habits.

HIT THE MOVIES EARLY

Instead of the traditional dinner-and-a-movie, go to the movie during matinee hours, then dinner. Matinee prices may be up to 50 percent off the regular adult admission price, even on weekends; check around.

While matinee tickets are a bargain, the concession counter is not. Save your appetite for after the film.

REPAIR IT YOURSELF

When an appliance goes on the fritz, the service call alone can turn into a major expenditure. Here's a secret few people know: Many home-appliance manufacturers offer over-the-phone repair instructions. A technician will analyze the problem, walk you through a few steps, then give you a test to conduct—all for no cost. If a faulty part is the culprit, you can order it.

- General Electric, Monogram®, RCA, Hotpoint major appliances: 800-626-2000
- Whirlpool, Roper, Estate, Holiday major appliances: 800-253-1301
- KitchenAid appliances: 800-422-1230
- Maytag: 800-688-9900
- Amana appliances: 800-843-0304
- Repairclinic.com

Keep a copy of these numbers handy in your phone book, on your bulletin board or in your warranty file folder.

BUY PRESCRIPTION DRUGS BY MAIL

These perfectly legal and highly reputable pharmacies often charge less than local druggists. Depending on the medication, you may be able to save up to 40 to 60 percent of the retail price.

Mail-service pharmacies cannot dispense prescriptions quickly in an emergency, but they are perfect for people who take medication for long-term conditions such as high blood pressure or heart disease. Buying in larger quantities could reduce the cost, so discuss the possibility with your physician.

- AARP Pharmacy Service (AARP membership not required): 800-456-2277
- Drugplace.com: 877-599-8050
- Smartchoicedrugstore.com
- Drugstore.com

$$ SAVER These companies will give quotes by phone, as will your local pharmacy. That makes shopping around a whole lot easier.

SHOP THE SALES, EAT THE SALES

Make it a rule to buy and eat what's on sale. That's the best way to consistently lower grocery bills. Instead of sitting down with your recipe box and developing your menu plan for the week, start with the weekly ads from the store where you shop. If chicken, ground beef and red snapper are on sale, build your dinner menus accordingly. Likewise for breakfasts and lunches. Following this one tip could slash your yearly food bill by at least 25 percent.

MORE SUPER SAVERS

- Switch from commercial window cleaner (18¢ an ounce) to club soda (2¢ an ounce). It works amazingly well.

- Add an extra can of water when you mix concentrated fruit juice. You'll achieve an immediate 25 percent savings on the cost of juice, and the difference in taste is nearly undetectable.

- All alkaline batteries (name-brand, store-brand and generic) perform equally well in most cases. Always opt for the cheapest.

- Add ½ cup baking soda (very inexpensive) to the wash cycle to reduce your liquid laundry detergent.

- If not stained, wool items may be professionally cleaned only once a year.

Be sure to hang them between wearings and air them out occasionally to allow the natural fibers to breathe. Consider hand-washing. Many natural fibers actually last longer when washed this way.

2. Painless Ways to Save $50 or More

Money may not grow on trees, but we can help it grow in your wallet. We asked people how to make saving $50 or more a no-brainer.

- Jennifer L. doesn't spend any $5 bill that comes into her possession. "My husband laughed at me, but I did this for five months leading up to a vacation and saved $485," says Jennifer, who lives in Tannersville, Pennsylvania. "And I didn't have to let go of any favorite luxuries like manicures, pedicures or Starbucks."

- Do without just one luxury for a month. It's more palatable. Mary C. of Hoboken, New Jersey, gave up taxis, eating out, clothes shopping and more—but only one at a time, and each for only one month.

- Lydie T. has found a way to make credit card companies pay her. "I pay for every purchase (groceries, books, gifts) with a Visa card that gives me one rewards point for every dollar I spend," says Lydie, who lives in Alameda, California. "I pay the balance in full at the end of the month, so I don't pay any interest. Last summer, I saved $1,000 by using the points to buy my husband's ticket to France to see our family."

- Instead of searching her purse for the exact change, Lori G. makes sure she receives change. "Every few days, I put my change in a container. I average $10 a week. It's so fast and easy, and adds up to $50 in no time."

- Eleanor C. does comparison shopping on the spot. "When I'm in a store, I use my BlackBerry's web connection to check if what I want is available for less from an online retailer. Sometimes my local store will match the best online price," says Eleanor, who lives in San Francisco. "Standing in line at Staples to pay for a camera, I checked prices at become.com. Staples was charging $449, but it was available online for $368. I saved more than $80!"

- Energy efficiency helped Kristen and Jamie S. save $60 in just two months. "We unplugged our second computer, microwave, radio, shredder, spare phone, toaster oven, second TV and numerous other appliances that we don't use daily. We plug them in when we need them," says Kristen, who lives in Grand Junction, Colorado.

- Monica T. and her husband, who live in Montclair, New Jersey, ditched their cable premium movie channels. Instead, they wait until the entire season of a show is on DVD and rent it. Savings: $50 in the first three months, $227 in a year (or $211 after renting the DVDs).

- Jane C. downgraded her landline phone account to bare-bones DSL service, combined her family's cell phones through the same company and chose a plan that lets them talk to each other for free. "This has cut nearly $80 a month off our bills."

- Michele H. of Madison, Wisconsin, shops off-season and buys in bulk. "Last year children's winter coats were on sale at JCPenney for $12 (originally $65). I bought one for each of my kids to use this year—and two coats a size larger for next year." Her savings? More than $200.

- Emily and Ivan S. of Hyde Park, New York, opt for cloth diapers over disposables and save nearly $1,800 a year.

- At a financial seminar Elaine W. attended, more than half the participants said they found mistakes in their monthly credit card bills. She's been diligently checking hers for errors ever since. "I've found a $35 dinner that was charged at $135," says Elaine, of Woodland Hills, California. "I have returned items that were never credited. This month, I found a charge for an appointment I'd cancelled two weeks earlier. They forgot to cancel the charge on my credit card."

- Angie A. frequently calls her service providers to make sure she's getting the best deal. "Many will match new-customer offers if you have the ad and ask for that rate. I have lowered my satellite TV, high-speed Internet and cell phone bills, usually by $15 to $20 a month, per provider. That's $50 to $60," says Angie, from Grand Junction, Colorado.

- Split costs with friends. Save $90 a month by going in with a like-minded foodie on a community farm share. Each get a box of fresh vegetables every other week. If your lawn mower and your neighbor's are both on their last legs, split the cost of a new mower ($200 plus) and share it.

- Some cell phone companies let you change your services without charge. If you're traveling a lot one month, you can switch to a plan that includes more minutes, free nationwide calling and no roaming charges. When you're back home, revert to your less-expensive local plan. Also change your Netflix rental options. This lets you order more movies during the summer when the kids are home from school. Then, scale back to just one or two a month when our lives are busier—this can save $50 a year during the cheaper months.

- "On payday, I withdraw a certain amount from the ATM, then use that cash over the next two weeks, whether at the gas pump or a dinner out. Anything that's left—usually $400 every two weeks—goes into savings," says Elaine K. of Kansas City, Missouri.

- A year ago, Judy G. of Eau Claire, Wisconsin, started taking advantage of her employer's offer of a free bus pass. The administrative worker at the University of Wisconsin estimates that leaving her car at home has saved her $40 to $60 a month in gas alone. It also inspired her to walk more and stay healthy.

- Diana R. switched to free computer-to-computer calling with Skype to cut high long-distance costs. "With in-laws in India, our long-distance bill was pretty high," says Diana, who lives in San Francisco. "We save about $50 a month now."

- Jeanne H. of Baton Rouge, Louisiana, has an unofficial hand-me-down network with several friends who have kids. They spread the word about needs and sizes, and everything from school uniforms to prom dresses magically appears. "My child's uniform jumpers are $35, so getting two that someone no longer needs saves me $70," she says. "The savings on clothing for my daughter will easily total $200 to $300 in a year."

- Just chatting about your plans can really pay off. Val wanted a cheap printer for her family's second computer. A friend gave her one she'd been planning to donate and saved her $75 to $100.

- Browse the "free" listings on craigslist.com or the Freecycle Yahoo Group, or look for local bargains in your area. You can find everything from exercise equipment to TVs.

- A few months ago Rita W. of New York City, realized that she was paying close to $50 a month (which was automatically billed to her credit card account) for three online memberships, even though she only used one of them regularly. That was an easy call. She canceled two and just kept the one she checks every day.

- Use those hefty coupon books that are sold for school fundraisers and save on purchases from drive-through restaurants to bowling. The monthly $5-off coupon for the grocery store can save you $60 a year alone. You can also get e-mail coupons from stores you frequent, like Barnes & Noble. Keep them handy so you don't forget to take advantage of them.

- "I always shop with coupons—for groceries, dry cleaning, haircuts, toiletries, you name it," says Dorothy B. of West Seneca, New York. "At the end of each shopping trip, I deposit my total savings for the day in the bank. It makes coupon-clipping so obviously worthwhile."

- Donna L. and her sister always use priceline.com when they go on vacation. They've stayed in four- and five-star hotels for as little as $60 instead of $150-plus a night.

If you're inspired to try to save more than $50, have a look at these techniques.

- Even when her family was "dirt poor," Jonni M. of Colorado Springs, Colorado had an automatic paycheck deduction for savings. "A mere $5 adds up to $260 per year," she says. Each year the amount increases steadily. "We never see it, so we never miss it," she points out.

- Making saving a social activity works for Elinor and Murray Y. of Bloomfield Hills, Michigan. "We joined an investment club as newlyweds over forty years ago. We're in our third club and have gone from investing $10 to $60 per month." Murray figures that a good portion of their net worth can be traced to this succession of clubs.

- To increase her savings, Lorraine M. of Decatur, Georgia, asks herself a series of questions before each purchase: "Do I already have one (or more) of the item?" "Is it worth all the time I'll have to spend at work to pay for it?" "Will this really bring me fulfillment?" "Discovering that I had enough, if not too much, of most items (clothing, shoes, books, dishes, lipsticks—you name it!) helped boost my savings considerably," she says.

- Sean F. of Norwood, Massachusetts, has the salary for his 40-hour workweek direct-deposited into his checking account. He puts the rest of his paycheck—which often includes overtime pay—into savings. With his "overtime" savings, he was recently able to purchase an engagement ring for his fiancée.

- "We add $150 to our savings every month and don't even feel it," says Kathy M. of Everett, Washington. The family's medical plan requires them to pay for their prescription drugs, then file for a reimbursement. Kathy writes a check for the insulin prescriptions her husband, Don, regularly needs, then deposits every reimbursement check into their savings account.

- A special "shirt account" might just provide for Bryan L.'s retirement some day. The Cambridge, Massachusetts, resident figured out that over the next 40 years he could save $12,000 by laundering his own shirts. Each month, he invests the $20 he saves in a growth mutual fund, where he's banking on finding $70,000 at retirement.

- When the days of the month fall so that they receive five paychecks instead of the budgeted four, Barbara and Gene O. see the "extra" checks as an opportunity for long- and short-term savings. The plan has helped them buy a new car and build their retirement fund.

- Her budget used to include monthly car payments, so Jennifer K. of Norwood, Massachusetts, found it no problem to continue making those payments (now to her 401(k) account) after her car loan was paid off. Similarly, when her car insurance fees dropped, Jennifer used the "found" money to increase her credit card payment.

- When Jean D., a senior account supervisor for a public-relations firm in Los Angeles, gets a raise, she continues to write her old paycheck amount as the deposit in her checking account. Then she records the raise amount in a slush fund on another page. When the time comes to balance her checkbook, she simply adds the two pages together. And every six months she deposits the slush-fund cash in an IRA or another savings account. At first she accumulated about $150 a month this way. But by now, she is able to sock away $300 to $400 each month.

- If you think that $50 a month is so insignificant why even try, think about this: Even stashing the cash in an account with no interest whatsoever, after one year you will have $600 in the bank, after five years $3,000. In an interest-bearing account or money-market fund these savings will likely be compounded by at anywhere from 5 to 10 percent a year.

3. Painless Strategies for Saving Thousands

How would you like to find a few thousand dollars? Now you can—in your own pocket. The best part? You don't have to become a penny pincher.

SAVE AT HOME

- **GET A BREAK ON PRESCRIPTION DRUGS.** You may be able to save big, depending on your prescription costs. People pay enormous sums for maintenance prescriptions. Most people stop at the most convenient pharmacy. But if you check several pharmacies, the Internet and mail-order pharmacies, you may find a price break.

- **INVEST IN A PROGRAMMABLE THERMOSTAT.** Several studies show that the average household can save $250 a year with this little piece of technology. The thermostat regulates temperatures when you're away or sleeping. This adds up to a nice bonus at year's end.

- **TAKE STOCK OF WHAT YOU'VE GOT.** According to an article in the *Wall Street Journal*, only 25 percent of mall shoppers were actually looking for a specific item. Before you shop, inventory dresses, slacks, blouses, sweaters, T-shirts, underwear, shoes, party clothes, suits, belts, scarves and so on. Do the same for your kids. That way, the next time you hit the mall, you'll be less inclined to buy something new on impulse. You'll know for a fact that you have it at home. Depending on your shopping habits, you could save hundreds, even thousands each year.

- **TAKE CHARGE BEFORE TROUBLE STRIKES.** Dusting refrigerator coils saves energy and could save your appliance. Regular oil changes extend the life of your car. If you ignore a headache, it will probably go away. If you ignore a funny noise in your engine, you could throw a rod, burn out a water pump or otherwise incur major—and costly—damage.

Think Ahead and Save

- **Hold off on that high-tech gizmo.** You don't have to be the first person on the block with that new DVD player or digital camera. Technology gets better and cheaper as time goes on. Be patient, things will simmer down.

- **Change your oil and save several cars.** Over a lifetime of driving—for most of us, about 60 years—each of your cars may last ten years, or a total of six cars. But if you consider pampering your ride by changing the oil every 3,000 miles, you might only have to buy a car every 15 years, or four cars. This means a net savings of "two cars"—and thousands of dollars in your pocket!

- **Always get bids before you buy.** When you're ready to make a large purchase, say a car, call four or five dealers and make them compete for your business. Let them know that you're talking to other people and that you'd like their bids.

Eat Well, Pay Less

- **Say no to drinks and dessert.** The two biggest moneymakers for restaurants are desserts and alcohol. If you skip these two indulgences (except on special occasions), you can save at least $20 a meal (per couple) each week. Times 52 a year, you could fund half your IRA.

- **Order from the appetizer menu.** You can have a nice meal without overeating (another plus) if you order soup and salad instead of a main course. The savings? About $20 per couple. If you do this once or twice a month, and pass on drinks and dessert at other times, the savings can really add up. Invest that money in a mutual fund or the stock market. You'll save thousands—and lose some weight!

- **Bring your lunch—sometimes.** There are so many little things that take a chunk out of your wallet, and eating out every day is one of them. If you spend $4 on a sandwich, 75¢ on a soda and $2 on a cup of gourmet coffee, you're spending almost $7 a day, or $35 a week, $140 a month and nearly

$1,700 a year. Even if you bring lunch twice a week, the savings add up to almost $700 a year. You might feel funny at first packing a lunch, but you won't feel bad when you're on a beach in Hawaii.

- **KNOW YOUR STORES.** Find out where your favorite stores display markdowns, closeouts and other specials. Do they have double coupon days or honor other stores' coupons? Policies for money back on scanner errors? Freshness guarantees?

- **WAIT FOR A PRICE BREAK.** When the items your family uses frequently—such as peanut butter, cereal and dishwashing liquid—are marked down, buy enough to last until the next sale, which is usually about three months later. With a family of four, you can save up to 30 percent, or $2,160 a year. Combine it with coupon clipping, and you can up the savings to 40 or 50 percent, or more than $3,600 a year. If you can leave your kids, or "little salespeople," at home, you'll spend less.

- **SHOP AHEAD, WAY AHEAD.** Stocking up on nonperishable clearance-priced seasonal merchandise, like holiday cards or canned pumpkin, can be a great way to buy gifts or necessities for next season. It's also a very inexpensive way to create fun gift packs for showers, weddings and birthdays. Work with a list. Go to stores armed with a list of items you need now or in the near future. This helps you avoid impulse buying and allows you to focus on finding the best deals. If you do shop ahead, keep a list at home of what you bought and where you stored it.

4. Stash More Cash: Simple Money-Savers that Really Work

Are you still waiting for that winning lottery ticket? The pot of gold at the end of the rainbow? Well, to tide you over until you strike it rich, we've collected money-saving tips from smart consumers across the country. These ideas are so simple, getting started will be a cinch. The payoff? More money in your wallet.

NEVER PAY FULL PRICE

- **GET A BETTER DEAL ON ELECTRONICS.** When Betsy L. of Bartow, Florida, wants to buy a camera, computer components or other expensive electronics, she buys factory refurbished items at a substantial discount.

"Refurbished" items were returned by a consumer or the box was opened by a retailer and could no longer be sold as new. They're then sent back to the manufacturer, inspected for quality and factory specifications and sold at a much lower price, usually with a warranty. For more info, visit tigerdirect.com.

- **TAKE ADVANTAGE OF REWARD PROGRAMS.** Denise K. of Tallassee, Alabama, does most of her on-line shopping through mypoints.com, a site that lets members earn vacations and frequent-flier miles, as well as rewards from merchants such as Blockbuster, Barnes & Noble and Bloomingdale's. Membership is free, and you can earn points by shopping, filling out surveys and visiting websites. "I use these points for purchases that are more of a luxury than a need," says Denise.

- **SAVE MONEY FOR COLLEGE EVERY TIME YOU SHOP.** Upromise is a free service that helps families save for college by offering them money back on everyday purchases and groceries.

   Companies such as AT&T, Toys "R" Us, Coca-Cola, Staples and McDonald's contribute up to 10 percent of the value of purchases. Each time you use a loyalty or credit card at a participating store or restaurant, deposits are automatically put into your child's college fund. You can also save for your own college education. Family and friends can have their savings rolled into your account, too. The savings are tracked online, so you can see how much you've earned. For more information or to join, visit upromise.com.

- **HAVE FUN AT A DISCOUNT.** Linda L., who lives in New York City, took advantage of the free Playbill Club membership offered at playbill.com and now buys Broadway and off-Broadway show tickets for 10 to 50 percent off.

   In addition, she can get discounts from local hotels and restaurants. You can also find great deals on everything from books to movies to travel at amazing-bargains.com. AAA (ouraaa.com) offers members discounted tickets to many attractions and movie theaters nationwide.

Save Money Every Day

- **Never spend $1 bills.** Jenn and Joe S. of Canton, Massachusetts, made a pact to never spend singles. If they need to buy something, they purchase the item with a $5, $10 or $20 bill. At the end of each day, every dollar bill they've acquired goes into a savings jar.

- **Keep the change.** For every purchase, pay only with paper money and put the change in a jar. "A five-gallon container filled with coins (even if three-quarters are pennies) yields almost $863," says Lisa I. of San Diego & Imperial Counties. Keep the jar in the back of your closet so you're not tempted to spend it before it's full.

- **Create a cushion in your checking account.** Jason and Stacie M. of Leominster, Massachusetts, round up when entering withdrawals in their checkbook and round down on deposits: A check for $25.74 is recorded as $26, and a deposit of $150.65 is recorded as $150. What you save also acts as overdraft protection.

- **Never tap into that interest-bearing account.** Kristen B. began having $50 a month directly deposited into a money market account. Because she never saw that cash, she never missed it. In one year she saved $600. The savings plan worked so well that Kristen, who lives in Los Angeles, has since doubled her monthly deposit.

- **Make a second register in your checkbook.** Whenever you use your credit card, deduct the amount from the total balance in your checkbook. This will keep you from spending more money than you have, unless it's a true emergency. When the credit card bill arrives, you'll have the money in the bank, saving you a lot in interest charges.

- **Keep making those car payments.** Bill B., from New Milford, Connecticut, paid $300 each month toward his car loan. Once the car was paid off, however, he continued to put the money into an account and used it for a down payment on a new house a year later.

- **Carry only $20 in cash at a time.** The less cash you have in your wallet, the less likely you are to pick up a snack or an unplanned purchase.

- **Go directly to the source.** Call manufacturers' toll-free numbers or check their websites to request coupons. You'll be surprised at what companies will give away to get you to try, or buy more of, their brand. And don't limit your choices only to grocery items. Lots of offers are available for cosmetics, restaurants and more.

- **LOOK FOR MORE AT WHOLESALE CLUBS.** Viveca W., a public relations consultant in New York City, needed a new pair of glasses. A pair she liked cost $320 (frames and lenses) at the doctor's office, but she found similar ones at Costco for $149. She also suggests checking out items such as digital cameras, photo developing, greeting cards and books.

- **WATCH YOUR SAVINGS GROW.** For eight years, Lila A. and her husband have been clipping and redeeming coupons during their weekly grocery and drugstore shopping trips. "When we get home, we add up the savings and write it on a calendar," she says. "At the end of the year when we change calendars, we add all the savings for a grand total, which has grown each year. Last year, we saved over $825." The couple rewards themselves with a special dinner or an overnight trip.

PLANNING MAKES PERFECT

- **GET STRATEGIC.** When Debrie W. of Birmingham, Alabama, wants to buy a big-ticket item, she finds out how much it costs, adds in the taxes and sets a goal date. "I divide the item's cost by the number of paychecks I'll get between now and my goal date, then I put aside that amount monthly." But only set realistic goals. Don't set a three-month goal when it will take six months to get the item. It will leave you stressed and anxious.

- **RESEARCH WHAT YOU WANT.** Comparing prices around town and on the Internet is the key to making sure you get the absolute best deal possible. Researching keeps you busy thinking about the item you want, so you're less likely to succumb to impulse buys.

5. Ten Questions That Save

All of us make at least a few purchases we later regret: a toy that is soon ignored, a skirt that adds ten pounds or a gadget that fails to meet expectations. Many of these items hide in the back of closets, drawers, attics and basements. Still, you can keep your spending regrets to a minimum—and save hundreds, even thousands of dollars every year—by playing this version of "20 Questions."

Is it a must-have item that I really love?

Sometimes we're just in the mood to buy—because we're on vacation, perhaps, or have simply had a bad day. And if you've driven an hour to visit a special store or outlet, you may feel obliged to make a purchase just so your trip won't be "wasted." Don't buy it unless you love it. It's better to return home with empty hands than an empty wallet.

Is it a perfect fit or match?

Never buy clothes that are too small as an incentive to lose weight. Most of those purchases will never leave the house. If two items must match, buy them at the same time.

Will it be easy to maintain?

You buy the car of your dreams—a flashy red convertible. But it costs so much to insure that you may drop the collision coverage—and fear of high repair bills will make you reluctant to drive it very often.

Cars aren't the only items with high maintenance costs. The same applies to dry-clean only items. A wardrobe limited to machine-washable clothes could be very boring, of course, but you'll get more out of everything you own if you consider what's involved in taking care of it before you buy.

Is it both flattering and comfortable?

Too many of us end up with garments that pinch, bind, scratch or otherwise make us miserable. Why? Because we neglect to perform the "sit-down test" or we believe salespeople who claim that tight shoes or pants will "stretch after a few wearings." Forget it! Don't buy anything that doesn't make you look and feel your best.

Could I find a better buy elsewhere?

If you have no idea what a product should sell for, shop around. You don't have to waste time and gas going from store to store; you can compare prices at home. All it takes is a few catalogs and/or advertising circulars, plus a telephone.

Would I be willing to pay full price—or 30 percent more?

Buying something only because "it's so cheap" is usually a mistake. Would you buy this for cash? There's something about forking over a stack of bills that makes us weigh purchases more carefully. We know our cash is limited, but it's all too easy to overlook the limits—and extra costs—of using credit cards. An item that's not worth the cash is likely to be even less appealing when the bills come in.

How often am I likely to use it?

Most of us can go into debt for one special occasion. These days, almost everything—including wedding dresses—can be rented or purchased for bargain prices at a consignment or thrift shop.

Can I really afford it?

This is a tricky one, for you need to consider more than the size of your bank account. Are you adequately insured, for example? Do you have ample savings for emergencies? Have you put money aside for your children's education and your own retirement? In short, make sure that you can buy the item in question without jeopardizing your future.

What would happen if I postponed this purchase?

When you look back, what do you regret most, spending opportunities you missed or items you bought impulsively? If it's the latter, try to keep one simple truth in mind: Virtually any deal you're offered will still be available the next day—or next week.

Will it fill a hole in my life or merely add to a collection?

There's nothing wrong with being a collector, but many of us amass inadvertent collections because we have a weakness for certain things. To fight this tendency to add to a collection, draw up a non-shopping list to keep in your purse. Search your home—including children's rooms, workshop, linen closet, pantry and freezer—for items that you're oversupplied with.

The Third Degree

Once you've asked yourself all the relevant questions, ask the salesperson a few before you plunk down your money or your credit card.

- **Is this your best price?** Don't negotiate prices only at flea markets and other secondhand outlets, you'll learn that your silence probably cost you hundreds of dollars. Ask for a better price in a shop, you may get a surprising reply: "It's today's best price, but if you can wait until Saturday, all our coats will be reduced 25 percent."

- **Would you put that in writing?** The majority of salespeople are honest, but they don't always have the power to make good on their promises. If that one-year guarantee, free delivery and installation are important to you, insist on having the terms put on paper and signed by a person with the authority to back it up.

- **Is it machine-washable?** You probably expect a wool suit to be "dry-clean only," but what about a child's playsuit or a polyester blouse? Some of those may also require dry cleaning, so it's smart to check the care labels before you make the purchase.

- **Does the price include assembly, delivery, installation?** Don't assume anything: always ask a salesperson.

- **Who pays the shipping costs?** When placing mail orders or buying large items, smart shoppers always clarify who will pay the shipping costs if repairs or replacement are needed. The cost of shipping a TV set or computer back to the factory (which many stores require) can turn "free repairs" into an expensive proposition. Retailers who cover all shipping costs may charge more, but it's usually worth it.

- **Is it guaranteed or warranted?** This is essential for anything that has moving parts or is subject to malfunction. Otherwise, you could spend as much money repairing your new car or computer as you did buying it.

- **Can I return it for a full refund?** Stores have a right to set limits on refunding your money, but it's critical to know all such conditions in advance. When the policy is to grant refunds only on items returned within a week, you certainly don't want to delay trying out your purchase. If goods can only be returned for store credit, be sure it's a credit you can use.

Ⓓ *Money Makeovers*

1. The Extreme Money Makeover

There's nothing like being laid off, getting a call from the bank saying that you've bounced some checks or, in my case, learning that our home was about to be foreclosed, to suggest that an extreme money makeover is in order. Few things feel worse than not being able to pay your bills each month. This is a season in your life that has come and will go. It's not forever. But it is time to face your extreme situation with an equally intense response.

Where do I start?

- **Snap a "before" picture.** Any makeover worth its salt needs a great "before" picture. A personal financial snapshot is called a net worth statement. Since we're talking in extreme terms, imagine selling everything you own, taking the proceeds (probably a lot less than most of us want to believe our stuff is actually worth) and paying off all debt, including the mortgage, then counting what remains. That will show you what net worth really means.

- **Get a plan.** Write down the steps you'll take to reach your goal. Keep in mind that a good plan is specific, reasonable, realistic, finite and has a way to measure results. Give yourself a date by which you intend to complete this makeover. You can handle anything as long as you know it's going to end. Then create stepping stones so you can measure your progress.

- **Freeze spending.** Yes, it's extreme, but then again, so is your makeover. Imposing a spending freeze for the next week or two will give you the jump start you need. Then move into a nonessential-spending freeze for the foreseeable future.

Where's it all going?

- **Track spending.** Starting today, keep a written list of where your money is going. If you spend it, write it down. This is absolutely essential for a successful extreme makeover. That also means you must stop using your

SAVING STRATEGIES   125 credit card to create more debt. This has to stop immediately because of its negative effect on your net worth.

- **START SAVING.** Even five bucks a week put aside consistently is going to change your attitude about living frugally. Money in the bank offers a kind of security that's difficult to describe. And the more you save, the more willing you are to find bigger and better ways to make it happen.

- **WRITE A PAYOFF PLAN.** Is credit card debt killing you? Now that you're no longer adding to that balance, create a written plan for getting rid of it altogether.

WHAT CAN YOU UNLOAD?

- **SELL ASSETS.** Unless you use it regularly or it's a cherished family heirloom, start selling assets to raise cash. Take a look at the online selling tutorial at ebay.com. Or contact a third-party firm like i-soldit.com to sell your stuff for you for a cut of the profit. Use the proceeds to catch up on your bills, to start an emergency savings account or to pay down debt.

- **DOWNSIZE.** If you're in over your head with a mortgage you just can't afford or rent that's beyond reasonable, consider moving to a cheaper place. Or get a roommate. It's not ideal, but it may be exactly what you need to do.

- **GET ANOTHER JOB.** It won't be forever, but for right now working nights and weekends may be the best step you can take toward fixing your finances. If a part-time job nets $400 a month, that's an extra $4,800 a year to apply to your situation.

- **GIVE UP SOME VICES.** At $12 a pop, a weekly manicure costs you $624 a year. Do it yourself instead: Emery boards and polish are cheap. Or just cut down to twice a month—you'll still save. Other vices like impulse spending on clothes and fancy coffee drinks are huge money drains.

- **SELL A CAR.** Add up what it costs you to operate that second car—gas, payments, maintenance, insurance, registration, taxes—and maybe it won't be so difficult to live without it, at least for a while. Find out if your city offers car-sharing programs (check out zipcar.com) or use public transportation.

- **GO PUBLIC.** Sure, there are reasons you want your kids in private schools. But if you're drowning in the sea of financial doom, none of those reasons hold much water. Did you know that the average annual cost of private school tuition is $4,689? Public schools in America are still free and mostly excellent. Take advantage of them for now until you can get back on your financial feet.

The relief you will feel after taking such extreme measures to deal with your financial situation head on will far outweigh the temporary discomforts along the way.

MARY'S PET PEEVE: *Come-ons from credit card companies*

The notice from the credit card company is surprisingly lovely, with a message that goes something like this: "Don't you have better things to spend your money on this month? Sure you do, so go ahead and take a payment holiday on us! You'll have more money to [fill in the blank] when you skip making your payment to us this month."

What looks like a gift can really be a trap to keep you in debt longer. Just read the fine print: The interest still accrues on the unpaid balance. But rather than you paying it, it converts to principal and gets tacked onto the back end of your debt. Next month you'll start paying interest on the interest you didn't pay this month—and again every month until you pay the balance in full.

It makes me crazy to know that so many people will take these skip-a-payment offers as some kind of good thing. And that means they're likely to take the bait again in the future.

2. Money Makeovers: What to Do When the Unexpected Happens

SUDDENLY SINGLE

Several years ago, elementary school teacher Sherrye C., 52, of Houston, and her husband had just built their dream house. Their children were grown and their combined incomes allowed them to live comfortably. They had few worries about their financial future. But when the couple divorced last year,

Sherrye was forced to rely solely on her income and on a small divorce settlement to pay for expenses, including her new home.

Like so many other Americans, Sherrye now lives from paycheck to paycheck and wonders if she'll ever be able to stop working and retire. Although she lives frugally, Sherrye has little left over at the end of the month, in part because the house payment eats almost half of her $2,400 take-home check. "I've just about topped out in salary based on my experience and education," she says.

If she teaches till age 65, she'll receive about $1,700 a month from the Teacher Retirement System—$700 less than what she lives on now. She's had the option to join a 403(b) retirement plan, but she hasn't because she can't afford any more paycheck deductions.

The $20,000 settlement from the divorce is currently divided between a savings account and a CD, earning minimal interest. And she's had to dip into it on a few occasions. "I had some dental work and car repairs I couldn't have paid for unless I borrowed from this account," she says. She's also helped her grown daughter with some college tuition.

Because she worries about depleting her nest egg, Sherrye puts money back in when she can. Last year, she received a little over $1,000 in a tax refund from Uncle Sam. It went right into the bank. And she's already cut back in several areas. "I give fewer holiday gifts, I buy very few new clothes, and when I do, I shop outlets. I've practically stopped going to the movies, which I love," she says. She's also decreased the amount of the pre-medical taken out of her paycheck. "This optional take-out covers my deductible," she says, "but I had to reduce it by $20 because I needed the money." She still doesn't see herself as being able to retire anytime in the near future. "I'd just like to know I could, at some point," she says. She also wants to know her emergency fund could carry her through an "emergency" without wiping out her savings. "I know this house is draining me," she says, "and though I love it, maybe staying here is not the best idea."

What Sherrye Needs to Do

Based on her current expenses—mortgage payments, upkeep on her house, and occasional gifts to her daughter and grandkids—Sherrye will need at least $3,600 a month in order to retire at age 65 and not change her lifestyle drastically. Her teacher's pension will provide her with $1,700 a month, leaving a balance of $1,900 that she must plan for now.

To do so most easily, she needs to add $800 a month to the school's 403(b) retirement plan. Where will this money come from? First, she might consider selling the house. She can take her appreciation and equity and add it to her $20,000 nest egg. Then she must deduct $7,500 to put in an easy-access emergency fund. She can invest the remaining dollars in a bond fund, which will provide her with additional monthly income right now.

By moving to a $750-a-month apartment, she'll save $365 a month in mortgage payments and another $75 to $100 in utilities.

She should also reduce the amount of withholding tax from her paycheck by $220, so instead of getting a big refund once a year, she has more cash to spend each month. If she takes these monthly savings and adds the additional investment income from the house profits, she will have the $800 to invest in a 403(b). She'll also lower her tax bracket and automatically have an additional $224 in saved taxes.

If Sherrye doesn't want to sell her house, she's got to increase her income other ways, maybe by taking in a renter or working each summer until she retires (averaging a gross of $2,000). She can also decrease the amount of withholding tax by $220. If she invested these savings in a 403(b), she'd still come up short each month when she's ready to retire, and she wouldn't be able to help her family to the extent that she has been able to in the past. At that point she'd have to find other ways to change her lifestyle.

A FAMILY NEEDS SPACE

Like many young couples, Tracy and Ann K., both 30, found it much easier to save before they had children. With the birth of Jordan three years ago, and Connor one year ago, the household's $2,400 take-home pay barely stretches to cover their monthly expenses. "Besides the added everyday expenses of diapers, formula and day care," says Ann, "we had to cover $2,000 of Jordan's birth expenses because of a high deductible on Tracy's health insurance plan through his job at a grocery store."

Shortly after Jordan's birth, Tracy needed surgery, and the family had to pay an additional $1,000. Add to those expenses an unexpected tax bill, student loans, and some "emergency" credit card bills, and the family was close to $10,000 in debt.

Though they took out a bank consolidation loan to pay the taxes, medical bills and student loans, and are making monthly payments on the credit cards, they cannot get ahead—which means getting out of debt and saving enough to buy a bigger house. "Our small house was fine for Ann and me," Tracy says, "but it's cramped with a toddler and a baby." Toys are stacked in a living room corner, and the kids' bedrooms only hold a bed and a dresser.

"We do what we can to save," Ann says. "I use coupons at the store, we cut our boys' hair, we do all the maintenance on our home." She adds that with Jordan getting potty-trained, she's also noticed a savings of $30 a month in diapers. They use credit cards for gas, diapers and baby food only. Still, their current balance hovers around $6,000. "If we could save $2,000, we could put a down payment on a place," says Ann, "but between our debt and our monthly expenses, how we're going to do that seems impossible right now."

The Can-Do Strategy

We recommend the family keep their bank loan at 10 percent and the auto loan at 8.6 percent, and then find a credit card with 6 percent interest to buy out the balances on their two existing cards (currently at 21 and 12 percent interest). The couple have already asked the bank if they can add a few months to their loan and thereby lower monthly payments by $60. They can begin a cash reserve with this savings.

By consolidating their credit card balances, they can handle all the loan payments and save for a down payment on a house. Here's how: They qualify for a wellness discount on their life insurance; wellness criteria include general good health and a healthy lifestyle, including no smoking, and moderate drinking in some cases. Combine that with some minor changes in coverage, and the family can save $900 a year.

By shopping for a new auto insurance company, they can lower their premium by $225 a year. Finally, by consulting their tax advisor about switching to four exemptions on their W-4s (Ann and Tracy take none now), they could take home $800 more a year and put it to work as savings.

Total savings? Almost $4,000 in two years—twice what they set as their initial goal.

SAVING SLIP-UPS

- **SAVING WITHOUT A CLEAR GOAL.** Most of us need a reason to put off enjoying the money now. Write down a goal, assign a money value and a date to reach it. Then figure what you need to do each paycheck, each month, each week to reach that goal.

- **CHOOSING THE WRONG SAVINGS VEHICLE FOR A PARTICULAR GOAL.** If you're saving for the children's higher education, for example, which is a long-term goal, don't put the money into a low-interest savings account, which is primarily used for quick and easy access.

- **PUTTING ALL YOUR SAVINGS EGGS IN ONE BASKET.** Don't count on that life insurance policy loan, that piece of real estate, that one stock to pay for the kids' college, a down payment on a house, or retirement. Diversification reduces risk.

- **NOT PARTICIPATING IN A "MATCHED SAVINGS" PROGRAM OFFERED AT WORK.** If your employer will match your contributions in a savings plan, you are automatically forfeiting "free money" if you don't sign up.

- **NOT SAVING BEFORE TAXES, RATHER THAN AFTER TAXES.** If you participate in your employee retirement fund, which is before taxes, you receive an immediate income tax savings, since amounts are not taxed until retirement.

- **NOT HAVING SOME MONEY IN A SHORT-TERM INVESTMENT VEHICLE** so you don't have to pay penalties to withdraw cash for emergencies. Advisers recommend having three to six months' salary available for emergency expenses.

- **NOT SAVING A LITTLE BIT REGULARLY,** but rather saving a chunk sporadically. Build savings into your budget and let compounding interest work for you. The earlier you put money into savings, the less you have to put in to reach a goal.

- **NOT TEACHING YOUR KIDS TO SAVE.** Don't assume they'll learn by osmosis. Help them set a goal, make a plan and then meet it.

- **BEING TOO CONSERVATIVE ABOUT INVESTING** in mutual funds when a long-term time frame is available. Mutual funds tend to do well in the long haul. If your goal is years off, allow a little risk.
- **PROCRASTINATING.** The time to start saving is now—not five years before the kids are ready to go off to college or ten years before you hope to retire.

COLLEGE FOR LISA'S KIDS

To Lisa B., 32, a medical assistant in a surgeon's office, the most important thing is that her kids, Natalie, 12, and Alex, 7, go to college. "I struggled for years as a waitress and then as a secretary," this single mom says, "and then at 28, I went back to college and got a two-year degree in medical assisting." Today she makes $15,000 a year working for a doctor and receives $375 a month in child support. Though the cost of living isn't terribly high in tiny Spencer, Iowa (Lisa moved here from Sioux Falls, South Dakota, a year ago to lower her living expenses), she still has nothing left at the end of the month to put toward her children's potential college funds. Part of what eats her paycheck is the $200 a month she pays for day care for Alex, since he goes to a half-day kindergarten. She also has a $75-a-month prescription expense for his ADHD (attention deficit hyperactivity disorder). To cut costs, Lisa shops for off-brands at the grocery store and buys in bulk. Her brother changes her oil and does minor auto repairs. Her sister-in-law cuts the kids' hair. Another brother mows her lawn.

She doesn't believe in using a credit card and hasn't carried one in five years. "If a major expense came along," she says, "I don't know what I'd do."

Last year, Lisa brought Natalie to her office on Take Your Daughters to Work Day. "She loved seeing what I do," Lisa says, "and I'm determined for her and Alex to go to college—not for two years like I did, but to a four-year school."

Lisa's Education

It appears Lisa could not possibly squeeze one extra cent out of her paycheck. But she does have some options. The most obvious is the $200 she's been using for day care, which stopped in September when Alex started full-day school. We recommend that she put $100 each month into a money-market savings account earmarked for emergencies. Then she should put $50 a month for each child into an investment college fund like Kids, Parents and Money (AmEx Financial Advisors; 800-986-9598). Were she to do this for Alex, in 12 years the $7,250 investment could be worth $21,166, based on this fund's past performance. The investment in seven years could be worth $6,000. Lisa might ask grandparents, aunts and uncles to contribute to the funds for birthdays and holidays. She will also have to investigate financial aid when the time comes.

When Lisa gets her next raise, which will probably be on her first anniversary on the job, she'll be eligible to put the increase into the company retirement plan. Last year, Lisa received a large federal tax return that she used to pay bills. She should consult her tax advisor about increasing her withholding exemptions, which could give her about $100 more each month Also, Lisa should get a credit card with a low interest rate and use it only for emergencies. Once she sets up an emergency savings account, she can easily pay off a balance if she has to use the card.

Savvy Saving Strategies

- **Pay yourself first**

  Once you've set a savings goal, figure out what percentage of your after-tax income will help you get there during the next 12 months. Each time you get paid, take out that portion and add it to your savings account. So, if your goal is $1,000 per year, and your take-home income is $20,000, you'd deposit 5 percent of each paycheck. Consider this contribution like an electricity bill or taxes, something that has to be paid no matter what. It can be done on your own, or through a 401(k) plan or any automatic payroll savings program.

- **Track your progress in a savings journal**

  Just carry a notepad and jot down the amounts you save by paying less or not purchasing something you used to buy. Then at the end of the week, write yourself a check for the total savings and add that amount to your "Keepsum" savings account. To stay on track, aim to save at least $20 weekly (this adds up to more than $1,000 annually).

- **Become your own financial guru**

  If you educate yourself, you're less likely to be taken to the cleaners by insurance companies, banks and credit card companies, and you'll become much more savvy about investments and retirement plans. If you check out a book on personal finance from the library every few months, you'll likely be 200 percent more knowledgeable by the end of the year, and you can save thousands both in the short and long run.

4. Home and Family

 Family Vacation

1. Take a Vacation Without Spending a Fortune

There's something magical about getting away from your regular routine, isn't there? Vacation time can bring the family closer together, and it's good for your health. Time off is medicine. Taking a vacation is as important as watching your cholesterol or exercising. In 2007 Americans forfeited an average of three vacation days each—at least 438 million days off from work that were lost, according to a Harris Interactive survey. So what's stopping you from using those extra days off? Perhaps it's the expense. AAA's 2007 Annual Vacation Costs survey says a family of two adults and two children can expect to pay an average of $269 a day for food and lodging. Still, you don't have to plunge into debt to have a great time. Somewhere between booking a suite on a luxury cruise ship and sitting 24/7 in front of the TV in your jammies, there's a vacation you can afford.

- **HAVE FUN FOR LESS.** Go off-season. For example, if you go to ski resorts, such as Keystone in Colorado and Smugglers' Notch in Vermont, during the summer, you'll find great outdoor activities (hiking, fishing, rafting, water parks, mini golf) and lodging that can be had for rock-bottom prices. Ditto for going to the Caribbean in summer—many people call it family season!

- **PLAN AHEAD.** Consider the money you have, then design a vacation that will realistically fit within that financial boundary. If you have a family of five and $500 to spend, you can probably forget about a couple of days at Disney World. Divide what you can spend by a reasonable daily budget to determine how many days you can be away. Think about all the costs—not only admission fees and overnight accommodations but food and gas, too. Instead of full weeks, consider day trips or a long weekend away.

- **THEMEPARKINSIDER.COM** Don't even think about going to Disney, Six Flags, Universal or any other theme park without checking this website first. The site has great info on deals, discounts, safety concerns and the best time to visit. There's also a discussion forum where people share their experiences, tips and advice.

- **VACATIONKIDS.COM** This is a good place to find reasonable prices for family- (and baby-) friendly resorts, cruises and all-inclusive vacations. It includes reviews of resorts and vacation spots by Sally Black, owner of the website.

- **AAA** Always pull out your membership card when paying for attraction tickets, parking, hotels or restaurants. You won't believe how many establishments will knock 10 percent right off the top. Check out aaa. com for current discounts and travel deals city by city.

- **CITYPASS.COM** With CityPass, you pay one substantially reduced price for a pass that gets you into a variety of main attractions for less. You'll find discounts of nearly 50 percent for museums and other attractions in many big cities such as New York and Chicago.

- **ENTERTAINMENT.COM** For a reasonable fee, you can buy Entertainment books for the city you're going to visit. You'll find excellent coupons for restaurants, car rentals and attractions.

TRAVEL CHEAPER

Booking a flight for a family of five can get pricey. But there are plenty of ways to find discounts.

- **BESTFARES.COM** Check out the last-minute deals. Often if you don't book at least 7 to 21 days in advance, the price may go up. But here you can make reservations with a few hours' notice and get big discounts.

- **SITE59.COM** Procrastinators, rejoice! This site was created with spontaneous travelers in mind. Named for the 59th minute, Site59 is a one-stop shop that takes the travel industry's last-minute inventory for the coming weekends and creates affordable getaways. Package deals include combinations of flight, car rental and a choice of hotels. You can save up to 70 percent if you're willing to book at the last minute.

- **KAYAK.COM** There are lots of websites where you can shop for the lowest fares, such as CheapTickets, Priceline and Expedia. Kayak.com is a very good one. It searches over 100 travel sites in real time for the best deals available and compares prices for airfares, hotels, rental cars and cruises. Follow the link it provides to the site with the deal. You don't buy through Kayak, so there are no hidden service fees.

- **COMBINE FREQUENT-FLYER MILES** Some airlines, like Delta, let members transfer SkyMiles to friends and family for a fee of one penny per mile plus a $25 processing fee. The miles you have, plus some from grandparents and friends, could add up to at least one free ticket.

- **COSTCO.COM** Costco members can get deals on rental cars through all the major companies.

- **DRIVE FOR LESS.** Road trips are a wonderful way to see the country and are an inexpensive vacation alternative for families with young children. Even if your goal is to get somewhere and stay there, make the drive itself special by stopping and visiting some historic sites along the way. When it's time to fill up, look for the good deals on gasbuddy.com and gaspricewatch.com.

- **TAKE A CRUISE.** You may find discounted fares when booking at the last minute on a family cruise, if your budget allows. Look for "Family Cruise specials" at competecruise.com. Disney Cruises publishes "Magical Rates" on its Specials page. Families love all the activities on family cruises, plus the (nearly) all-inclusive price.

- **MAKE YOURSELF AT HOME.** Home exchange is the vacation alternative in which two families swap homes for a free vacation. You get to live like a local, not a tourist. And a home is usually more comfortable than a hotel. Is a swap right for you and your family? Find out at homeexchange.com.

CUT THOSE HOTEL EXPENSES

It sometimes takes a little digging to get the best deal possible on your hotel rooms. Find family-friendly hotels, that offer at least a complimentary breakfast can be a good option.

At Hilton's Homewood Suites (homewoodsuites.com) you get a two-room suite with a full kitchen, and the rate includes a daily hot breakfast and light evening meal Monday to Thursday evenings—perfect for families.

- QUIKBOOK.COM This site often has good deals. If you find the same room at the same hotel, but it's cheaper than the one you purchased at Quikbook, it will refund you the difference (up to three days after purchase).

- SENIOR DISCOUNT Many hotel websites have senior discounts (55+). Ask about it when making reservations.

- HOTELDISCOUNT.COM Another good search engine for hotel rates and deals. Book through the site for discounts of up to 70 percent.

2. Family Vacation Money-Savers

—MARY HUNT

When I was a kid, family travel meant four children crammed into the back seat of a sedan, poking and elbowing one another while counting the miles between rest stops.

Things have changed dramatically since then. But even in this day of onboard DVD players, spacious minivans, more affordable air travel, cruises and theme parks, family vacations can be either delightful or disastrous. It all depends on the time and care you devote to research and planning.

- INVOLVE THE KIDS. Talk about how much you can spend, then show the kids what it costs to eat at a restaurant, spend the night in a hotel or buy tickets for an amusement park. Dawn R., 41, who lives in Baltimore, allowed her teenager to plan their vacation with the money they had to spend, including the cost of overnight accommodations. "Our spendthrift daughter became Ms. Frugality because she wanted to parasail," she recalls. "She had us fix meals in our room and watched expenses like a hawk." Dawn says it was the best vacation they ever took. And the real bonus? "We went home with cash in our pockets and the priceless accomplishment of having taught our child the value of money."

- CALCULATE YOUR SPENDING POWER. When it comes to family vacations, quality is more important than quantity. Instead of trying to stretch your available cash over the time you can be away, always consider how much money you have available to spend first. Then divide by a reasonable daily budget to determine how long you can stay.

- **GAS UP THE CAR.** Road trips are an American tradition and a wonderful way to see the country. Before you go, log on to gasbuddy.com or gaspricewatch.com for insider tips on where to find the cheapest gasoline prices in your area. These sites are updated daily by local volunteers.

- **ENJOY THE GREAT OUTDOORS.** Camping can be nearly as affordable as staying at home, provided you have the equipment or can borrow it. Visit nps. gov to search affordable destinations within the National Park Service. Some campgrounds now require reservations, so don't wait until the last minute. Expect to pay about $15 a night, on average, for a campsite.

- **SEE IT LIVE.** There are at least 2,000 living-history museums around the country where the past seems as real as the present. Start with a virtual visit where you can "tour" many of these attractions online. Go to alhfam.org, the site of The Association for Living History, Farm and Agricultural Museums. Jamestown Settlement and Yorktown Victory Center (historyisfun.org), The Greenfield Village at the Henry Ford Museum (hfmgv.org) and Conner Prairie (connerprairie.org) are just a few living-history museums that make learning fun at any age.

- **HAVE FUN AT HOME.** A little short on cash? No problem. Turn a tent in the backyard into a memorable camping experience. Change all the rules for your stay-at-home vacation: stay up really late, unplug the phone, sleep in. During the day, visit the attractions right in your own town.

- **GO IN A GROUP.** Vacationing with another family can cut costs on rentals, food and transportation. This is an especially good choice for single-parent families who agree to pool their energy and resources. "Make sure you discuss expectations and budgets ahead of time," advises Sally Black, founder of VacationKids.com, an online travel agency devoted to family travel. Cruises are a good choice for group travel: They're semi-inclusive, so you know your costs before you leave.

To this day, my favorite childhood memories revolve around those crazy road trips. Just being together was so much fun, it made all the elbowing that went on in the back seat worth it. Now that I have my own family, I'm more convinced than ever: There's just nothing like a family vacation.

B *Save at the Supermarket*

1. Slash Your Food Bill

—MARY HUNT

Food prices have increased so dramatically in recent years, a trip to the supermarket is enough to ruin your appetite. With food weighing in as the second biggest monthly expense for many families, we all need to find clever ways to save. I've got some great tips for driving those costs down.

FIND THE DEALS

- **HIRE HELP.** Would you fork over $1.25 a week for someone to scour the aisles of your supermarket for the week's best sales, figure out which coupons go with those sales, tell you exactly where those coupons are, figure out the net cost, show you how much you'll save and then hand it to you in a tidy list? Then you need to check out The Grocery Game (thegrocerygame.com). I've been a big fan of founder Teri Gault since the days she shared her handwritten shopping list with just a few friends. Now Teri's List is available for major supermarkets nationwide. Tip: Try the 4-week trial for $1. *(For more information, see "What You Should Know About Coupon Shopping," page 146.)*

- **GET MORE THAN BOOKS.** Amazon Grocery (amazon.com/grocery) offers more than 14,000 nonperishable grocery items, with free Super Saver shipping on orders over $25. I was amazed at the selection of name-brand items, including cereal, spices, baking supplies and an extensive line of natural and organic products. Be prepared: in exchange for competitive pricing, you'll be buying in larger quantities than at a traditional grocery store. But here's the fun part: For the products it stocks, Amazon offers plenty of varieties. Where else can you find all 70 Jell-O products and more than 35 different types of mustard? Amazon Grocery also carries diapers, pet supplies and laundry products. Scroll down to find new arrivals.

Shop the sales

- **Go cherry picking.** A great way to save money is to handpick the loss leaders from several stores in your area. Loss leaders are items priced lower than the store's cost. My Grocery Deals (mygrocerydeals.com) is a cherry picker's dream come true. Register at the site, then select the stores in your neighborhood and watch all the sales pop up. As you check an item, the site creates a shopping list for you, arranged by store, with subtotals for each and a grand total. Print it out and you can see at a glance the regular price, the price you'll pay at checkout and the amount you'll save. Tip: If your spouse passes those stores on the way home, e-mail him the list.

Check it twice

- **Pay attention.** Grocery store scanners are not always reset with current sale prices. Your chances of being charged the full price on a sale item are high. To get the right deal, stay alert and watch the scanner—and speak up if you see a discrepancy. Tip: Some grocery stores will give you the item for free or at a discount if it scans higher than advertised.

- **Get a rain check.** Advertised sale items can sell out quickly. But don't despair if you get to the store too late. Simply stop at Customer Service and ask for a rain check. That's all you need to get the sale price when the stock is replenished, even if the sale is over. Tip: Make sure the rain check specifies how many items you can purchase at the sale price. Six is typical.

Here's the best thing about cutting the cost of food: The savings happen right now. Think about it: If you normally spend $125 a week for food and by using clever cost-saving measures you get the same amount of food for $100, you save $25 instantly. You don't have to work overtime, wait for payday or even pay taxes on it. It's the best kind of instant gratification.

Fast money-savers

- Go to Boodle (boodle.com) and input your zip code. Check the coupons you want and hit "Print." It doesn't get any easier than that!

- Check the websites of the companies that make your favorite products for special coupons or rebates. When an item you like goes on sale, you can save even more by using the coupon or rebate.
- If you store opened containers of items like cottage cheese upside down in your refrigerator, the contents will remain fresh far longer than if stored right side up because gravity helps keep spores from growing as quickly.

2. Print Your Own Money: Fresh Ways to Find Coupons for Almost Everything

There was a time when coupons showed up in the Sunday paper and that was about it. Now they're available online, in magazines, through the mail and directly from some manufacturers' websites. Locating the really great coupons is the challenge. There are coupons for everything from airport parking to flowers to office supplies at the free website, thecouponmom. com. Another helpful site, thecouponclippers.com, allows you to select the exact coupons you want and mails them to you for a nominal handling charge. They show up in your mailbox in just a couple of days, too. If you're not that good at collecting and clipping coupons, this service is a real bargain.

Are you renovating your home? Stephanie Nelson, "The Coupon Mom," found a coupon that got her over $700 off the price of new kitchen cabinets. You'd be surprised at what you can find on this and other coupon websites. Spending as little as possible on purchases involves having both a coupon collection and a coupon redemption strategy. The trick is to gather free coupons from a variety of sources. But what's even more important is how you use them.

MAXIMIZE, MAXIMIZE
- SUPERMARKET MAGIC. Don't let checkout slips slip away. At the register in some supermarkets, you'll find machines that print out strips of coupons for future purchases, based on what you've just bought. The coupons are frequently for competing products, but you can get big savings if you're willing to switch brands. Also look on the back of your receipts for coupons good at area restaurants, liquor stores, car washes, cleaners

and other service providers. Another reason to join a warehouse club. Members of Costco and BJ's Wholesale Club receive regular mailers containing coupons for products that are redeemable at the issuing store. (Sam's Club, however, never sends out coupons.)

- **DOUBLE OR NOTHING.** Never shop where they don't double coupons. And watch for special notices when supermarkets triple the value of coupons. Also use the store's advertised sales as a guide for what to buy and keep your eyes peeled for special shelf tags indicating a manager's special or inventory reduction sale. Combining a discontinued product with a doubled coupon can often net a savings of 50 percent or more.

- **JOIN A COUPON TRAIN.** The idea? An envelope of coupons shuttles from person to person (groups usually consist of between two and ten people) by mail. You take out coupons you want, replace them with some you don't need and mail it to the next person on the list. To get started, check out mothersnature.com/frugal/coupons.

- **SCAN THAT PACKAGE.** Manufacturer coupons can be easily missed unless you're looking for them. Look inside, on top of, or on the back of product boxes and cans. Some coupons are good on the current purchase, while others are meant for your next shopping trip.

- **DO THE MATH.** Sometimes buying less gets you more. For instance, buying several small bottles of shampoo, with associated coupons, will result in a smaller cash outlay than buying one economy-size bottle. And stock up when a product you buy regularly is significantly marked down. Such sales occur only every few months, so plan ahead and buy in bulk.

- **READ THE FINE PRINT.** Everyone knows to look in the Sunday newspaper for coupon inserts, but don't ignore the rest of the paper. Manufacturers frequently print coupons inside the newspaper on a particular day each week, such as when supermarket sale prices change. Some grocery stores also sell leftover coupon inserts on Monday at a reduced price, while others just give them away. It never hurts to ask.

- **LOOK AROUND.** Keep an eye out for coupon dispensers at the grocery store. Mounted on supermarket shelves, these little coupon-generating machines spit out coupons on demand for the product above them.

Bargain Shopping on the Web

- **Check auction sites.** Consider visiting ebay.com or livedeal.com to bid on sets of coupons up for auction, especially if you're looking to save on high-price items such as diapers and formula. Paying money for coupons others have collected is considered questionable by manufacturers, however. Some coupons say in the fine print that they cannot be sold. It's not illegal, but you could make the coupon void. Counterfeit and expired coupons are also a concern.

- **Before you head to the mall...** Visit your favorite retailers' websites to generate savings on future purchases, either by downloading available coupons, registering or providing information.

- **Jump on the Welcome Wagon.** Whether you're new to the area or not, look for savings at businesses in your area at welcomewagon.com, which is set up to introduce new residents to local stores and service providers.

- **More coupon surfing.** Download online coupons for products and services at websites such as hotcoupons.com and coolsavings.com. You'll find printable coupons as well as coupon codes for websites that result in savings off orders.

Looking for More Bargains?

- **Let your fingers do the walking.** Don't forget to check your yellow pages directory for coupons good at area service providers, restaurants, house-cleaning services and video stores. You'll usually find a special coupon section in the middle of the book.

- **Pick up the phone.** Call the 800 number of the manufacturer whose products you can't live without. Most manufacturers are happy to send coupons if you request them. Use the 800 number directory at 800-555-1212 to find the number of the company you're interested in contacting.

- **Eat out for less.** Look closely at materials on your table the next time you eat out at fast-food or chain restaurants. You may find coupons printed on a paper placemat or on the side of takeout bags.

- **Put a little fun in your life.** Every fall look for a new Entertainment Book at local bookstores or at entertainment.com. For about $30 you get a coupon book that can save several hundred dollars. Although the guides vary by area, most include dollars off grocery store purchases, dry cleaning, car washes, restaurant meals, movie rentals and museum admissions.

- **CONSULT YOUR DOCTOR.** Put waiting-room time to good use by scanning the materials your doctor or vet has displayed. You're likely to find product samples, introductory flyers and brochures about services.

CHECK YOUR MAIL

- **HEAD TO THE POST OFFICE.** Pick up a change of address kit at the post office. In addition to instructions on how to forward your mail to a new home, you'll find a packet of coupons for moving- and home-related purchases. Also, putting yourself on the mailing list at your Lowe's or other major retailers may net you a coupon for 10 percent off your next purchase.

- **BECOME A PREFERRED CUSTOMER.** Shoppers who have a store credit card at large retailers such as JCPenney, Lord & Taylor and Old Navy receive regular coupons for savings off purchases. Lord & Taylor, for example, prints them right on the credit card statement, while Old Navy inserts a bill stuffer worth $5 every time you spend $100.

- **AND THE ENVELOPE, PLEASE.** Some of the biggest names in the business, such as ValPak, Advo, Money Mailer and SuperCoups, regularly mail envelopes full of coupons for area restaurants, home and garden stores, and grocery stores. You might also go to their websites, which offer local coupons as well: valpak.com, moneymailer.com, supercoups.com.

- **FOR MORE BARGAINS.** Approximately 100 million homes receive *Clipper* magazine in the mail around seven times a year (and even more often in some areas) at no cost. It's filled with coupons and special offers at area retailers and restaurants. Visit clippermagazine.com for some coupons.

KEEP TRACK OF WHAT YOU HAVE

Making the most of the coupons you have is just as important as tracking down new ones. That means being able to find the coupon you need, when you need it and before it expires.

- **HAVE A CENTRAL COUPON REPOSITORY.** Some shoppers like index-card holders with tabs to divide the various categories of coupons, such as paper products or breakfast foods. Others like plastic cancelled-check file-folders that accommodate oversize coupons.

- **ORGANIZE YOUR COUPONS EFFICIENTLY.** Instead of filing coupons alphabetically behind tabs, organize your coupon file compartments in the order of your supermarket aisles to save time.

LET'S SWAP

Avid clippers may form refund groups or exchanges that meet regularly to trade coupons with each other. Ellie Kay, author of *A Woman's Guide to Family Finance* and a well-known coupon queen, advocates establishing a swap box, where shoppers put unwanted coupons and pick up castoffs.

One idea is to put plastic zippered bags inside a cardboard box in a public place such as a church, library or community center. Each participant places coupons she doesn't need in a plastic bag, writes her name on a 3x5 card and then puts it in the front of the bag (this marks which bag is hers so she doesn't have to go through it). Then she can look through the other bags for coupons she does want.

3. What You Should Know About Coupon Shopping

—MARY HUNT

Most people I know are careful shoppers. They limit their weekly grocery purchases to what they'll need for the coming week. Invariably they end up paying full-price for at least some of the items in their cart.

I want to introduce you to a different method of shopping. Instead of buying just what you need for the week, you purchase what's on sale, even if you don't need it right now. Teri Gault, CEO and founder of TheGroceryGame. com, calls this "stockpiling."

"The secret for getting sensational supermarket savings every time you shop is in knowing how to use a store's sales cycles to your financial advantage," says Gault. "Adding manufacturers' coupons to the process takes the prices even lower."

Before I tell you how simple it is, I need to disclose that I am not an organized person. Trying to clip and keep track of all the coupons that come in the Sunday paper makes me crazy. Sound familiar? It's the reason that very few coupons are ever redeemed. Still, I've become an avid coupon shopper. I routinely walk out of my supermarket with savings of 50 percent (my all-time high was 74 percent). And you won't believe how easy it is.

Each week I start out at TheGroceryGame.com, where I click on my favorite supermarket. Up pops a shopping list of the week's best sale items and a list of the specific coupons that I need to go with them.

While The Grocery Game does not issue coupons, it does match up what's on sale that week with the coupons that people are receiving in their newspaper. So if Keebler Crackers are on sale for 99¢ this week at Kroger, The Grocery Game goes through its vast database and figures out that three weeks ago you received a coupon for 50¢ off Keebler Crackers.

I zip through the list of products on sale in my area, eliminating items that don't interest me. Then I hit "print" and out comes my shopping list, specific and detailed, laid out by aisle for my supermarket. It shows me, to the penny, how much each item is going to cost before and after the coupon amount is deducted. Isn't that fabulous? It's like having a secretary do all the footwork for you.

Once I have my list, it's time to round up the coupons. I collect the circulars in my Sunday newspaper each week, but I don't clip the coupons. I just write the date on the front and stick them in a drawer.

When I need to find a specific coupon, I use the Virtual Coupon Organizer at thecouponmom.com. This free online tool is an electronic index of every coupon that comes out in those circulars each Sunday. And there are thousands. So if The Grocery Game says that I should buy Keebler Crackers this week, I could search for hours to find the coupon and still not be successful. But if I simply type "Keebler Crackers" in the Virtual Coupon Organizer, it tells me the coupon is in the Valassis circular dated September 24. I pull out my drawer, flip to V 9/24 and go right to the coupon. I cut it out and move on—no filing involved. In a matter of minutes I have all the coupons that I need, good to go.

Not every person lives in an area that is covered by The Grocery Game or has access to a metropolitan Sunday newspaper, but they're not out of luck. Kathy K. of Rochester, New York, gets savings similar to mine by using The Coupon Clippers, a service that mails out all the coupons available from Sunday papers across the country. She checks her store's sales circular on Sunday, orders the coupons she needs on Monday and has them in hand by Friday—in plenty of time to take advantage of the sales. The coupons are subject to a nominal handling fee plus postage. Kathy reports, "Last week, my $3.87 coupon order knocked $30 off my grocery tab. I think that's a pretty good return on my investment!" I've been stockpiling for so long, I have the equivalent of a small grocery store in my pantry. Sometimes we live off the stockpile for weeks at a time.

> In 2006, households reduced their collective grocery tab by about $2.6 billion with coupons. But $331 billion worth of coupons went unredeemed and found their way to the landfill.

4. Save at the Supermarket and Leave the Store Smiling

GROCERIES

- **BREAD WINNERS.** Buy day-old bread from the bakery section for making French toast, bread crumbs (cheaper than packaged), stuffing and such. If you have freezer space, stock up!

- **BUY AMERICAN.** Most domestic dried pasta is just as good as imported, and almost always cheaper.

- **JUICE.** Forget fresh-squeezed (squeeze your own if you must) and single-serving juice boxes.

- **THE BIG TIME.** If you have storage space, consider buying those giant-size packages of rice, detergent and other nonperishables. You'll probably save, but always check the unit price to be sure.

- **SOUP'S ON.** Nothing's easier (and cheaper) to make. Keep bags of ramen noodle soup on hand; you can even add leftovers to make a meal.

PRODUCE

- **OVER-THE-HILL ITEMS.** Check the "overripe" bin for bananas (for banana bread), tomatoes (tomato sauce)—anything you're not going to recognize once it's cooked.
- **IN THE FREEZER.** Opt for poly-bags, not boxes. You can use what you need, then reseal the bag (and you won't pay for packaging).
- **BUY THE BAG?** Except for bulk items prebagged by the pound, such as potatoes or oranges, it's usually cheaper to buy just the amount you need.
- **IN SEASON.** Don't buy out-of-season. If there's something you must have, go for canned or frozen.

MEATS

- **EXPAND YOUR REPERTOIRE.** Stews, pot roasts and other slow-cooked dishes use cheaper cuts (pricey ones dry out). They tend to stretch into more than one meal, too.
- **BURGER BARGAINS.** Use ground chuck for hamburgers. They'll be juicier, tastier and cheaper, and much of the extra fat will cook out.
- **DON'T WING IT.** Got a recipe for chicken wings? Substitute drumsticks. There's more meat and less skin, and you can cook them the same way. (Before wings became so popular, they were the cheaper of the two.)

DANGER ZONES!

- **THE ENDS OF AISLES.** Just because there's a big, flashy display doesn't mean the items there are on sale.
- **CONVENIENCE ITEMS.** Beware the words "ready-to-eat." Be careful of seasoning mix-ins for rice, pasta, vegetables and such. Flavor your own.
- **LUNCH MEATS.** Be judicious. Yes, they're convenient, but you get incredibly little for your money. Even if you buy a ready-to-eat roast chicken and cut it up yourself, for example, you'll save plenty.

Shoppers' Secrets

- **Buy essentials.** If need be, star those items on your list. Allow only a few nonessential purchases per shopping trip.

- **Read all about it!** Use the newspaper not only for coupons, but to comparison-shop. Don't drive to different stores to bargain-hunt—you'll spend anything you save on gas.

- **Don't run out.** Quick trips to convenience stores will bankrupt you. Plan ahead.

Supermarket Supersavers

Too busy to dash from store to store for specials or cook everything from scratch? You can still cut your food bills down to size!

The Basics

- Shop alone, so you don't blow your budget on extras that catch your husband's eye or keep your children quiet.

- Bring a list and stick to it. (You can switch to save on specials, but the idea is to make substitutions, not additions.)

- Don't go when you're tired, hungry, rushed or the store is very crowded. You'll care more about getting out than saving money.

- When choosing between comparable products or different sizes of the same product, check the unit-price stickers on the shelf below. Bigger isn't always better.

- Look on the top and bottom shelves for good buys. The middle shelves are often stocked with the most expensive brands.

- Check the tape before you leave—scanner errors can cost you.

Worst Bets

- Coupons for things you don't normally buy.

- Coupons that require multiple purchases you couldn't possibly use up. What you don't eat is never a bargain.

- Individually wrapped and single-serving items—too much of your dollar pays for fancy packaging, not food.

- Vegetables frozen in butter sauce; they cost nearly double what you'd pay for plain.

Super Strategies

- Compare the cost of freshly sliced cold cuts and cheese at the deli counter to that of packaged products before you buy.

- Buy cheese in chunks and shred or grate it yourself. (If you have a food processor, this takes no time at all.)

Down the Aisles

- Consider edible weight when buying fruit. You can eat almost all of an apple, but the seeds and rind of a melon go into the garbage.

- Use the scale to lock in the best values; one head of lettuce may look larger but weigh less than another.

- Prebagged or fill-your-own? It's usually cheaper to buy only what you need, except for big bags of potatoes, onions, oranges. (But again, if you won't be able to use these produce staples before they spoil, they aren't a true bargain.)

- Canned fruits and vegetables often cost less than fresh or frozen, and can be terrific timesavers too. (We're thinking of beets, tomatoes, peaches, pumpkin, sweet potatoes—but you probably have your own favorites.)

- Take advantage of the lower prices for generics and store brands on items where there's no quality difference, such as sugar, corn oil, vinegar, etc.

- Figure the cost of iced-tea mix not by weight, but by yield—the number of quarts you'll end up with.

- Don't be tempted by toppings displayed near ice cream. You probably have less expensive toppers, such as chocolate and fruit syrups, already on hand.

- When a recipe with many ingredients calls for a large amount of broth, the most economical choices are bouillon cubes, powder or granules.

- Greek or Spanish olive oil is a better buy than Italian, and just as flavorful.

- Buy "salad" olives to use in dips, salads and cooked dishes. They're slightly broken, but who'll care?

- When lettuce is pricey, make salads with spinach, cabbage or whatever's reasonable.

- Marked-down day-old bread is ideal for stuffings, bread puddings and French toast. Buy extra and store in your freezer.

- When a recipe calls for an unusual cut of pasta, substitute a less expensive shape.

Ⓒ *Kids and School*

1. Save on Back-to-School Expenses

If the thought of busting your budget on back-to-school expenses makes you quiver, have we got good news for you. This year, most parents will spend an average of $363 per child on school gear, according to the American Express Retail Index Survey—but you don't have to. These cost-cutters will really add up.

FASHIONABLE, YET FRUGAL

Off-price stores are just the tip of the iceberg when it comes to savvy clothes shopping.

QUALITY COUNTS. One way to stretch your clothing dollar is to buy from companies that offer satisfaction-guaranteed policies. "If at any time a customer is not satisfied with a product, she can return it for a refund or exchange," says an L.L. Bean spokesperson.

LOYALTY HAS ADVANTAGES. Mega-retailer Sears rewards its repeat customers with the Kidvantage program. Parents who register get a 15 percent discount every time they spend $100 on kids' clothing. Likewise, parents who buy from cataloguer Hanna Andersson can return their kids' gently used clothes and receive a credit for 20 percent of what they paid.

UNIFORM APPEAL. Sometimes local retailers give discounts to parents who get together and order school uniforms in bulk. Ask your principal if there's already such an arrangement in place, or try negotiating with uniform supply companies you find in the Yellow Pages.

MAJOR RETAIL STORES SOMETIMES OFFER SPECIAL SAVINGS, TOO. At Montgomery Ward, parents who buy at least two articles of a school uniform get a discount. To find out if your favorite retailer has such a program, ask at the customer service desk.

SAVINGS BY ASSOCIATION. If you're affiliated with a charitable or social organization, you might also be able to defray clothing costs. For instance, Mervyn's California, in conjunction with the Kiwanis Club and other groups, runs ChildSpree, in which kids who qualify are given from $25 to $100 to spend on clothes.

SWAP 'N' SHOP. Organize a clothing exchange at school and bring in garments your kids have outgrown. In return, you'll get gently used clothing from other parents. No money changes hands.

STOCKING UP

One of the best ways to save on school supplies is to buy in bulk at office-supply superstores.

BUILT TO LAST. Most major school-supply companies will stand behind the durability of their products. Take advantage of lifetime warranties.

GOOD AS NEW. Why not recycle last year's school binder? Hot-glue a pocket from an old pair of jeans to its cover.

FABULOUS FREEBIES. You can also find free school supplies through store giveaways.

AFTER THE (SCHOOL) BELL

Keep extracurricular activities' costs to a minimum:

MUSIC TO YOUR EARS. Stores that sell used instruments, such as Music Go Round, offer big price breaks. Just ask Anne T. of Mukilteo, Washington, who bought her son Sam a refurbished saxophone for $400—which is $600 less than a brand-new one.

WINNING STRATEGY. You can find savings on used sports equipment at stores like Play It Again Sports, where secondhand hockey skates ($99 new) can cost as little as $30.

PRICE POINTS. When buying brand-new sports equipment, shop in a superstore like JumboSports, which gives customers 5 percent off if they find an item is cheaper elsewhere.

WORTH MENTIONING. Ask relatives and friends if they have an old flute or baseball glove they no longer need. Your child's coach or bandleader might also know families willing to lend or sell you their used equipment.

Food for Thought

Kids can eat you out of house and home, but only if you let them. These tricks keep grocery bills down.

Cheap eats. See if your school district sells hot lunches in advance at a discount. Or, find out if your children are eligible for either free or reduced-cost lunches.

In the bag. For brown-bag lunches, it's worth investing in the U.S. Department of Agriculture's cookbook, *Food, Family & Fun*, which is full of money-saving recipes such as this: Save on fruit-flavored yogurt by buying a tub of plain or vanilla yogurt and mixing in puréed fresh fruit or jam.

Smart drinking. Buying commercial juice boxes can be expensive, so Denver mom Pam L. invested in Rubbermaid containers (about $1.30 each), refills them daily, and saves about $95 a year. Or simply wash and reuse 20-oz soda bottles.

Munchies makeover. You'll save at least $5 a week if you substitute cut fresh veggies or apples for expensive processed junk food. And the health savings is priceless.

High Tech, Low Cost

Getting your kids access to a computer doesn't have to be an overwhelming expense.

Pay as you go. Copy shops like Kinko's often rent on-site computers by the hour. (An Ann Arbor, Michigan, branch lets you use a PC or a Mac for a few dollars an hour.)

By the books. See if your local library or school has computers available for public use.

Super seconds. If you want to buy a computer but find brand-new prices too steep, consider buying used equipment from a reputable reseller. Just be sure you get a full warranty.

Software savvy. You can save on software if the computer you buy, new or used, comes preloaded. And take advantage of shareware websites, which let you download software for about a third of the retail value.

Healthy Savings

Cheaper checkups. If your pediatrician's office staffs a nurse practitioner, seeing her for well-child visits may cost a lot less. Paying in cash may also mean a price break.

Sure shot. Call the National Immunization Information Hotline (800-232-2522) to find information on free or low-cost immunizations.

Patient plus. Some doctors offer incentives for referring new patients. A Framingham, Massachusetts, dentist rewards his patients with a $20 credit and a $20 gift certificate to a local restaurant. Their friends get $50 off their first exam. Ask your doctors if they'll do the same.

Expand Your Child's Library

Easiest ways: Catalog-shop with book clubs such as the Children's Book of the Month Club (cbomc.com), which offers both hardbacks and paperbacks.
Also, most schools have book-ordering programs through companies such as Scholastic. Usually, a teacher or librarian provides order forms, and the books are delivered to the child at school.

Cheapest ways: If you're willing to bargain-hunt, chains like Barnes & Noble and Borders discount children's books. Used bookstores are an even better bet.
Otherwise, check yard sales and sales at local libraries. Mention to friends and relatives that you're looking for hand-me-down books, and that books are welcome holiday gifts.

Best ways: Ask a librarian which books have won awards, such as the Newbery Medal or Caldecott Medal. Go to a library and read reviews from the *New York Times Children's Book Review* or the *Horn Book Magazine*.
The Association for Library Service to Children offers three pamphlets—for preschool, early school and middle grades—on "Building a Home Library." For information, write to: ALSC, Home Library Pamphlets, 50 East Huron, Chicago, IL 60611; tel: 800-545-2433. Specify which pamphlets you'd like. Or find them online at ala.org/ala/alsc/alsc.htm.

Living in the Material World

There was a time when kids interested in photography got toy cameras. Now they receive expensive digital ones. Little girls playing dress-up coveted play makeup; now they want department store cosmetics. Some kids even have opinions on what make the family car should be. What's going on?

Marketers and advertisers have begun targeting children directly, rather than their parents.

In fact, the amount spent on advertising to children has increased nearly eightfold since 1999.

This is dangerous because kids aren't sophisticated enough to analyze these messages and are likely to believe everything they hear, then yearn for expensive products they simply don't need or their parents really can't afford.

But you can beat the advertisers and protect your kids.

- **LIMIT TELEVISION.** Bedrooms should be TV-free. The less television kids watch, the fewer opportunities marketers have to get their messages across. Likewise, websites are rife with ads, so monitor computer use.

- **MAKE SURE YOUR KIDS UNDERSTAND YOUR VALUES.** Watch television together and discuss the commercials, speculating about whether the products are as much fun as they're made to seem, or if they're worth the money.

- **GET AWAY FROM IT ALL.** Help children understand that happiness doesn't come from stuff. Playing outside makes kids happy, too.

- **JUST SAY NO.** Stand firm and recognize that your child will survive even if he is the only one without the latest, hottest, coolest new fashion or toy.

- **WATCH FOR UNEXPECTED ADVERTISING SOURCES.** Advertisers have even found their way into schools and youth organizations through sponsorships and vending machines.

- **GET INVOLVED.** Many national organizations are supporting bills in Congress to limit advertising to children. Log on to commercialalert.org or commercialexploitation.org to learn more.

Ⓓ *Mortgage Savings*

1. Have a Mortgage? Here's a Smart, Simple Way to Save a Bundle

Thirty-some years ago when Marc Eisenson was young and houses were cheap, he took out a 25-year mortgage on a $35,000 house with a one-acre plot and a pool in Croton-on-Hudson, New York. Marc, who worked as an electrical contractor, knew he'd gotten a good deal on the house. But he wanted to be debt-free. So he began adding whatever he could each month to his mortgage payment. "By the time I was 27, we had paid off the mortgage," he recalls.

His house wasn't the only thing that came out of Marc's debt-free strategy: He turned his philosophy into a book, *The Banker's Secret.* In it he makes a compelling argument for getting out of debt. By adding a little bit to each mortgage check you are "investing in your mortgage," he says. Your return is whatever your interest rate happens to be. And you can save thousands of dollars over the life of the loan.

Suppose you have a $100,000 mortgage at 8 percent. If you pay an additional $25 a month, you would save $23,337 in interest and cut nearly four years off the life of your loan. If you pay an extra $100 a month, you would save $62,456 and cut nearly ten years from the life of your loan. "Where else can you invest $25 and get a guaranteed return of 8 percent?" Marc asks.

If you've invested in your tax-deductible retirement fund, paid off your high-interest credit card debt, and taken care of your regular monthly obligations, it may be time to consider prepaying your mortgage. Some financial planners argue against prepaying a mortgage because you lose the tax-deductible interest. In addition, they say, you use money that you could invest elsewhere at a higher return. But Jonathan Clements, personal finance columnist for the *Wall Street Journal*, doesn't buy that.

Clements, who has a 7.7 percent mortgage, began making extra payments on the principal more than four years ago. This is how he compares investing in your mortgage to investing in stocks and bonds: "If you have a balanced portfolio of stocks and bonds, you might get a 10 percent return on your stocks and 7 percent on bonds. That gives you an average 8.5 percent return," Clements says. "So I have a choice. I can invest in a balanced portfolio and hope I get 8.5 percent. Or I can invest in a sure thing and get 7.7 percent." As for the taxes, Clements says it's a wash if the alternative is to put the money in a taxable investment account. "If you prepay your mortgage, you lose the tax-deductible interest," he says. "But if you put the money in an investment account, you pay tax on the earnings."

Prepaying on your mortgage is also a painless way of saving. Most of us could afford to add an extra $25 a month to our payment. But if we don't prepay, how many of us would put the same $25 into a bank account or mutual fund? Most of us would fritter it away. Every extra dollar reduces your long-term cost. "The average person's mortgage check is for an odd amount of money. Why not just round it up? If you owe $673, pay $700," Eisenson says.

Be sure to check with your mortgage lender first to make sure there is no prepayment penalty on your loan (such penalties are rare, particularly after the first year of a loan). Note the additional principal payment, plus the regular, monthly payment on the memo space on your check. Then, look on your mortgage coupon for a space marked additional principal. That's where to enter the extra amount you are adding to your regular monthly payment. If the coupon has no such space, or you're confused by the process, contact your mortgage lender for directions.

One final word of advice: Avoid consumer products that have been designed to capitalize on the prepayment idea. For example, some companies have developed elaborate kits that range in price from $100 to $300 to help you figure out how to prepay your mortgage. What do experts like Eisenson recommend? "Don't pay anyone else to help you figure out how to pay off your mortgage. It's too simple."

First Things First

Like any good idea, paying down your mortgage has a couple of caveats. Investing in your mortgage doesn't make as much sense as investing in a tax-deductible plan such as a 401(k) at work or a tax-deductible individual retirement account. Be certain that you've put as much as you can into these plans before you consider prepaying your mortgage. Second, pay off your high-rate credit card debts before you prepay your mortgage. "If you pay $5 extra on your credit card balance, you will be earning a return of 17 or 18 percent," says Marc Eisenson.

2. Pay Off Your Mortgage Early

—MARY HUNT

I have a warm spot in my heart for the person who came up with the concept of the 30-year home mortgage. Like many Americans, my husband and I would never have been able to buy a home without a mortgage. The 30-year feature allows for affordable payments, but also fits nicely into the typical working career. Still, as grateful as I am to have a mortgage, I'm even more anxious to get rid of it. Who wants to drag a big pile of debt into retirement?

Whether you are currently a home owner or you plan to buy in the future, the right knowledge and repayment strategies will help you look forward to the day when you can kiss your mortgage lender goodbye forever!

MAKE THE FIRST PAYMENT COUNT

When you buy a home, many lenders require one month's interest to be prepaid as part of the closing costs, with the first payment due in the second month after closing. If you choose to make your first payment in the initial month, that entire amount will go to reducing the principal. Making this one payment at the start lops off $7,394 in interest and six months from a $200,000 30-year mortgage at 6.5 percent interest.

LESS IS MORE

Let's say you qualify to buy a $250,000 home with a $200,000 mortgage at 6.5 percent interest for 30 years, payable at $1,264 per month. A better strategy would be to buy a $150,000 house with a 30-year $100,000 mortgage at 6.5 percent ($636 payments). By paying the larger amount each month ($1,264), you'll pay this mortgage off in 8.5 years. Sell and upgrade to a $250,000 home, use the entire $150,000 as a down payment and repeat.

Get fixed

Even though interest rates are creeping upward, if you have a primary mortgage and home equity loan with variable rates of interest, refinancing both into a fixed-rate mortgage may be a wise move. With a fixed rate you always know what to expect. Caution: As tempting as it is to cash out some of your equity (the current market value minus what you owe on your mortgage) as you refinance, leave all of your equity alone so it can appreciate.

Pay it down faster

BIWEEKLY IS GOOD. Paying half of your monthly payment every two weeks (26 half-payments each year) turns out to be 13 full monthly payments in a year. That extra payment is the secret behind the power of the biweekly payment schedule. But unless you join a biweekly program that charges steep fees and locks you into that schedule, your mortgage company is not likely to accept half-payments.

You can do the very same thing yourself. Each month when you make your regular mortgage payment, write a second check for one-twelfth of one payment and designate it for "Principal Prepayment Only." Send the two checks together. Do this every month and in one year you will have made the equivalent of 13 monthly payments—with no fees, no obligations and no lender approval required. This strategy will drop about seven years from your payback term (depending on the other terms) and save you thousands of dollars in interest.

DON'T CASH OUT. The equity in your home is a precious commodity because it is an appreciating asset, providing the housing market keeps going up in your area. Taking out cash through home equity loans widens your debt and increases your monthly payment. You risk owing the lender more than the home is worth. If that equity is money you really need for some other purpose, consider selling your home now and downsizing to a cheaper area. Your goal is to achieve 100 percent equity before you retire. If you keep taking out cash to pay off credit cards or pay for college, you'll never pay off that mortgage.

Expand your profit

Widen the gap. You need to maintain a healthy gap between the amount your home is worth and the amount you owe—never less than 20 percent is my advice. Concentrate on widening that gap by paying off your mortgage early and you'll sail through any market downturn.

Spruce up. While you have no control over housing market values, you can keep your home at the top of your neighborhood's value by performing routine repairs and maintenance. Even in a down market your home will be more likely to stay at the top of its class when it reflects your pride of ownership.

Keep paying it down. It doesn't matter if you plan to be in your home for two years or for 20. No matter when you sell this house, your goal should be to come out with your original down payment, plus lots of equity for the next down payment. You want to use all of that money to make the largest down payment you can and take out the smallest mortgage possible. And you want to do that every time you buy. That's the way to build wealth on an ordinary income.

You can buy and sell a dozen times in your homeownership career, and if you're careful to move your equity into the next home—just as you move your furniture and other possessions—you should be able to own the last one free and clear, in time for retirement.

What's it worth?

You know how much you owe on your mortgage. But what is your home actually worth? Go to zillow.com to get a "zestimate" of its market value today, based on current sales and other factors in your local area. Now subtract your current outstanding mortgage. Voilà! Your present equity.

Ⓔ *Save on Utilities*

1. Ways to Cut Your Utility Bill: Do Your Wallet— and the Environment—a Favor

Leave the water running when you're brushing your teeth? Forget to turn off the TV when you leave the room? You could be wasting hundreds of dollars a year. Read ahead for energy-saving tips you can begin to use today.

GETTING STARTED

Nearly everyone can practice energy conservation on a daily basis and reap significant dollar rewards. By shaving just 10 percent off your utility bill, you can save $180 a year on an average monthly utility bill of $150 (gas, electric and water combined). Here's how to plug the energy leaks throughout your home.

BRIGHT IDEAS

- Use one large bulb instead of several small ones that add up to higher wattage.
- Take advantage of low settings on three-way lighting fixtures.
- Replace your regular bulbs with compact fluorescent bulbs, they have a longer rated life and use less energy.
- Consider installing dimmers or high-low switches.
- Keep lightbulbs and fixtures clean; dust absorbs light.
- Remove any lightbulbs that are not truly needed. Taking out just one 100-watt lightbulb can save over 200 kilowatt-hours (kwh) of electricity every year, plus the replacement costs of the bulbs. That averages out to $18 per bulb.
- Try 4-watt nightlight bulbs with clear finishes in regular lamps. They're almost as bright as 7-watt frosted bulbs but use half the energy.
- Use 50-watt reflector floodlights in directional lamps (such as pole or spot lamps). These lights provide about the same amount of light as standard 100-watt bulbs.

- Consider installing high-efficiency sodium lamps for outdoor security lighting.

Room Service

- Save electricity by concentrating lighting in reading and working areas and reducing it elsewhere.
- Turn off your radio, TV, stereo or CD player when you're leaving the room for more than five minutes.
- Stop drafts under doors by using draft stoppers. Rooms will stay nice and warm in cooler months.

The Temperate Zone, Heating

- Set your thermostat as low as possible in the winter. Often, 68° to 70°F is recommended as a reasonably comfortable and energy-efficient indoor temperature. However, some older or ailing people may require higher indoor temperatures at all times.
- Clean or replace the filter in your forced-air heating system each month-during the fall and winter.
- Consider the advantages of using a clock thermostat for your heating system.You program it to automatically turn down the heat at night while you're sleeping.
- If you have an oil-heating system, have your serviceman look to see if the firing rate is correct. A recent survey found that a large majority of oil furnaces checked were over-firing.
- In the fall, have your central heating/cooling system, whatever its energy source, checked out by a professional.
- Think about installing ceiling fans with reversible motors. In winter, ceiling fans push warm air that collects near a high ceiling up, around and back down again. In summer, they help circulate cooler air around the room as well.
- Dust or vacuum radiator surfaces frequently to ensure free flow of heat.
- Use kitchen and bath vent fans sparingly in cool months, since they can blow away warm air quickly.

Cooling

- Depending on where you live, set your thermostat as high as possible in the summer. Often, 78°F is recommended as a pleasant temperature for indoors.

- Don't set your thermostat at a colder setting than normal when you turn on your air conditioner. It won't cool the room any faster, but it does use more energy.

- Keep strong light sources a sufficient distance from the thermostat to prevent inaccurate warmer readings.

- Set the air-conditioner fan on high except in very humid weather. Low fan speeds remove more moisture from the air.

- Clean or replace window air-conditioner filters at least once a month during the warmer months. Use ceiling fans. They lower air temperature by about 4°F.

- Delay using the dishwasher, dryer and other heat-spewing appliances until cooler evening hours.

- Turn off lights when you don't need them. Slowly—but just as surely—they add heat to a room.

- Turn off the AC when walls are cool to the touch. Use fans to move air instead.

- Block sunlight, especially through east- and west-facing windows. Use drapes with light-colored linings, or light-colored blinds, to reflect warm sunlight right back outside.

- Shade east and west windows with awnings or trees—and spruce up the outside of your home.

- Make the most of breezes by opening windows or using air conditioning during the hottest hours of the day only. If your area lacks consistent breezes, create a steady flow of air by opening windows at the lowest and highest points in your house.

- Replace broken or cracked windows. If you're replacing them frame and all, look for double- or triple-pane, low-emissivity models.

Keep Your Cool

Do...

- Install room air conditioners on a north wall, if possible, or a wall that's shaded outside. The south wall is second best.

- Use a room air conditioner appropriate for the space being cooled. Too large a unit wastes energy; too small doesn't cool properly and taxes the compressor. As a rule of thumb, you'll need 5,000 BTUs to cool a room of 100 to 150 square feet. Figure 1,000 additional BTUs for every 50 extra square feet, up to 450 square feet.

- Be certain the outside condensing unit of a central air conditioner is shaded from direct sun for more efficient cooling.

Don't...

- Cool rooms you're not using. Some new central-air systems provide zone cooling, which enables you to cool designated rooms to desired temperatures. Or you can simply close the registers in unused rooms. However, don't shut off too many registers in a central system. It may harm the compressor.

- Use a dehumidifier at the same time as an air conditioner. Dehumidifiers increase the cooling load, forcing an air conditioner to work much harder.

- Run attic or window fans when the air-conditioning system is on. You simply blow the cool air outside.

Window & Wall Units

PROS

- They occupy a small amount of space, either mounted in a window or built into a wall.
- Room air conditioners cost just a few hundred dollars and don't require extensive installation.

CONS

- They're limited in the amount of space they can cool—usually just one room.
- Window air conditioners block views, light and natural ventilation. Wall-mounted units are often a better choice, but they're more expensive to install.

MAINTENANCE

- Air filters should be cleaned monthly. Some newer units have washable filters that slide out so they can be washed, dried and returned to the unit.
- The condenser should be cleaned every 18 months to two years by a professional. During servicing, refrigerant should be checked to see if it needs recharging.

Central Air

PROS

- They're out of the way, quiet and convenient, and they tend to be more efficient than window air conditioners. Plus, if you already have a forced-air heating system, you may be able to tap into existing duct work.

CONS

- These systems are not cheap. They also need an exterior space for the condensing unit.
- If you don't have duct work, the cost of installing it can range from $2,000 to $5,000 or more for a 3-ton system, the most commonly used.

MAINTENANCE

- The exterior condensing unit should be kept free of debris such as grass clippings and leaves, which can clog the unit.
- The system should be inspected, cleaned and tuned by a professional every two or three years.

What to Think of When Buying an Air Conditioner

Best Buys

- Before buying a room air conditioner, shop around. You may find a difference in price of hundreds of dollars for the same unit.

- Consider buying a floor model with a slight imperfection—a scratch or dent—and offer to pay about 75 to 80 percent of the retail price.

- Typically, the best time to buy a unit is in winter, when a store's sales are slow. But if you're looking in the heat of the summer, ask if any of last year's models remain in stock. They may come cheaper.

- When reviewing bids for central air conditioning or a heat pump, consider the terms of the warranty and any service plan that may be part of the package. When you look at the whole picture, the lowest bid may not be the best deal.

- Carefully read labels when shopping for new appliances or a new heating/cooling system. Compare energy-use information and operating costs of similar models by the same and different manufacturers.

Hot Tips & Cool Features

- Be certain to buy a high-efficiency room air conditioner or central air conditioner when you replace an old unit—an inefficient model will only lock you into high electric bills for years. The Energy Efficiency Rating (EER) should be above 9 for a room unit, and the Seasonal Energy Efficiency Ratio (SEER) should be above 12 for central air conditioners. (Those that bear the Energy Star® label are government-certified for the unit's energy efficiency.)

- Other energy-saving features to look for include a fan-only switch, which lets you use the unit for nighttime ventilation; a filter check light; and timers that turn the unit on and off automatically.

In the Kitchen, Appliance Aid

- Be sure your refrigerator is located in the driest, coolest part of the kitchen, well away from the range or oven.

- Don't keep the refrigerator or freezer too cold: 37° to 42°F for fresh-food compartment, 5°F for the freezer section. If you have a separate freezer for long-term storage, set it at 0°F.

- Don't allow frost to build up more than a quarter inch in manual-defrost refrigerators and freezers. It lowers energy efficiency.

- If you have an electric stove, develop the habit of turning it off several minutes before the allotted cooking time is up. The burners stay hot long enough to finish the job without using more electricity. The same principle applies to oven cooking.

- If you have a gas stove, make sure the pilot light is burning efficiently, with a blue flame. A yellowish flame may indicate an adjustment is needed.

- Don't use a pan that's too small for the burner—it wastes heat.

- Use a timer or watch the clock carefully when operating the oven. Opening the door lets heat escape.

- Don't preheat the oven unless required for the proper baking of foods such as bread and cake.

Clever Cleaning

- Fill a sink or pan when washing or rinsing dishes instead of using a constant stream of water. Rinse the dishes in cold water.

- When using a dishwasher, let your dishes air-dry. If you don't have an automatic air-dry switch, prop the door open a little after the final rinse.

- Don't use the "rinse hold" on your machine for just a few soiled dishes unless you really need it. Rinse hold removes stuck-on food, and it requires about 1.5 to 7 gallons of hot water each time you use it.

- Use cold water rather than hot to operate your garbage disposal.

- Install an aerator in your kitchen faucet to reduce the amount of flow and hot water used.

Laundry Lessons

- Don't use too much detergent—it makes your machine work harder.

- Separate drying loads into heavy and lightweight items. Since the lighter ones take less drying time, the dryer doesn't have to be on as long for these loads.

- Dry your clothes in consecutive batches. Stop-and-start drying uses more energy because a lot goes into warming up the dryer each time you begin.

- If the dryer has an automatic dry cycle, use it. Overdrying wastes energy, which costs you money.

- Keep the lint screen in the dryer clean by removing lint after each load. A dirty screen forces the machine to use more energy.

- Keep the outside exhaust vent of your clothes dryer clean. A clogged exhaust lengthens the drying time.

Shower Power

- Take showers rather than baths, but limit your showering time. It takes about 30 gallons of water to fill the average tub. A five-minute shower uses only 15 gallons.

- Consider installing a flow controller in the showerhead. These inexpensive, easy-to-install devices restrict the flow of water to an adequate 3 to 4 gallons per minute.

- Don't leave the water running when you brush your teeth, wash your face or shave your legs. A running faucet puts 3 to 5 gallons down the drain every minute it's on.

Water-Heater Hints

- Be sure the water heater (which accounts for 20 percent of all energy used in the home) and the hot-water pipes are sufficiently insulated.

- Set the water heater at 120°F unless you have a large family and use vast amounts of hot water or have a dishwasher. Reducing the temperature from the usual 140°F to 120°F could save over 18 percent of the energy used at the higher setting.

Tool Talk

- Do not allow gasoline-powered yard equipment to idle for long periods of time.

- Maintain electrical tools in top operating condition. They should be clean and properly lubricated.

- Keep cutting edges on tools sharp. A sharp bit or saw cuts more quickly and therefore uses less power. Also keep them oiled; this will reduce friction, which will cut down on the power required.

- Remember to turn off shop lights, soldering irons, gluepots and all bench heating devices right after using them.

Smart Savings

- Use the new, screw-in fluorescent bulbs in lamps and small, open fixtures throughout your home (they're available at lighting specialty stores). They save $30 of electricity over the life of the bulb and last up to ten times longer. Fluorescents are costlier initially, but more than pay for themselves over time.

- Plant deciduous trees and vines on the south and west sides of your home to provide shade in the summer and sunshine in the winter.

The Biggest Saver: Proper Insulation

This can cut 20 to 30 percent off your monthly energy bill. When purchasing insulation, compare the R-number on the packages. The higher the R-value or numbers, the more effective an insulator is. You can install the insulation yourself in only a couple of days.

Drafty windows and doors, or the cracks where plumbing or electrical wires go through walls, floors and ceilings, can be deadly to the budget. Caulking and weatherstripping are simple ways to prevent these air leaks. Materials cost between $40 to $50 for the average house (12 windows, 2 doors). Savings in materials costs between $40 to $50 for the average house (12 windows, 2 doors). Savings in annual energy costs alone may range as high as 10 percent.

If you suspect you have a draft, use your hands to test the area. Or, construct a simple "draft detector" by taping a piece of tissue paper to a coat hanger. Hold the coat hanger in front of or over a suspected crack and watch for any movement.

The attic is the biggest secret entrance for heat. To add insulation to attic flooring, determine the total square footage as well as the distance between joists. Ask a building-materials supplier the proper R-value (resistance to heat flow) for your climate. (The higher the R-value, the greater the insulating capacity.) Then, simply lay insulation between joists according to instructions.

 Pet Care

1. Cut the Cost of Pet Care

—MARY HUNT

No one was more surprised than I when my first granddog, Sir Boddington, nuzzled a place in my heart. I knew I was smitten the day I loaded up on toys, milk bones and other doggie delights. I blame it on "Boddie" that I so willingly became a member of the U.S. population who last year spent $38.4 billion on food, supplies, services such as grooming and boarding, and medical care for their 358 million pets.

So how can you afford to care for your furry friend—in sickness and in health? Make prevention maintenance your top priority as a pet owner and you'll save later on.

STICK WITH THE BASICS

RESTRAIN THEM. "A fence or some other reasonable restraint is the best way to avoid big vet bills," says David T. Roen, D.V.M., board-certified veterinarian and owner of the Clarkston Veterinary Clinic in Clarkston, Washington. "I see more dogs in my office because of injuries sustained while unrestrained than for any other reason. Dogs should always be leashed, fenced or supervised."

CHOOSE THE RIGHT FOOD. Dr. Roen advises pet owners to skip all the fancy premium foods sold by vets. Use name-brand pet food from the supermarket labeled "complete and balanced." Or look for the seal of approval of AAFCO (the Association of American Feed Control Officials). Stick with the same brand. Switching abruptly can cause health issues for some animals. And less is better, as slightly underweight pets have fewer health problems.

KEEP THEM HEALTHY. Make wellness routine, some pet supply stores offer in-store clinics and special events. Humane societies and veterinary schools offer low-cost clinics where inoculations and wellness exams are administered by professionals. Keep good records of the inoculations and treatments your pet has.

SPAY AND NEUTER. Reproductive issues aside, spayed and neutered dogs have fewer health and behavioral problems.

FORGET HEALTH INSURANCE. "Pet insurance will probably cost more money than it saves," says Dr. Roen. But you should anticipate future medical bills. "Instead of sending premiums to an insurance company, put the amount you'd pay in premiums into a savings account."

CONSIDER PREPAID. Scott G., who has three dogs in Atlanta, enrolled in the discount wellness plan offered by Banfield The Pet Hospital (banfield. net), a national chain of pet care facilities. "I pay a set fee each month so that all of my wellness exams and inoculations are covered. With enrollment comes deeply discounted office visits and services should they be necessary."

GO FOR SECOND OPINIONS. Even if it's an emergency, if the estimate is for more than a few hundred dollars, get a second opinion. "If the estimate is for $800 and you can only afford $400, speak up," says Dr. Roen. There may be less aggressive and cheaper alternative treatments.

SHOP AROUND FOR MEDICATIONS. Ask your vet for prescription drug samples to get started. Then call around to retailers such as Wal-Mart or Costco pharmacies (many meds are the same for humans and animals) to compare prices. Search websites like discountpetmedicines.com or petmeds.com.

THE COST OF LOVING FIDO

ANNUAL COSTS FOR SMALL DOGS		ONE-TIME COSTS FOR SMALL DOGS	
Food	$160	Spay/neuter	$75
Medical	$150	Collar/leash	$25
Toys/treats	$60	Carrier	$30
License	$15	Crate	$60
Grooming	$200		
Misc.	$35	Total first year: $810	

5. Shop and Buy Smart

 General Shopping

1. How to Save on Big-Ticket Items

—MARY HUNT

I couldn't help noticing that the lady in front of me had about the same mix of milk, cheese and frozen chicken as we waited in line at the warehouse club one Saturday morning. Only she needed an industrial-strength cart because she had a couple more items: a sofa and matching love seat! The man behind me had his groceries, plus a big-screen TV.

We laughed because both said they had no intention of making these big-ticket purchases before they got to the store—they just couldn't pass up the deals. Standing there, I recalled similar decisions I've made in my life for items that didn't last as long as the payments.

Thankfully, it's not every day you are faced with a major purchase like a refrigerator, a computer or tires for the car. But with the right information and a healthy dose of planning, you can avoid making a purchase you'll live to regret, and slash the cost of buying the big things in your life.

ANTICIPATE

Nothing lasts forever. Take your refrigerator: You can expect about 14 years of service. Beyond that, you're probably on borrowed time. Anticipate by giving yourself time to save for a replacement.

WAIT

That horrible clunking sound may mean the washing machine is on its last leg. But a temporary repair job or just putting up with the annoyance may buy you the time you need to save for a reasonable replacement. So hold out for as long as you can to avoid making an impulsive decision.

Pay cash

If at all possible, pay cash for things that depreciate, such as major appliances. Offers of "nothing down, no payments and no interest!" are tempting, but these deals are often confusing and may be filled with pitfalls. If you do sign on, make sure you pay the balance in full before the deadline, or you may have to pay double-digit interest retroactively to day one. Better idea: Skip the hype and buy what you can with the cash you have.

Three-year rule

Only buy an item on credit if it has a life expectancy of more than three years and you will pay it off in less than three. If you stretch the payments any longer, you'll regret it when that computer is obsolete and you're still paying for it.

Quality vs. need

Match the quality of the item to your needs. Sometimes you need the best quality you can afford, but not always. You might need the highest-quality computer for your graphic-design work, while a lightweight mattress in a little-used guest room would be ideal.

Nearly new

There is a huge secondary market of gently used appliances, furniture and electronics, if you're willing to look. Consider consignment stores, estate sales, rental returns, classified ads and auction houses. Craigslist.org has become a hot secondary market for everything from furniture to appliances and beyond. Click on your city and check out the deals.

Furniture

Looking for a new couch? Most of the furniture manufacturers located in High Point, North Carolina, dubbed the Furniture Capital of the World, sell direct. I cut the full retail price of our family room furniture, including shipping, by buying direct. A good place to start your research is highpointfurniture.com.

On sale now

Don't waste time (and gas) driving from store to store looking for the best deal. Visit one store so you can actually see, touch and measure the item, then go to ciaro.com, a site that makes it easy to compare this week's sale prices at most retail stores, including Best Buy, Circuit City and Sears.

Last year's model

Each year, appliance manufacturers come out with new, souped-up models of refrigerators, dishwashers, ranges, washers and dryers with bigger price tags. Last year's model may be perfectly adequate for your needs. Current-year models typically go on sale toward the end of the year.

Discount clubs

The big three (Costco, Sam's Club and BJ's) routinely undercut the competition on appliances, electronics, computer hardware and mattresses, but selections are limited. Search their respective websites. You don't have to be a club member to search online.

Go ahead and ask!

Make an offer on the floor model. If you can get the warranty intact plus a big discount, it merits your consideration. It never hurts to ask.

TIP: NEED A NEW MATTRESS?

FORGET THE PILLOW-TOP. It can add upwards of $100 to the cost of the mattress and flatten long before the mattress shows any wear. Instead buy a great mattress pad. When it flattens out, get a new one. Your mattress will last for many years longer.

TRY LIFTING IT. Determine whether a mattress is light or heavy by trying to pick it up at one corner. For a guest room seldom used or a small child, lightweight is just fine. For adults, opt for the heaviest mattress you can afford.

Attention Shoppers: Find the Best Bargains Ever with These Simple Tips

- Get to know the salespeople at your favorite stores and treat them like gold. They can usually give you 10 or 20 percent off if you're a regular customer and you purchase more than one item.

- Look for clearance signs for deals on end-of-season merchandise. Check the sale racks often because the good stuff turns over fast.

- Keep your eyes peeled for preseason sales. Some stores put their new arrivals on sale to drive up business and meet their sales goals.

- Hit stores in suburban and rural areas instead of shopping in the city. You're likely to get a better price because the store overhead tends to be lower and retailers don't have to mark up as much.

- Ask about floor models for low prices on appliances. Shop electronics outlet stores for deals on last season's models and freight-damaged or returned items. If a box says "factory refurbished," it's usually in excellent shape.

2. A Savvy Shopper's Secrets for Buying in Bulk: How to Tell a Bum Deal from a Real Steal

Buying in bulk is an article of faith in these cost-conscious times, and judging by the boom in discount warehouse paradises and mega-markets, the trend is showing no sign of slacking. But is bulk buying really the answer to our prayers?

That depends. When you first visit a discount warehouse, it's stunning—aisle after aisle of giant packages at seemingly low, low prices. How can you afford not to buy? Even the carts are super-sized, and you feel downright insufficient if you can't fill one to the top. So you become a bulk hulk. You spend a couple hundred dollars, drive home and load your cupboards, freezers and the basement with those glorious deals. And three months later, lots of them are still around, only now they've spoiled, gone stale and gathered dust. Welcome to the seedy side of bulk shopping.

How do you cultivate bulk smarts? Start by tearing out this guide and hanging it on the inside of a cupboard door. And do it now, before it's too late.

Do...

- Take an inventory of family standbys, bearing in mind that not everyone may be willing to commit to using the same shampoo for the next six months.

- Make a list, remember to bring it with you, and stick to it. If it's not on your list, don't buy it. It's that simple.

- Establish a buddy system: Maybe you get starry-eyed over the low price of dishcloths in bulk, but do you really need 20? Divide great deals with a friend to really save.

- Shop with a conscience and you're likely to boost your savings. If your kids drink more boxed juice during warm weather, instead of doubling your standing inventory, consider a 32-oz can of presweetened lemonade mix. Needless packaging costs money—especially in bulk.

- Watch for rebates. Manufacturers often offer rebates on large institutional packages. Check the front of the store for coupon displays before you shop. When you get home, promptly remove the proof of purchase and save it with your receipt to return with the rebate coupon.

- Be on the lookout for post-season bargains. Look for racks of reduced-price clothes and bins of seasonal goods such as holiday wrapping paper and accessories.

Don't...

- Outshop your space. Yes, you'll eventually use up that toilet tissue, but 48 rolls stored on the basement floor is an open invitation to all manner of nasties—from floods to creepy crawlies. By the way, don't even think of installing a shelving system to hold all your "wise" buys. The idea is saving money, remember?

- Buy perishable or fashionable. No one can eat an entire case of prune yogurt in two weeks. Period.

- Forget to comparison-shop to be sure you're getting the best deals in your area. Bring along your last grocery or discount store's itemized cash register receipts to check against bulk prices.

- Buy before you try. If you've not tried a product before, for heaven's sake don't buy 50 of them. Most warehouse stores offer samples or single items.
- Buy more than you can store safely. Large quantities of flour, soup and biscuit mixes can host insects and their eggs. If you live in a damp climate or store your goods in a moist place, buy realistic amounts so you don't have to deal with bugs.
- Buy food that others may have inadvertently contaminated. If you buy from a bin, do so only in stores where there's a lid on each bin, a tethered scoop for each product and plenty of bags.
- A sale item at the supermarket may cost less than at a membership warehouse club. Combine a supermarket sale price with a coupon and the per-unit price will almost always be lower than at a warehouse.
- Ask a local grocer or retailer if they'll give you a per-case discount. Supermarkets, unlike most warehouse clubs, can accept coupons; if you have 24 separate coupons, you can significantly lower your net price.
- Frozen foods are great deals in warehouse clubs because they're packaged for commercial use. But partner-shop with friends if you're buying a lot more than you can use.

3. Hey, Big Spender: How to Save More on Major Purchases

Today the Internet, telephone and mailbox bring plenty of shopping options 24/7 for most anything you want. Do your homework before making any purchases, especially big-ticket items. These tips will help you shop big, shop more and avoid big-ticket mistakes.

MAKE A SMART CHOICE

DON'T: Talk to the wrong guy.
DO: Negotiate with the person who can make a decision.

A manager might have the authority that salespeople don't for negotiating prices or offering discounts on flawed items. But getting to know anybody on the selling floor over time can be helpful. "Building a relationship with a particular salesperson or dealer can help you get better deals on future purchases," says Beverly B., from Austin, Texas, who often learns about upcoming sales this way.

Don't: Disclose too much information up front.

Do: Be vague when a salesperson asks about your budget for an item.

After all, you don't go around telling friends and coworkers how much money is in your wallet, so why tell a salesman? Just tell him whether you want to see the $100 toaster or the $10 model, whichever browns your bread better and suits your needs.

Don't: Assume you're being told everything you need to know.

Do: Ask the seller questions.

When buying anything, from a collectible item to a home to a used car, order any available reports or take along your own expert for advice. Don't make assumptions about missing information. For example, auction specialists represent the seller, not the buyer. While they may not purposely mislead you, they won't necessarily call your attention to a particular flaw or condition rating that you may have overlooked either in ignorance or because you took an advertisement or catalog photo at face value.

Get the Best Price

Don't: Accept the first offer.

Do: Call around.

When Hilda B. of Atlanta fell in love with a wrought-iron headboard several years ago after seeing it in a magazine, she immediately priced the piece at a local store. It was an unaffordable $1,200. Then she saw ads for furniture outlets in North Carolina. "I called three of them, and to my amazement, the price got lower with each call," Hilda says. "I finally landed the headboard for about $650, which included $100 in shipping costs." Looking for more ways to get the best deal on furniture? Check out the online version of *The Furniture Factory Outlet Guide*, at smart decorating.com for advice on how to shop like a pro.

Don't: Accept a price at face value.

Do: Always compare sticker prices—and then compare some more.

A sign that reads, "Regularly $569—Our Price $450," may not be a good deal. Harried shoppers sometimes accept these price advertisements at face value and assume that they're getting a good deal, but that's not necessarily so. The item could be had for the same price or even a better price elsewhere. To find the best price, read the newspaper sales circulars at salescircular.com and use online shopping sites, including mysimon.com and shopper.cnet.com.

Don't: Shop only fixed prices.

Do: Bid at auctions.

And we're not just talking about eBay. To bid for new, seized and surplus items from the government, including cars, boats, SUVs, computer equipment and real estate, visit first gov.gov/shopping/shopping.shtml for details. To find excess or surplus items, go to gsaauctions.gov, the government's centralized electronic clearinghouse. It's often a good idea to try police auctions too. Pat C., a mother of two in Watkinsville, Georgia, says her husband bought a four-year-old Ford Crown Victoria from a police auction for $1,600. "If he had been buying a new car, he wouldn't have chosen a Crown Victoria because it would have cost too much," she says.

Don't: Think bigger is always better.

Do: Buy only what you need.

An appliance that's too big for your home, or its intended job, will cost you money eventually because it will use more energy or operate inefficiently. That's why the government-backed Energy Star program guidelines (energystar.gov) suggest your new furnace, boiler, refrigerator or air conditioner be sized to fit your home. Oversizing shortens the equipment's life span by causing it to use more energy unnecessarily (which also raises your bill) than a properly sized unit.

Be a Little Flexible

Don't: Automatically buy what's in style at the moment.
Do: Go for the less popular color or style if you can get a price break.

Always ask the dealer if there's a particular item or brand he's trying to sell at a discount. Five years ago Beverly B. bought a Ford Explorer Eddie Bauer Edition loaded with special features instead of a less well-equipped SUV because the dealer had one in stock he really wanted to sell, and the price was right. "It was a reddish brown—something we hadn't even considered but ended up liking very much," she says. Beverly recently went back to the same dealer for a new model.

Don't: Buy only perfect items.
Do: Look for new items with minor cosmetic damage.

When aesthetics aren't a big priority, try opting for products labeled "as is." Juliet M. of Brooklyn, New York, enjoyed significant savings when she bought a new Whirlpool self-cleaning electric range and oven last year for less than $200. "You would have to be on your knees and nose to nose with it to see the dent," she says. Look for stores or outlets selling marred appliances. Factory warranties may still apply.

Don't: Ignore the "R" words.
Do: Look for items labeled "remanufactured," "reconditioned" or "refurbished."

This basically means that the item, such as a computer, television or digital camera, may have been a floor model or a customer might have returned it. The products are then thoroughly inspected and restored, if necessary, to their original operating conditions and put back on the market at a lower price than new items of the same make and model. However, be sure to read the warranties, which may be limited.

Do You Really Need It?

Don't: Buy extended warranties to avert trouble later.
Do: Choose reputable products and stick with the standard warranty.

Salespeople often suggest you take an extended warranty when you make a big-ticket purchase. But items such as refrigerators and computers usually come with a standard warranty that covers parts and labor for a period that's often long enough to have any major problems become apparent. And even an extended warranty won't necessarily cover a problem that has been caused by negligence.

DON'T: Choose an item solely based on the rebate.
DO: Take advantage of any rebate that's offered.

Many buyers forget to redeem rebates, even on larger ticket purchases such as computers and televisions. Go home and complete the rebate right away. The longer you wait, the less likely you are to redeem it.

SHOULD YOU REPAIR OR REPLACE APPLIANCES?

No one rule of thumb can help you decide whether to repair or replace your malfunctioning appliance, such as a refrigerator or dishwasher.
Ask yourself these questions:

- Can you afford to buy a new one? If your budget shouts no, repairs may be the way to go.

- Have your needs changed since you purchased the appliance? For example, maybe you have a bigger family. If so, replacing your broken appliance with a bigger one may be necessary.

- Could the energy-saving features of a newer model save you money in the long run? Do the research and the math.

- What's the cost of repairing versus replacing? If the cost of a professional repair exceeds half the cost of buying a new appliance, consider replacing it.

What are the hidden costs of replacing versus repairing? For instance, in addition to the price of a new dishwasher, you'd want to consider any costs related to disconnection, removal and disposal of the old dishwasher, plus installation of the replacement.

---

4. How to Shop the Outlets like a Pro

Some say shopping is a sport. If it's your sport of choice, you know that outlet centers present a particular challenge. They've become the new malls, and are often crowded with people who shop nowhere else. And while you may still find A-list bargains that somehow got passed over in retail stores, spotting these gems gets trickier every year, because now the shelves may also be filled with flimsier merchandise made specifically for outlets.

ON YOUR MARK...

- **CHECK OUT THE COMPETITION.** Cruise a mall and look through catalogs. The best bargain hunters are aware of retail prices, so they can recognize the real deals.

- **STUDY QUALITY.** Visit the finest section of a department store and see what the stitching, lining and fabric is like on full-price designer clothing. Try on a few things (they can't stop you from looking). Then try to find that same fit and feel in clothing from the bargain racks.

- **KNOW WHAT YOU WANT.** Keep a running list of gift ideas, plus a list of things you can always use more of, such as socks or giftwrap. Also update your list of family members' sizes and preferences.

- **KNOW WHAT YOU DON'T WANT.** Make a mental note of things you shouldn't buy, such as "no more T-shirts at any price!"

- **TRACK DOWN YOUR FAVORITE STORES.** There are about 350 outlet centers to choose from. One fast way to locate the stores you like is by doing an Internet search (outletbound.com), or try using the index in books about outlet shopping. Another hint: Often the best outlets aren't at vacation destinations; they're near the actual factories in small towns.

GET SET...

- **MAKE A DAY (AT LEAST) OF IT.** Breeze through the stores one evening, plan your purchases at dinner that night, then shop the next day from early morning until late afternoon.

- **DRESS FOR THE JOB.** Wear slip-on shoes, a lightweight T-shirt that fits under blazers and sweaters and pants without a belt to make try-ons easier.

- **LEAVE YOUR HANDBAG AT HOME.** A fanny pack, a backpack, either way, they keep your hands free.

- **BRING SUPPLIES.** Marathon shoppers should carry tissues, pen, paper, a hair scrunchie or a barrette, aspirin and a calculator. If you're looking for home furnishings, bring a tape measure and wallpaper or fabric swatches. And, like any athlete, you'll be thankful for bottled water and healthy snacks.

- **DON'T BRING THE KIDS OR YOUR HUSBAND.** You'll be faster and more efficient without them.

GO!

- **DON'T LIMIT YOURSELF TO CLOTHING.** We found plenty of great housewares outlets. Furniture outlets sell assembled pieces at lower prices than you would usually pay for those you have to assemble yourself.

- **TRY CATALOG FACTORY OUTLETS.** Check the factory stores for catalogs such as J. Crew. They often overstock and then send perfectly good leftovers to outlets.

- **NEVER PAY FULL PRICE FOR KIDS' CLOTHES.** Children's wear is inexpensive at outlets and because kids grow fast, you don't have to be as concerned about durability.

- **BE PICKY ABOUT QUALITY ON ADULT CLOTHING.** For instance, on a jacket or shirt, are the pockets stitched at the corners so they won't rip? Are suits or jackets lined for sturdiness? If you bunch some of the fabric in your hand and squeeze, does it fall back into place?

- **LOOK FOR ITEMS MADE IN THE UNITED STATES.** Use this as a general guideline. Because manufacturing in this country costs more than it does in some other countries, it's usually not skimpy stuff.

THE REWARDS

- **CONSIDER EACH PURCHASE CAREFULLY.** If you're going to buy it, you should love it. Even bargains add up.

- **THEN CONSIDER SOME MORE.** Ask yourself, "Would I pay twice as much for this?" If not, you should pass. "Would you pay $20 more?" Then try to visualize the new item in your closet, as well as where you would wear it. If it seems out of place, walk away.

- **TABULATE THE FINAL COST.** In some stores, you have to remember that everything is half off the ticketed prices. In others, you can take a percentage off some racks. If you're uncertain about the bottom line, ask.

- **DON'T BE DAZZLED BY QUANTITY.** Just because you can afford to get nightgowns in every color doesn't mean you should.

- **NEGOTIATE.** Ask store clerks if there is any way to get a lower price, there sometimes is.

- **NOTE RETURN POLICIES.** At most outlet stores, all sales are final. A few give store credit.

- **PUT YOUR NAME ON MAILING LISTS.** Of course, you may not want more advertising filling your mailbox, but it is nice to be notified of sales and special events.

LABEL SPEAK

- Original price is a sign that an item was once on sale in a retail shop.
- Compare at… usually means that the item is a knockoff and made for the outlets.
- Overrun means that the company made too many of the item and needs to get rid of leftovers.
- Irregular clothing or "factory seconds" have small imperfections that shouldn't prevent you from buying them.
- Damaged items may have more serious flaws—check carefully.
- Samples may have been on display or were used during sales pitches. They may be available in limited sizes.

B Fashion

1. Dress Better, Spend Less

—MARY HUNT

Wouldn't it be fabulous if one day the Shopping Fairy smiled on you and gave you back all the money you've ever spent on clothes you didn't wear? How much would you have? Enough for a new car, maybe even a summer cottage? For sure, I could start a nice retirement fund with all the money I've wasted on back-of-the-closet mistakes.

Here's the problem: We head for the racks with no particular plan in mind. If it fits, it's a candidate. If it's also on sale? Done deal. That kind of shopping just wreaks havoc on your bank account and can fill the dark side of the closet fast.

Cutting the cost of clothes is less about finding bargains and more about knowing what to wear, where to buy and when to stop buying.

WHAT'S RIGHT FOR YOU

YOUR UNIFORM. Everyone needs one. It's your look, your signature style. It addresses your body type and shape, your image and color palette.

YOUR SHAPE. Clothing is always designed for silhouette first and measurements second. Your measurements can change, but your essential frame remains the same—that's your silhouette.

A simple way to describe your shape uses letters and a number: If you are an A, you're smaller at the top than the bottom; a V is just the opposite; H is straight up and down; while 8 is curvaceous. The properly shaped garment for your silhouette creates an unbroken line, which means that the item fits properly. Once you identify your silhouette, you'll be amazed at how easy it is to spot that same shape in clothes on the rack.

An item of clothing that is not cut to your silhouette will never fit your shape—no matter the size, how it's cut or how many times it's been marked down. When you start learning how to make the right choice for your body type, you'll stop wasting money on clothes that look great on the hanger but are all wrong in the mirror.

YOUR COLORS. Each of us has natural coloring. It's in our DNA and shows up in our hair, eyes and skin. Certain colors will make you look healthier, radiant and more alive, even without makeup. The predominant tone or color just under your skin is what dictates the colors you should wear. For example, if you have yellow undertones and wear yellow, you will appear yellow. But wearing colors with blue undertones balances the yellow, resulting in a beautifully radiant appearance. Go to stylemakeovers.com for a simple, free online analysis, or consult the classic book, *Color Me Beautiful*, by Carole Jackson.

TAKE ACTION

YOUR PLAN. Creating a written plan for exactly the number of pieces you need for your lifestyle is invaluable. Why? Because without a specific plan, you won't know when to stop buying and will just keep spending mindlessly. Generally, suits are the foundation of a wardrobe. Whether yours are business suits or running suits depends on where you are in your life. *(See "Your Fashion Essentials," page 191.)*

CLOSET SWEEP. While there are likely many items in your wardrobe you need to purge, you may be surprised to discover how many pieces you already have to plug into your wardrobe plan. Take everything out of your closet. Audition the clothes you own by trying them on. Only those that fit your shape, style and color palette—and fill a slot on your written plan—earn a place back in your closet. Everything else? Sell what you don't want at a yard sale or an online auction site like eBay. Or donate it to charity and take a tax deduction for the fair market value of each piece.

MIX AND MATCH. If you stick to your style, shape and color palette, you'll probably be able to come up with new outfits by mixing and matching what you already have—and it won't cost a dime. Look to inexpensive accessories to keep up with trends and fads. But when investing in classic pieces like slacks, suits and skirts, always try to go for quality.

FIND A TAILOR. A good tailor can take a garment down by as much as two sizes. This means a jacket or pair of slacks that is perfect in every other way may still be a candidate for your wardrobe plan.

Smart shopping

Time the sales. Waiting for sales is a great way to stretch your clothing dollars, particularly if you are ready to invest in a few high-end pieces. Typically stores discount spring and summer clothes in June and early July, and then put fall and winter items on sale in January and February.

Each store also has its own sales cycle. One reader says her local Target marks down clothes every Tuesday night. That makes Wednesday morning her favorite time to go shopping. Find out how your favorite store operates, then time your purchases. If an item you need isn't on sale, ask the staff when it will be. Try requesting that a particular item be held for you pending the markdown.

Other places to buy. There's a whole new world of opportunity in consignment, vintage, discount and thrift stores, warehouse clubs, outlets and eBay.

Shop online. This can be a bit tricky. But if you're familiar with how a specific brand or item fits and are confident about the color, you can find some great bargains online. Just make sure you know the website's return policy and factor shipping charges into your final cost.

What's your style?

Your clothing personality is that "look" to which you are drawn most often. Stumped? Your favorite outfits hold the clues. Consider what you like to wear, then stick with that look.

Romantic Ruffles and lace, soft luxurious fabrics, gently curved lines, dainty patterns, draped silhouettes.

Sporty All kinds of sportswear, from casual to chic; comfortable, versatile and practical clothes; when appropriate, slacks instead of dresses.

Classic Separates and traditional, tailored pieces that are always in style.

Dramatic Distinctive or theatrical clothing in bold prints and designs.

> ## YOUR FASHION ESSENTIALS
> This sample plan for a career woman provides the basic framework for a functional wardrobe.
>
> - 3-piece suit (skirt, jacket and pants) in navy or black
> - 3 basic skirts (taupe, gray and black)
> - 2 dresses (one should be a basic black dress)
> - 5 or more blouses or shirts
> - 2 blazers or jackets
> - 3 pairs of classic slacks
> - 3 coats (trench or rain, between-seasons and winter)
> - 2 or more pairs of casual slacks or jeans
> - 1 tunic-type top
> - 2 sweaters or cardigans
> - 1 evening dress or gown

2. 32 Ways to Look Great on Less

- Don't shop at stores that have a store-credit-only return policy.
- Wrap credit card receipts around your card so you'll be reminded of what else you've bought that month.
- Return items you're not 100 percent happy with.
- Keep a list of needed items in your wallet so you always have a mission when shopping.
- Give yourself two days to think about an item you want. If you still want it then, buy it.
- Use those personal shoppers that stores employ. They are being paid to help you. Even if you don't buy anything, they'll still give you advice and spend as much time with you as you want.
- Paid full price and it's on sale a week later? Don't get mad; simply bring back the receipt for a price adjustment.
- Buy maternity wear at large-size stores rather than a maternity store.

- Shop drugstores for your makeup and save big. The trick? Find products that do double duty.
- Use a puff to apply (and reapply) powder. A powder brush collects lots of excess that literally goes to dust.
- Always warm up a pencil between two fingers before using. It will glide on smoother so there's less wear and tear.
- Use a brush (yes, for cream shadows, too) to apply and blend. Cotton swabs and sponge-tip applicators absorb (and waste) too much.
- An all-time favorite beauty basic: Vaseline Petroleum Jelly. Use it on everything from lips, cheeks and eyebrows to chapped hands, elbows and feet.
- Check out mass retail stores for great basics.
- Dilute shampoo with an equal amount of water in an empty bottle. Cover, then shake well before each use.
- To get the last squeeze of toothpaste, gel or lip balm, snip the flat end off with a pair of scissors. After using, cover the end with plastic wrap to maintain freshness. You're guaranteed to get two or three more uses!
- Several drugstores now take back makeup you're not completely satisfied with (as long as you keep the receipt), so there's no risk involved.
- The cheapest hairstyle helper we've found: giant foam rollers that create glamorous waves.
- To get that new haircut you've been after, take advantage of training nights at your favorite salon. The stylists are always supervised and if you don't get a good vibe, just get up and walk out.
- Professional makeup brushes help cosmetics go further since they blend well—and they're not as expensive as you think.
- The best end-of-season buy: shoes and handbags. There's little difference between spring and fall shoes. A black pump is always a black pump.
- Look for seasonless items that you can wear for ten months out of the year, such as wool gabardine and blends (rayon, cotton).
- Look for top-notch ingredients in drugstore products. They really work!

- Consignment shops offer real deals (up to 50 percent) before the holidays. The stores want to get rid of these items, because if they don't sell them they'll just get donated.

- Always ask for discounts, even at major department stores. Say to the manager discreetly, "I really love this skirt, but it's a little above my budget. Is there anything you can do about it?"

- Shop for special-occasion dresses in vintage clothing stores or rent-a-gown stores, or borrow from friends whose taste you like.

- You don't need to join a fancy gym or buy expensive equipment to get in shape: walk, play with the kids, even jump rope.

WHEN YOU'RE OUTLET SHOPPING, REMEMBER THESE HELPFUL HINTS

- Find out if you can return items through the mail. This is especially helpful if the mall is far from your home.

- To shop till you drop at the outlets, wear comfortable shoes and clothing. Dress in neutral colors for trying on a variety of clothes.

- Inspect garments for irregularities. Weigh the discount versus any flaws.

- Contact Outlet Bound (at 888-OUTLET2 and online at outletbound. com), ask for a VIP Voucher. It's good for a coupon book for even greater discounts on already marked-down items and brochures on outlet malls nationwide. Outlet Bound can also give you directions to the discount mall nearest you.

- Don't waste your money following all the latest trends. A good sense of style is always your best fashion asset.

3. An Insider's Guide to Getting the Biggest Bang for Your Fashion Buck

Bringing home clothing bargains used to mean hitting the department stores at sale time—period. That's still a good idea, but you have many more options today. Head for discount or off-price stores for luxe labels at low prices. Order wearable classics from catalogs, stock up on basics at one of the giant mass chains, or check resale shops for unexpected treasures. Looking great for less is easy if you know the ropes.

MASS RETAILERS

Giant retailers like Target, Wal-Mart and Kmart carry clothes for the whole family and almost everything for the home. They can offer great prices because volume is huge.

BEST FOR: Basics like jeans, T-shirts, sneakers, lingerie, though many also carry stylish clothing.

LOVED BY: Women who like the convenience of being able to pick up paper towels and pleated pants on a single shopping trip.

STRATEGY: Go armed with lists of the needs and sizes of everyone in the family and you can really save time. Keep an open mind—you might find even better buys on sweatshirts or jeans for yourself in the men's or boys' department.

OFF-PRICE STORES

Off-price stores like T. J. Maxx, Marshalls, Filene's Basement and Loehmanns carry name-brand clothes at prices 20 to 60 percent below department store prices.

BEST FOR: Separates, dressy clothes, outerwear, shoes and accessories.

LOVED BY: Women who enjoy the thrill of the hunt and have the time and patience to sift through racks.

STRATEGY: Go often and go with a goal (a good blazer, a dressy top) so you won't be tempted by bargains you don't really need. If you can, check out department stores at the beginning of each season so you'll know how current and how much of a bargain your off-price finds are.

CATALOGS

Catalogs sell everything from lingerie to outerwear, and usually offer a wide range of colors and sizes.

BEST FOR: Knits, classics, items that are sized S-M-L, styles with an easy silhouette (A-line dresses, raglan-sleeved coats, etc.) or that have looked good on you in the past. Catalogs are not the place to buy your first fitted jacket if you can't stand the hassle of making returns.

LOVED BY: Women who hate to shop, or don't have time for it. Most catalogs take orders around the clock.

STRATEGY: Know your measurements and use the size charts, then allow for the fact that items are usually a bit bigger than you'd expect. Ask questions—operators often have access to more information and can tell you what a fabric looks like or what color "thistle" really is. Take advantage of quantity discount offers by ordering with a friend, but be sure to factor in shipping and handling—it can sometimes offset savings.

RETURNS: Who pays for shipping? Usually you do, but it's a good idea to ask the operator when you place your order. Although they don't advertise the fact, many catalog companies will foot the bill if you ask. If it's company policy to pay the cost of returning things, take advantage of it when you're unsure of your size by ordering several; return what doesn't fit later on.

RESALE SHOPS

Resale shops carry previously owned garments, usually of high quality.

BEST FOR: Classic suits, coats, dressy items and luxury pieces like leather jackets, cashmere sweaters, wedding gowns and evening bags.

LOVED BY: Women who appreciate upscale clothing but don't want the hassle of hunting for it at off-price stores.

STRATEGY: Never buy without trying on—the previous owner may have altered her size 10 in surprising ways. Make friends with salespeople so they can keep an eye out for things you'll like.

6. Health Care

 ## A *Get Better Health Care for Less*

Medical costs were the last thing anyone worried about when MarySue B., 48, suffered critical brain damage in a car accident. "We had good insurance," says her daughter, Lisa S. "We thought we were fully covered."

MarySue's insurance did pay her hospital bills. But she also needed nurses around-the-clock at home, and insurance provided little for nursing care or medical supplies. The Pasadena, California, family's out-of-pocket expenses totaled about $17,000 a month—and continued until MarySue died a year and a half later. "The medical bills forced us to sell our family home, which we loved," says Lisa.

Similar stories are all too common these days. And you don't have to be critically ill to run up devastating medical bills. In the United States, health care costs now average $3,510 per person each year, according to a recent study published by Project HOPE, a health education organization.

Despite these grim statistics, however, you can still get good medical care without going broke. The key is to become well informed and learn how to work the system so you won't be tempted to take risks with your health just to save money.

KNOW THE RULES

When a New Jersey pediatrician ordered a skull X-ray for an infant, the baby's parents raced to a nearby radiologist. The receptionist said their insurer would accept the charges, so they paid in full and filed for reimbursement later. That's when they discovered that although their plan "accepted" the $100 X-ray fee, it counted toward a $500 deductible for out-of-network providers. Had they been more familiar with the details of their insurance, the family could have found a network radiologist and saved $100.

As this case illustrates, it's important to review your policy's "explanation of benefits" before seeking treatment. Ask your benefits department or the insurer's customer service representative to explain anything you don't understand. If you're in a managed-care network, ask for an updated list of approved doctors and hospitals. Find out when you need insurer approval before having a medical procedure.

If you do not have health insurance, call your state Medicaid office. You may qualify for government-funded coverage even if you have a job.

NEGOTIATE DOCTORS' FEES

They're more variable and negotiable than many patients realize. Sometimes, discussing your financial concerns upfront is enough to get a reduction. That's what Elizabeth S. of Pelham, New Hampshire, did. Pregnant and uninsured, she was dismayed when her physicians recommended extra procedures. She asked if they could lower the fees—and they did. She also discovered that her dentist and chiropractor offered discounts to patients who paid cash.

Patty W., a medical billing manager in Fort Lauderdale, has seen doctors cut fees in half when patients ask for reductions. "They set prices high because insurance companies pay only part of the fee," she says. Her advice: Ask your doctor for the appropriate procedure code, then use that to obtain quotes from other physicians in the area.

Patty followed her own advice when her toddler had emergency surgery. The bill was $3,000, which she considered exorbitant. Her insurance company paid only $2,100, so Patty acquired the surgery's procedure code and compared prices. When she told her surgeon that other physicians were charging much less, he cut his fee by the $900 she still owed.

You don't have to be uninsured or facing major bills to negotiate reductions. Ask for fees to be waived for brief office visits or to combine several services under one fee. Every time the insurance company is not billed for a medical procedure, it saves you money (by holding down insurance costs).

LOBBY FOR BETTER COVERAGE

Nora L. of Erie, Colorado, needed expensive medications for herself and her daughter. Although her husband's employer-sponsored health plan covered the whole family, it didn't cover drugs. Nora decided to ask other employees if they'd be willing to pay extra for drug coverage. Many said yes, so she took her case to the company's owner, who agreed to set up a prescription plan.

"We received a marginal increase in our premiums," Nora says, "but we're saving $120 a month on drugs."

Ask your employer to offer flexible spending accounts if they're not already available. These allow you to have money withheld from your salary to cover unreimbursed medical costs, including insurance deductibles and co-payments as well as vision care and other uncovered services. Since the money you put aside is not subject to income taxes, the savings can be considerable. If you're in the 28 percent bracket and put aside $1,000 a year, for example, you'd save $280 in federal taxes alone.

It's important, however, to estimate your unreimbursed costs carefully before deciding how much to put into a flexible spending account. Any money left in the account at the end of the year is forfeited.

CUT HOSPITAL COSTS

One way to fight high health care costs is to scrutinize medical bills, especially those from hospitals, which are notorious for making mistakes. Keep a record of all procedures and doctors' visits during your hospital stay, then compare it with your charges. If you're too ill to do the paperwork, ask a friend or relative to help you.

Reject services you don't need (such as the routine chest X-ray), if your doctors allow it. Then make sure the hospital business office doesn't charge you for them anyway. Take any medication you use regularly along with you because hospitals charge premium prices for drugs. Always ask what every medication is for—and decline anything you don't need. One New York woman reported: "Hospital nurses came around every night handing out sleeping pills and painkillers. Although other patients took them without question, I refused them—and saved myself hundreds of dollars."

It also pays to choose your hospital carefully. Try to avoid going to an expensive teaching hospital for minor procedures that can be handled at a community facility or an outpatient center. And be sure to ask what time the hospital's new-day room rate begins, so you can leave in time to avoid extra charges. If your insurer refuses to pay for something that is medically necessary, speak up. According to Lisa S., such decisions can often be reversed. "I fought with the claims adjuster for three weeks, but I finally got them to pay for a hospital bed for my mom to use at home because she couldn't sleep in a regular bed."

REDUCE DOCTOR VISITS

When one of Ginger C.'s three children gets sick, she consults a medical guidebook. It not only suggests home treatments, it also explains when to take the patient to a pediatrician or an emergency room. Ginger and her husband, who live in Denham Springs, Louisiana, have also consulted the book for their own illnesses. "The $20 guide has saved me a lot of doctor visits," she says.

When choosing a doctor or medical group, ask if they offer free telephone consultations. Many will suggest a home remedy or advise you to wait a day or two before making an office visit. See specialists only when absolutely necessary. A family practitioner can treat many of the same conditions as an internist, gynecologist or cardiologist—often at lower fees. Limit visits to costly emergency rooms to true emergencies.

SHOP AROUND FOR INSURANCE

If you don't have employee health insurance, you may qualify for lower group rates by joining a business or trade organization, a union, an alumni group, or a religious or professional society. Self-employed people may be eligible for group coverage through the Chamber of Commerce. *The Encyclopedia of Associations*, available in many libraries, can aid your search.

CUT PRESCRIPTION COSTS

Ask your doctor if a cheaper medication will work as well. A generic drug has the same active ingredient as its name-brand counterpart, but costs less. A therapeutic substitute has a different active ingredient but may be equally effective. Get a list of your medical plan's approved drugs. Don't wait until you go to the pharmacy to find out if your medication is covered. Give your doctor a copy of the list to refer to when he writes prescriptions.

Be wary of free samples. Those that doctors receive are often the most expensive medicines. If your supply runs out before treatment ends, you may have to pay a high price to continue. Samples are a good deal, however, if you're taking a drug for only a short time or want to make sure you can tolerate the side effects before you buy a large quantity. Consider mail order for medications you take daily. For long-term use, ask for price quotes from several mail-order companies, compare them, including mailing costs, with local pharmacies before ordering. And plan ahead; mail orders may take several days to arrive.

SAVE ON BASICS

- Call first. If you discuss your problem with a doctor or nurse-practitioner, you may find that you don't need an office visit.
- Make doctors' visits count. Make a list of concerns and ailments so you won't have to visit the doctor again for problems you forgot to mention.
- Choose a high deductible. Your premiums will be much lower if your deductible (what you pay before coverage begins) is $500 or more.
- Schedule checkups carefully. You can maximize your reimbursements if you schedule checkups and other preventive care for years in which you've already met your insurance deductible.

Ⓑ *Money-Saving Guide to Health Care*

Good health is one of the best things in life, but it usually isn't free. You can save on a host of health services and products without sacrificing your family's well-being. Here, we offer strategies that really work, some to consider and others to avoid

Medical Insurance

Plans differ dramatically in terms of what they cover and your co-payments and monthly premiums. Before making a choice, review the policy very carefully to make certain it matches your needs and your budget.

YOU WILL SAVE

- Drop duplicate policies. For instance, you don't need cancer or other disease-specific insurance if you have a comprehensive policy. There's also no advantage to you and your spouse each carrying family policies, since you can't be reimbursed twice for medical costs or (in most cases) use one policy to pay the deductibles and copayments of another.

- If you aren't insured through your job, join an organization such as a trade association or alumni or fraternal group that offers members group insurance rates. Some places of worship also apply for group rates. You can save up to 60 percent over what you'd pay for the same plan as an individual.

- Get preapproval from your insurer for any procedure or test your doctor suggests and for emergency room visits, whenever possible.

You May Save

- Look into a health maintenance organization (HMO) or preferred provider organization (PPO). Typically cheaper than traditional reimbursement policies, most of these plans carry no deductible or high co-payment. However, access to services and specialists is key. If you require special care, make sure you will be able to see the experts you need.

- Consider buying disability insurance. To keep your premiums low, purchase a policy that begins paying benefits after you are out of work for 90 to 180 days. One company highly rated by the Consumer Federation of America for its low premiums is USAA Insurance (800-531-6396).

- If you are on Medicare, which covers 80 percent of the "reasonable or allowed charges," consider buying extra coverage to make up the difference. Supplemental Medigap policies are one choice; a cheaper option is a Medicare HMO. These plans cover 100 percent of your medical costs if you use approved physicians. Monthly payments range from nothing (beyond your Medicare premium) to about $40.

- If you are married with no children to insure, buying two individual health plans may be cheaper than a family plan.

- Find out whether your employer offers medical spending accounts. These allow you to set aside a portion of your pretax pay to cover uninsured medical costs. But only deposit as much as you intend to spend, since you lose any balance that remains at year's end.

You Won't Save

- Don't go without health insurance coverage, one accident or hospital visit could wipe you out financially. At the very least, purchase a high-deductible "catastrophic" policy.

- Don't buy hospital indemnity coverage policies, which usually pay $100 or $200 per day spent in the hospital. That won't cover much, since the average hospital stay costs nearly $1,000 a day.

Hospital Stays and Tests

If you need to go into the hospital, it's crucial to ask key questions in advance so you can avoid overpayments later on. Although feeling in control is tough if you're really sick or hurt, you're still a customer paying for a service.

You Will Save

- Try to keep your stay as short as possible. Hospitals are hotbeds of infection and the longer you stay, the higher your risk of contracting something. The People's Medical Society, a nonprofit consumer advocacy group, reports that 10 percent of hospital patients become infected during their stay.

- Always ask for itemized hospital bills and review them carefully. Auditing firms report that 90 percent of hospital bills contain errors.

You May Save

- Always ask your doctor why a test is required, what risks are involved and what treatment would be necessary depending on the results. Ask whether you can skip any preadmission tests. One recent study reported that 60 percent of "routine" tests such as X-rays and blood and urine analyses are not needed.

- Consider a birthing center within a hospital complex, and functioning under the obstetrics department. These homelike settings, which cater to women with low-risk pregnancies, are staffed by nurse-midwives. Birthing centers lower the cost of deliveries by about 40 percent.

- Inquire about having procedures and tests done on an outpatient basis.

This way you won't be formally admitted or charged a room fee ($500 per day on average).

You Won't Save

- Don't agree to be admitted to the hospital between Friday and Sunday. Few tests or procedures are done on weekends, so you end up paying for wasted days.

- Don't use a for-profit hospital if you can avoid it, because such hospitals tend to be more profit-conscious and beholden to their stockholders.

Prescription Drugs

Brand-name medication prices have risen faster than inflation in recent years. Often, though, you can keep costs down by shopping around.

You Will Save

- Check prices with mail-order companies. Those that sell to the public include: American Association of Retired Persons (800-456-2277), Action Mail Order Drugs (800-452-1976) and Medi-Mail (800-331-1458).

- When your doctor prescribes a medication, ask for the names of other drugs that could be used as alternatives. Shop around to see which is cheapest, then ask your doctor to order the prescription as long as it's a safe and effective substitute.

- Comparison-shop. Drug prices vary from store to store and sometimes from week to week. Large discount retailers tend to be cheapest.

You May Save

- Ask your pharmacist for generic formulations after getting your doctor's OK. Generics (drugs that have lost their original patent) are cheaper.

- If your insurance doesn't cover prescription drugs, ask your pharmacist whether your prescription is available in a cheaper over-the-counter (OTC) version, which often is simply a lower dosage.

You Won't Save

- Never stop taking medication or lower your dosage without asking your doctor.
- Don't continue using OTC medicine if your problem persists or worsens. Visit your doctor immediately.
- Don't take leftover prescription medications. Drugs lose their potency over time.

Supplements

Overblown claims and scam artists abound in the largely unregulated supplement industry. Follow this advice to get a good product at a fair price.

You Will Save

- Buy no-frills vitamins. Fancy designer versions and heavily advertised brand names are no more effective than store varieties. The Center for Science in the Public Interest, a Washington, DC, consumer advocacy group, suggests spending no more than $10 per month on supplements.
- Look for supplements that meet standards set by the U.S. Pharmacopoeia (USP) for quick dissolving. Vitamins don't work well unless they can be dispersed into your bloodstream.

You May Save

- Don't put too much faith in claims made on the label. For instance, the label on one multivitamin formula says, "Vitamin A is essential for the normal function of vision." This does not mean that taking supplemental vitamin A will improve your eyesight.

You Won't Save

- Never rely on pills to replace a healthy, balanced diet.
- Don't spend extra for "natural" vitamins—they're no more effective than synthetics. (There is some evidence, however, that the body prefers vitamin E in its natural form.)

Eye Care

Many health policies no longer cover routine eye care or glasses, so you need know-how to cut costs.

You Will Save

- Consider seeing an optometrist for routine vision tests or to change your eyeglass prescription. You'll pay about $20 instead of $60 to $100 for an ophthalmologist. However, it may be better to see an ophthalmologist for vision problems or more serious eye symptoms.

- Schedule eye examinations only every two to three years unless you have a particular problem or are over age 60.

- Shop around for glasses. Eye doctors are required by law to give you a copy of your lens prescription after an exam.

You May Save

- Check prices on mail-order contact lenses. Try Contact Lens Discount Center (800-780-5367), Factory Direct Lens (800-516-5367), or 1-800-CONTACTS (800-266-8228).

- Don't take your prescription to a pricey one-hour service center unless you need glasses that quickly.

You Won't Save

- Don't automatically go for the cheapest eye examination. Make sure it includes vision screening as well as a glaucoma test and an evaluation of your inner eye, done by dilating your pupils with drops.

- Choose sunglasses that protect against the sun's ultraviolet rays (which can cause cataracts), even if they cost a bit more.

Dental Care

Preventive maintenance, including regular cleaning and flossing, is the key to keeping costs low in the long run.

You Will Save

- Get a comprehensive examination and cleaning at least once a year, suggests the American Dental Association (ADA). Many dental problems don't cause pain until they're serious and quite expensive to treat.
- Skip annual full-mouth dental X-rays unless a problem warrants them. The ADA recommends X-rays once every three years to detect underlying cavities, bone loss or nerve problems.

You May Save

- Use the clinic at a local dental school. Student dentists typically offer everything from low-cost teeth cleaning and fillings to braces and oral surgery under the guidance of faculty dentists.
- Have sealants applied to the chewing surfaces of your molars and bicuspids, where trapped food and bacteria tend to cause adult decay. At $20 to $50 per tooth, this is 100 percent effective in preventing cavities and lasts up to ten years. Fillings cost more than twice as much and need to be replaced eventually.

You Won't Save

- Your toothbrush should not be used for longer than two months. Scraggly bristles can wear away gum tissue and cementum, the soft material between tooth enamel and roots.
- Pass up at-home bleaching as an alternative to professional bleaching. Although at-home kits cost less—$30 to $50 compared with $100 to $400 for a pro job—in some cases they do not whiten teeth significantly and can cause blotching and nerve damage if used incorrectly.
- Don't buy expensive electric or ultrasonic toothbrushes. You can clean your teeth just as well by properly using a manual brush with soft, staggered, rounded-end bristles, and dental floss.
- Never postpone having a cavity filled. Cavities continue to grow, leading to larger, more costly fillings and possibly root canal. If you can't afford a filling, tell your dentist before the procedure; you'll probably be able to pay in installments.

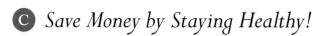 *Save Money by Staying Healthy!*

The biggest payoff for healthy living is, of course, better health. What you may not realize is that changing your lifestyle can also help save a lot.

STAY UP TO DATE ON SHOTS

- Chicken pox, measles, mumps and other "children's" diseases can be dangerous and costly ailments in adults. Spare yourself the misery and expense by getting immunized against illnesses you haven't had. You may be able to get low-cost vaccinations at clinics, churches or stores through organizations such as the Visiting Nurses Association. Also, keep in mind that Medicare covers flu and pneumonia shots.

FOCUS ON HEALTHY FOODS

- Many people have the notion that a healthy diet is expensive. But if you focus on fresh ingredients instead of low-fat frozen dinners or junk food, your bank balance won't suffer.

- Packing a small bag of potato chips—at about 33¢ each—in your child's lunchbox each day costs about $60 per school year. Instead, try carrot or celery sticks with nonfat ranch dressing at 17¢ a serving.

- Try substitutions for expensive, high-fat meat. Two cups of pasta with tomato sauce costs about 67¢, compared to $1.46 for a 5-oz pork chop. Substitute tofu for ground beef, and halve the fat and the price.

CHECKUPS

- The latest government figures show that half of all American women (and 59 percent of men) are overweight, many at levels increasing their risk for heart disease and diabetes. Choose a diet low in saturated fat, include plenty of fruits and vegetables, and exercise.

SNUFF THAT SMOKE

- Every year, more than 400,000 Americans die from diseases caused by smoking. Lung cancer outranks breast cancer as the leading cause of cancer death among women.

- Quitting is tough, but adding up the money you'll save can give some incentive. At more than $2 a pack, a pack-a-day habit costs minimum $800 a year. Some life insurance companies penalize smokers. For example, a 40-year-old woman who smokes is charged $127 more each year than a nonsmoker for a $100,000 policy. Nonsmokers often pay up to 5 percent less on their auto and homeowner's insurance as well.

LAY OFF THE BOOZE

- Serious liver disease is not the only risk for women who consume more than two drinks a day. Alcohol can also contribute to breast cancer, ulcers, heart irregularities and high blood pressure. Drinking heavily during pregnancy can permanently damage a fetus.

- Drunk driving can cost you thousands in legal fees, towing charges and higher car insurance rates. But even moderate drinking strains your budget. If a bottle of wine costs about $9, two glasses every evening comes to nearly $1,100 a year. Instead, try club soda with a splash of fruit juice. Two glasses cost about 15¢.

FITNESS, ABSOLUTELY FREE

- Pull on a pair of comfortable shoes and start walking. To stay safe, join up with a friend or a walking club, or try a mall during non-peak hours.

- Check out a couple of beginner exercise videos at your public library. Work out with friends to boost the fun factor.

- Consider cycling to work—2.6 million Americans do it. A 12-mile round-trip takes an hour or so, burns up to 600 calories and can save about $260 a year in gas and wear and tear on your car.

NEW WAYS TO PAY FOR ALTERNATIVE CARE

- Some 34 percent of American adults seek relief through unconventional health therapies like acupuncture. A new law in Washington State requires all health plans to provide access to alternative practitioners; some large insurers also offer comprehensive coverage of nontraditional care.

THE LATEST ON ASTHMA INHALERS.

- If you have mild asthma and use your bronchodilator inhaler on a regular schedule, ask your doctor if you can cut back. A new study found that inhaling the most common type of bronchodilator medication only as needed relieves symptoms just as effectively.

7. Holiday Savings

 51 Ways Not to Go Broke This Christmas

From October to Christmas Eve, this guide gives you a month-to-month plan to organize every aspect of your holiday for the most stress-free, money-saving and festive holiday ever.

Tis the season to be jolly, but that doesn't mean you have to go for broke. With a dash of planning, a pinch of creativity and a large sprinkle of resolve, you can enjoy the holiday season without wasting time or money.

OCTOBER OPPORTUNITIES

- Create a budget that includes not only your gift list but also items like paper, cards, even postage—anything that goes into gift-giving and holiday well-wishing. Make sure the bottom line is affordable, then stick to it!

- Ask family members for wish lists that include both big and little items— and make it clear nobody will get everything on his or her list. Then make a master list to take on every shopping trip; keep an eye on the sales. Also, jot everyone's sizes on an index card and carry it with you when you shop to eliminate unnecessary returns.

- While it's too early to buy your tree, it's not too early to think about where to get it. If you live near a national forest, call the closest regional office of the Forest Service and see if they'll be selling permits to cut your own tree. Permits in some parts of Colorado, for example, cost $10.

- At a garden-supply store, buy paper white narcissus (about $1 a bulb). Ask how long the bulbs will take to flower and place them in a pot full of stones and water on a sunny windowsill in time to make a stunning holiday centerpiece.

- Check antique stores for great gifts—jewelry, heirloom plates, an unusual lamp—at bargain prices. If you shop now (before the holiday rush), you'll have a better selection.

- Cruise garage sales and flea markets for "gently used" toys. Kids under five generally don't know the difference between used and new, and you can pick up a near-new toy for a few bucks.

- Is there someone on your list with a very specific hobby or interest? In the reference section of your library, look for *The Catalog of Catalogs* by Edward L. Palder, which lists specialty catalogs for everything from barbecuing to art supplies and theatrical memorabilia. Send for some catalogs now so you'll have time to order something unique.

- Many mail-away film processors offer low-cost and unique gift items such as coffee mugs displaying your favorite photo, photo T-shirts and personalized calendars. Call your processor and ask for a catalog.

Pre-Thanksgiving

- Between now and Turkey Day, watch grocery store ads for sales on big-ticket items, such as turkey or ham or special cuts of beef. Buy on-sale meats and desserts for Christmas, Chanukah or New Year's dinner now and stock the freezer.

- If you're the Christmas hostess, provide the main dish and a salad and ask guests to bring the side dishes and dessert.

- Many subscriptions to children's magazines cost under $20. Order now to ensure arrival by Christmas. Consider *Ranger Rick*, *Sports Illustrated Kids*, *Boys Life* or *Highlights for Children*.

- Talk to siblings about a group gift for your parents, and to coworkers about a joint gift for your boss. Collecting $10 from five to six people buys a much nicer gift than you could afford to buy on your own.

- Review your Christmas card list and eliminate every person who merited only your signature last year, not a personal note. If you can delete 20 names, you've saved the cost of a box of cards plus postage.

- Keep all gift purchase receipts in a envelope, in case of returns. The $25 blouse you buy now may be reduced to $15 in a few weeks or after Christmas. Without a receipt, you've lost $10.

Post-Thanksgiving

- Shop first thing in the morning on Mondays, Tuesdays or Wednesdays, when traffic is generally lighter. Pay only by cash or check. Research shows that people spend up to 30 percent more when they use plastic. If you must charge, use only one card and keep track of what you've charged.

- Two books offer great cheap send-aways for kids: *The Official Freebies for Kids* and *Free Stuff for Kids*. You can order several low-cost stocking stuffers (you pay postage and handling) such as a rubber stamp with your child's name on it or a beaded earring set. After you order your stocking stuffers, give the books as presents to a child who loves to send away for free merchandise.

- Remember, necessities also make good gifts. If your daughter needs new sheets or your son, new pajamas, give them as gifts rather than buying them in addition to presents.

- How about giving your child a U.S. Government Series EE savings bond? For $25, you can buy a $50 bond. But order now because it takes approximately three weeks for the Federal Reserve to mail the actual bond to you.

- Avoid buying battery-run toys and appliances. Why? Because batteries not only add to the immediate cost (four AA batteries, for example, add $3 to the price), but research by a battery manufacturer revealed that over the lifetime of a $90 handheld game, throw-away batteries added another $199 in operating costs.

- Clean out closets and drawers. Not only might you find potential gifts, but you can also get one more tax deduction for the year if you donate the items you no longer use.

- As you clean out those closets, look for a piece of your grandmother's jewelry or a favorite aunt's purse that your sister loves more than you do. Wrap it up and give her a gift that's invaluable but free.

- Keep paper and card costs reasonable. Brown paper lunchbags make great wrapping paper. Use stamps or markers to decorate.

- A roll of white paper from an office-supply store also makes an inexpensive wrap. Cut to fit, and let the kids customize the wrapping with colored markers or rubber stamps.

- Instead of wasting paper on an unwieldy gift, put that trike or CD player in a white or green trash bag and tie the top with ribbon. (Afterward, use the bag to collect trash.)

- Some department stores wrap gifts for free if you spend a certain amount. Find out which stores offer this service, then shop there.

- Cut the fronts of old or unused Christmas cards and use as gift tags.

- Use old Christmas cards to make tree ornaments. Cut out all the Santas, for example, punch holes through the tops, tie ribbon loops and you're ready to hang some new "ornaments."

- Add a new ribbon or fresh glitter to old ornaments and make them good as new. You can buy both for under $5.

- Instead of buying high-priced wreaths, trim your own evergreens, buy an 18-inch plastic foam or wire frame plus some wiring and a hook (total around $10) and make your own wreath. Decoration is extra, of course.

- Set up a cookie exchange with five other people. Each of you bakes 12 dozen of one kind of cookie and then exchanges two dozen with everyone else. Buy ingredients in bulk and save. Also, making only one type of cookie can reduce prep time and cleanup time.

- Make one extra batch of cookies for kids to decorate as ornaments. Before baking, stick a toothpick in the dough to create a ready-made hole for hanging. (Leave it in until the cookies come out of the oven.)

- Shopping by catalog? Check out the shipping and handling charges. Can you save money by ordering several items at once? Usually shipping is determined by weight. For example, if you order two 4-pound items at different times, you'll pay $17 for shipping. If you order them at the same time, you'll only pay $11.

- Avoid crowds and save time by shopping in unexpected places: the hardware store for a tool-lover, an Oriental grocery store for your friend who loves Chinese cooking.

- Don't forget paint and craft supplies for those who love making things by hand, and unusual baking pans and utensils for the cooks on your list (check flea markets and antique stores).
- Many schools have pre-Christmas fundraisers, selling magazine subscriptions, boxed oranges and candy. Help your neighborhood school (and save time shopping) by calling and asking what they are selling.
- Now is the time to check out church bazaars and holiday craft shows for hand-crafted items (sweaters, patchwork baby quilts, hats and mittens) that sell for much less than retail.
- Books always make great gifts. To simplify your shopping and save time, call the bookstore to see if they have every title you want. Ask them to gather your selections and put them on hold for you. (Many bookstores also gift-wrap free!)
- For the hard-to-please, make a donation to a favorite charity. The charity will send a card to the honored person and whether you give $5 or $50, no dollar amount will appear.
- If your family has decided to reduce the number of gifts you give, replace the presents with a family ritual. Visit the library for ideas.
- If your child is dreaming of a big-ticket gift, maybe a train set or bicycle with all the accessories, break the gift down into its affordable parts—a length of track, a caboose; a basket or pump for the bicycle—and ask grandparents, aunts and uncles to each contribute an item.
- Rather than ordering holiday event tickets by phone and paying a service charge, pick them up at the box office and save about $10.
- Stuff a child's stocking with a $2 bill, which a child is unlikely to have seen. Order from your bank now.
- Ask your family to forgo one gift each and replace it with a donation of your time: volunteering at a soup kitchen, visiting sick kids in the hospital, delivering food to shut-ins.
- Pick up some $5 or $10 gift certificates from movie theaters or bookstores to give as stocking stuffers.

- Plan to mail your gifts by December 15, while you can still pay Priority mail rates. If you wait until the week of Christmas, you may be stuck with Express mail rates. (The difference between Priority mail and Express mail service can run as high as $15 on a 5-pound package.)

START TODAY

Vow to put away $1 a day from now until December 23. You'll give yourself some extra cash to pay for those last-minute gifts. Make a list of everyone you usually exchange gifts with. Are there people who might enjoy a holiday get-together for eggnog and conversation rather than exchanging presents? Ask them.

MERRY ME!

- The perfect gift for someone on a limited budget? A long-distance calling card.

- Did you have a favorite book or game as a youngster? Get it for your child. Share your memories as you read or play together.

- If the whole family agrees, take the money you would've spent on gifts and spend it on a family getaway.

- Instead of buying a pet for Christmas, buy a bird feeder and seed to encourage birds to visit your yard. Or adopt an animal from a local shelter.

- Don't fight with your kids to write thank-you notes. Give them a fun box of stationery (under $10), personalized address labels and pretty postage stamps.

- Use your computer to personalize stationery as a gift. Pick a special font and a design, even use colored paper. A print shop can bind 100 sheets into a pad for around $5.

B *Cut Holiday Food Bills*

Grocery bills can pile up during this season of eating, drinking and merrymaking. Before you head to the stores, consider the following:

IN THE SUPERMARKET

- Buy nonperishables well in advance. At holiday time, when turkey prices plunge to get you into the store, the costs of stuffing ingredients, cranberry sauce and traditional trimmings often rise.

- Check the small print on supermarket flyers. You'll be out of luck if you shop on Wednesday for a sale item limited to "Friday only" or "starting Sunday."

- Compare prices of different forms of the same food. If there's little difference between the price of fresh and canned sweet potatoes, and you plan to mash them anyway, buy canned. (You pay for the skin on fresh.)

- Rolls made with refrigerated dough or roll mix are less expensive than bakery rolls.

- If you're planning to serve a tossed salad, but the price of lettuce has soared, substitute spinach, cabbage, cucumbers and other vegetables.

- When buying corn, check the drained weight of canned. Frozen may cost less.

- Don't feel obliged to make every side dish from scratch. Some convenience foods may actually cost less—and there's no waste: canned beets, frozen squash, pearl onions and many other unsauced frozen vegetables (especially in large bags).

- Be flexible. If the price of broccoli is up, choose something else.

- Check out supermarket specials the day after Thanksgiving and stock up for Christmas. But make sure anything you buy on special at Thanksgiving and plan to keep for Christmas won't spoil in the meantime.

- Buy frozen pumpkin, mincemeat and apple pies a month or so before the holidays, when many markets put them on sale.

- Though you pay a membership fee, warehouse shopping can save you big bucks. In a supermarket, pure vanilla extract costs almost five times more; ground black pepper four times more; shelled walnuts and semisweet chocolate chips more than twice as much.

- If there's an ethnic market near you, chances are you can save on items such as nuts, tea, ground spices and rice.

Meat and poultry

- Why buy a whole turkey if your family will eat only dark or light meat? Buy a turkey breast or legs instead.

- Prices slashed on sausage you could use in your stuffing? Check the expiration date, especially if it's an unannounced or unadvertised special.

- No wonder turkeys are so popular for feeding Thanksgiving crowds— they're the least expensive form of poultry. Based on yield of edible meat per pound (minus skin and fat), they're about 46 percent edible. Chicken yields 41 percent edible meat, duck and goose about 22 percent.

- Ham, beef, pork and lamb roasts also grace tables at holiday time. Compare yield per pound with cost: 1 pound boneless meat serves 3 to 4; with a minimum amount of bone, 2 to 3; and a large amount of bone, 1 to 2.

- Instead of buying cocktail franks, save about $1 a pound by buying regular franks and cutting them up for pigs-in-a-blanket and other hors d'oeuvres.

Dairy case

- Follow this rule when buying eggs: If there's less than a 14¢ difference between two sizes of the same grade of eggs, the larger is a better value.

- When your cake recipe calls for 1 cup buttermilk, there's no need to buy a whole quart. Substitute "sour" milk made by stirring 1 tablespoon lemon juice with enough milk to equal 1 cup and letting it stand 5 minutes.

- Whipped cream in a 7-oz aerosol can can cost more than twice as much as buying 8 oz of heavy cream and whipping it yourself.

Produce

- A pound of one kind of fresh vegetable (as purchased) can yield a different number of servings than a pound of another. For example, you get 5 to 6 servings per pound of green beans, 4 to 5 per pound of Brussels sprouts and 3 to 4 per pound of broccoli.

- If you're planning a fruit bowl centerpiece, check the cost of similar fruits: compare tangerines to Clementines, Delicious apples to McIntosh, Comice or Bosc pears to Bartletts, green grapes to red.

- An inexpensive holiday dessert is Ambrosia: traditionally, layers of sliced oranges, bananas (and sometimes pineapple), sugar and sweetened flaked coconut. Buy the heaviest oranges, which are the juiciest, and compare prices for coconut in cans versus bags.

- If you're paying for fresh greens by weight, shake off the excess water before you take them to the register. You'd be amazed how much may be hidden in the leaves.

Staples

- Compare pie crusts for the best buy: frozen, refrigerated or mix, or make your own.

- Use bouillon cubes instead of canned broth in gravies, soups, stews and homemade flavored rice mixes.

- Those little bags of shelled walnuts, pecans and almonds can be very costly. Buy large bags around holiday time and store them in your freezer.

Entertaining

- Use seasonal fresh fruit and vegetables instead of flowers to make edible centerpieces for holiday meals.

- Buy bargain-priced day-old plain cake and turn it into a festive, quick-to-fix trifle: Soak the cake with fruit juice or sherry, layer with vanilla pudding and garnish with whipped cream and spoonfuls of jam.

- Make your own flavored coffee by adding ground cinnamon or a few drops of almond or vanilla extract to the grounds before brewing.

Good Old Common Sense

- Read the unit-price sticker near each item. It shows the name, retail price and cost per unit—quart, pound or ounce, for example. This makes it easy to compare the costs of different-size containers. Bigger isn't always a better buy, particularly when a smaller item has been specially priced.

- Impulse buying can wreak havoc with your budget. Go with a shopping list and stick to it unless you can substitute a less expensive item for one on your list.

- Get in and get out fast. Surveys show that shoppers spend close to $2 for every extra minute in the market.

- When comparing costs, look at the high shelves and low, as well those in the middle. The more expensive brands are often displayed at eye level.

- Scanner errors cost customers millions of dollars annually. Use a calculator to figure your costs as you do your shopping. Or check the register tape carefully, preferably before you leave the store.

- Enjoy free samples, but resist the temptation to buy.

- When you clip coupons, check the minimum purchase requirements. If you have to buy three but can only use one, it's no bargain.

- No space to store large-quantity specials? Shop with a friend or neighbor and share.

- A small bunch of fresh herbs can cost a mint. Grow herbs in a sunny window. The pots make a handsome table decoration, too.

Ⓒ *How to Rein in Holiday Spending*

Stick to a Budget Without Being a Scrooge

- Agree to set price limits on presents. Your siblings, for instance, will probably be thrilled to set spending caps on niece and nephew gifts.

- Make a list of everyone you're buying for, including how much you can spend on each. Carry it when you shop, keep a running total as you go.

- Don't compete. Just because your sister spends $100 on your parents doesn't mean you have to. Spend what you can afford.

- Set aside money for stocking stuffers and buy them all at once. You won't nickel-and-dime your way to the poorhouse.
- Decide what you can donate to sidewalk charity collectors and keep the money in a separate wallet.

Give Sensibly

- Give a family one large gift that everyone can use.
- Buy gift certificates. There's no chance of overspending on a whim.
- Find something terrific and affordable? There's nothing wrong with choosing the same gift for more than one person.
- Consider the size and weight of gifts you have to mail.
- Eliminate gifts to pets altogether.
- Give neighbors and coworkers cookies in a festive tin instead of presents.
- Have lunch with your friends in lieu of gifts.

Cut Out What You Won't Miss

- Scale back decorations that need electricity such as outdoor lights.
- Break the new-holiday-outfit habit. Buy just one piece of new clothing or an accessory.
- Don't buy poinsettias or mini-pine trees that will just go in the trash after the holidays.
- Forget "traditional" food like fruitcake, eggnog, fancy nuts or peppermint candy if it never gets eaten.
- Buy a little less than you think you need for holiday meals—chances are you've overestimated.

Conquer the Mall

- Shop alone unless you're just browsing.

- Make major purchases before the Thanksgiving stampede.

- Don't go on crowded weekends when you're bound to become too frustrated to bargain-hunt.

- See something you want for yourself? Wait for an after-Christmas sale, or add it to your wish list.

- If you feel tired, leave before you start making lazy (i.e., expensive) purchases for the sake of convenience.

- File receipts in an envelope as you shop and put them in a safe place you won't forget once you get home.

Avoid Pitfalls

Post offices. Go early so you don't have to pay for Express Mail or wait in long lines.

Convenience stores. Avoid them. It's convenience you'll pay extra for if you pick up batteries, film or anything else.

Grocery stores. 'Tis the season to stick to a shopping list and resist those hyped-up holiday specials.

Saved money? Pay off lingering bills and put some dollars in the bank for next year.

PART III

Building Wealth

1. Invest in the Future

 How to Finance Your Dreams

Most women have big dreams, but many of us can't see our way around the biggest obstacle to achieving them: lack of cash. But it is possible to raise the money you need to make your fantasy a reality. These women have done it, and you can, too.

SAVE AS A FAMILY

HER DREAM: To relocate so her family could enjoy a better quality of life
HER BIGGEST CHALLENGE: Accumulating enough savings to make the move
BEST TIP: "Learn to live on what you earn. Using credit cards to finance your life is a sure way to get into debt."

Jacqueline, who worked as a phone company administrator, knew she couldn't afford to give her two young children a good-quality life in New York City. "I had visited Las Vegas once for my job," says Jackie, who is divorced. "When I saw how clean it was, how you could get a nice place for a little money, I kept dreaming of moving there."

The problem? She owed too much on student loans, car payments and credit cards to save the money she needed. "I knew I couldn't move until I paid off my debts, and I couldn't pay them off while paying such ridiculous rent."

Fortunately, her family had a way of saving together for big-ticket items. Every week, 20 relatives each kicked in $100 to a communal fund. And each week, one person got the whole pot. While no one got back more than he or she invested, the savings plan, widely known as "pardna," helped keep them from frittering away their money. Jackie waited patiently for her turn. She used her initial $2,000 to pay off the last of her debts. "I took my next $2,000, piled the kids into the car with all I could carry and headed to Las Vegas," she recalls. "Within days, I found a townhouse to rent; within weeks, I had a job."

Eight years later, Jackie, 33, is the southwest regional coordinator for the National Association of Female Executives, and publisher of the *Women's Yellow Pages of Las Vegas*. Not only are her kids, now 10 and 12, thriving, but she also owns her own home. "I never would have been able to do this without the forced savings and the encouragement of my extended family!" says Jackie.

RAISE A FEW DOLLARS AT A TIME

HER DREAM: To make a documentary film

HER BIGGEST CHALLENGE: Getting grant funding

BEST TIP: "Little bits add up. If you can't find all your funding from one source, ask multiple lenders or donors. Even the smallest additions to your dream fund will add up."

As a nurse in the neonatal intensive care unit at Saint Vincent's Hospital in New York City, Claire was constantly moved by the daily drama of struggling babies and their families. She decided to make a documentary film about their triumphs and travails.

Her first step was to apply to dozens of private philanthropies and corporate foundations. "But I fell between the cracks because arts funders didn't understand the idea of a film about a hospital. And health-care foundations usually want to give their money to things that provide care and services."

Then, the nonprofit organization she was working with folded, taking money she and several other filmmakers had given them. "I had to start all over again," she says.

Unwilling to give up, Claire expanded her grassroots fundraising campaign. With sponsorship from the Center for Independent Documentary, which agreed to allow donors to get tax deductions for their contributions, she wrote to public officials and private citizens about the project. She scoured corporate directories and the Internet for addresses, and wrote to long-lost high school and college buddies. She made lists of parents she had dealt with in her years as a NICU nurse and sent them a letter describing her project.

Claire, now 38, raised more than $80,000, mostly from $25 or $50 donations. One family, whose daughter had been in the NICU for a cleft palate, sent her $10. "That meant a lot to me, because I saw how important this film was to people who had gone through the experience of having a very sick newborn," she says, "and how it could touch others."

Her documentary, *A Chance to Grow*, aired on the Discovery Channel (as *A Baby's Battle for Life*). The widely acclaimed film has been shown at several prestigious film festivals around the country.

KEEP YOUR DAY JOB

HER DREAM: To switch careers

HER BIGGEST CHALLENGE: Getting clients when she had no track record

BEST TIP: "If you want to switch fields, consider a lateral transfer within your current company and create a network of contacts to help build a base for your new career."

Stacey wanted to start her own business as a personal coach. Her goal: to help clients formulate and reach their personal or career goals.

But after years working in organization development for a health-care system, she was terrified of quitting her job cold turkey. "It was very frustrating to feel I had identified my dream but couldn't chase it. I needed the income my job provided," says Stacey, who lives in Houston with her husband and new baby.

Instead of giving notice, she approached several in-house department heads at her office and offered them her coaching services. Because they knew and trusted her, the fact that she was new at coaching was less of a handicap than it might have been with new contacts.

"My company let me develop new skills at my existing job," she says. "It became part of my job description."

The experience Stacey, 34, gained gave her the confidence to start her own business. Today, she is self-employed.

TAKE THE MORNING SHIFT

HER DREAM: To start her own business

HER BIGGEST CHALLENGE: Finding the startup money

BEST TIP: "Don't think small. If you're not willing to do what it takes to bring in money to take care of yourself, then your dream is not compelling enough to see it through. Make it bigger."

Like many fledgling businesses, Chrissy's public relations and special events firm had large startup expenses and not enough income to cover them. To get her business up and running, the former advertising executive got herself up and running, delivering *The Boston Globe* every morning before sunrise.

She used her paper-delivery time to listen to books on tape, which gave her ideas and inspiration for her business. And the best part? "I was home in time to shower and work the phones all day," she says.

When she needed more cash, she cleaned houses in the evenings, exercising aerobically as she dusted and vacuumed. Soon she had enough money to grow her business, which became a big success.

Now Chrissy, 47, who is married with two stepchildren, has set her sights on fulfilling her biggest dream yet: to launch a nationally syndicated television show that combines entertainment, humor and personal development. "If you're willing to think creatively, you can finance anything," she says. "It costs more to ignore your dreams than it does to go for them."

TRY TO GET SERVICES FREE

HER DREAM: To write a book on personal finance

HER BIGGEST CHALLENGE: Planning ahead enough to have the financial resources to accomplish her goal

BEST TIP: "Start building your financial security today. So whenever an opportunity presents itself, you can pursue it full tilt."

When Deborah first sat down to write a book on personal finance, she went from a hectic job at a marketing consulting firm to hours on end in a desk chair. "I spent more time at the refrigerator than the computer," she says. "I put on five pounds with the first chapter alone!" To get back into shape, she cut a deal with a personal fitness trainer, swapping money advice for workout time. It's win-win for both dreamers, without a penny's cash outlay. "Why buy when you can barter?" asks Deborah, 36.

She has found creative ways to finance other dreams. By investing her savings in a rental property, she earned money to buy a private home. She also received a Rotary Club scholarship to finance her graduate school education.

Find the Right Bank

Her dream: To find funding for a restaurant

Her biggest challenge: Getting a bank loan

Best tip: "Your business may be a dream, but treat it like a business. Have a detailed business plan and cost projections. It's especially important for women to show that their plans are well thought out."

Margo and her husband bought a landmark restaurant in Salt Lake City, planning to turn it into their home. But they were flooded with letters from former customers begging them to restore the place to a restaurant. "People said they used to come to Log Haven with their mom or grandmother," Margo recalls. "I quickly saw I had the opportunity to keep people's memories alive."

She wrote a detailed business plan for renovating and operating the restaurant. "The first banker I approached gave me a verbal guarantee, so I started construction and hiring."

Four months later, however, the bank rescinded its loan offer. By then, she was knee-deep in renovation expenses and debt. She'd maxed out her credit cards and liquidated her retirement fund from her former job at a health-care company. She threatened to sue, convincing the bank to give her a bridge loan. Then, she negotiated with creditors for a few months' grace and scrambled to find funding.

Major local and national banks all rejected her. "They were pretty up front about the fact that they would not lend money to a woman restaurateur because the failure rate for restaurants was so high."

Then a lawyer friend referred her to a small local bank outside of town. The bankers, all men, had memories of Log Haven, too. They looked at how the renovation was going, pulled her credit history, and asked questions about her business plan. Satisfied, the bank gave her the biggest loan in its history. "They made me feel like they believed in me," says Margo, 50.

The key, she adds, is establishing a personal relationship with a lender, so a banker invests in you rather than just a business profile. In this case, it was a good investment. Log Haven received the DiRoNA, one of the most prestigious restaurant awards in North America.

Ⓑ *How to Retire Rich*

When the road to riches seems long and hard, keep in mind that there's more than one path you can take. Choose the one that best suits your spending and saving style, and let it lead you to a financially secure future. It doesn't matter how much (or how little) money you make. What counts is what you do with it. Success story after success story proves that almost anyone can coax an impressive nest egg out of a modest income. Build your savings strategy on this plan and make your dream of retiring rich come true.

• **SET A TARGET DATE.** You have to name your goal to reach it, and the first step is deciding when you want to retire. If it's five years away and you haven't saved a dime, you'll know what you're dealing with. Roughly 60 to 70 percent of the population lets retirement sneak up on them with no savings plan at all.

- **CALCULATE YOUR NEEDS.** Once you've marked your calendar with a retirement date, decide how much money you'll want to live on. Start by calculating the bare minimum for your future needs. To do so, take inventory of your current annual living expenses, inflate that number by 3 percent per year for the number of years until retirement, then adjust for expenses that might change in retirement. Inflate that number by 3 percent per year for the number of years you will live in retirement (using 85 as the average life expectancy). The total is what you'll need to save to live comfortably.

- **CONSIDER YOUR WISH LIST.** Assign a dollar figure to your dreams—vacations, a boat, whatever—and add it to the above total. Then compute how much you'll have to save per year to amass this amount. (Use a reasonable rate of return, such as 8 or 9 percent.)

- **FIND THE WASTE.** Now you know how much you should be saving. But where are you going to find the dollars to do it? People may say "I don't have a dime," but everyone has a level of waste. If you spend $3 a day on coffee, after a month you've wasted $60. Compound that over 20 years and you've got a lot of savings. Keep ledger sheets on every item you buy—a self-scrutiny that stops them from throwing money around. Try this for a month to find ways you can pocket a few extra bucks to invest. One often-overlooked area is coupons—an average family of four can save as much as $1,000 a year by clipping coupons regularly.

- **INVEST IN THE BEST.** The first place to put any extra money is into your employer's 401(k) plan. Contribute the maximum allowance if you can, since you're often rewarded in two ways. First, your employer will usually add to it, and that's free money. Second, Uncle Sam's giving you a tax deduction. If you invest in a mutual fund, you'll see a hearty 9 or 10 percent return.

- **GET AN IRA I.Q.** After you've maximized your 401(k), start an Individual Retirement Account (IRA). Consider a Roth IRA, which lets you pay taxes on the money you first invest rather than on the much larger sum it becomes when you cash it out. Unlike traditional IRAs, you can pass this kind along to your children—tax-free. You may even want to convert any traditional IRAs you have into Roth IRAs, since the benefits are so good.

- **PLAN AHEAD.** Don't save just for retirement; also save for upcoming big-ticket items. When you buy a new car, for example, you begin to invest cash for its replacement right away. Start to put money into a mutual fund or money market account. Then you can buy the next car with a check and not pay interest.

- **PREPARATION PAYS OFF WITH SMALLER SHOPPING, TOO.** Drive the extra mile to the discount store, or scan the paper for sales. It takes extra time to live like this, but ultimately, you're richly rewarded.

CONSERVATIVE SPENDER & SAVER

Twenty years ago, Odette A. was struggling to start over after a divorce left her practically penniless. For Odette, going broke once was enough. So she set out to build a more secure financial future for herself. Odette admits that she "doesn't like change," which is why she sticks to a routine of selecting the safest and most conservative investments. When Odette retires from her job as an administrator at an engineering firm, she'll be able to rest easy, knowing she's put away more than enough money to meet her needs.

ODETTE'S STRATEGY:

- Odette calls a financial adviser a few times a year. (He gets a small percentage of her profit in exchange for counsel.)

- In 1980, she began saving 4 percent of her income and also invested in an IRA. Today, she contributes 8 percent of her income to a 401(k). The money is automatically deducted from her paycheck and deposited in the account. It's then invested in both stocks and bonds.

- Odette also contributes $100 a month to her tax-deferred Roth IRA.

- She puts $50 a month into a regular savings account, which usually holds six months' worth of living expenses. When she has an overflow of a few thousand dollars, she buys aggressive mutual funds or contributes more to her Roth IRA.

- Odette knows her comfort zone when it comes to investing—she likes to keep her emergency fund a bit larger than necessary. So even though she could get a better return on her money by investing in other ways, Odette holds back some of her cash overflow and buys Certificates of Deposit (CDs) that mature in nine months. These have a higher interest rate than her savings account, but still keep her money readily accessible.

If, like Odette, you occasionally find you have some money left over, contribute it to a mutual fund that will automatically debit your checking account each month. Historically, both stock and bond funds have outperformed CDs.

Comfortable with Taking Risks

Home: Splits her time between St. Paul, Minnesota, and Tucson, Arizona.
Income: Retired (previous income: $9 an hour or about $15,000 per year)
Saved: $575,000 (also owns a condominium worth $75,000)

When Dorothy divorced and had to go to work for the first time at age 43, she knew she'd have to be bold if she wanted to build savings for retirement. Since she had never gone to college, Dorothy felt her earning potential was limited. "The only kind of financial growth I could get was in the stock market." So Dorothy formed a plan: She'd save as much as possible before she retired, then afterward invest the bundle and live off its return.

True to her plan, when Dorothy stopped working in 1986, she had $65,000 in her 401(k) and $17,000 in company stock. She took that money, plus a $10,000 inheritance, and poured it into Wall Street.

Dorothy's strategy:

- She never seeks counsel from financial advisers. "As long as you do the homework," she says, "they won't know any more than you do."

- She's ridden out any dips in her stock prices. "If you don't rush to sell when you get nervous, your stocks will most likely rise again."

- Dorothy invests in corporations with diversified offerings. That way, if one of the product lines fails, the company is sure to stay in business.

- Before she buys any stock, Dorothy reads up on the company in *Money,*

Forbes and *Fortune* magazines or in the local newspaper. She watches the PBS show *Wall Street Week in Review* and calls the firm for an annual report to make sure it is prospering.

If you're going to invest in stocks, first join an investment club, where you can learn from people with experience. Also, Dorothy's approach is best tried while you're young, since retirement isn't a good time to take financial risks.

Ⓒ *Easy Ways to Save and Invest: Expert Strategies on How to Grow Your Nest Egg*

There's never been a better time for you to take control of your financial future. A woman can put herself on the road to economic security simply by setting aside as little as $5 a day, no matter what her age, status or situation. Saving and investing on a regular basis is easier than you think. Use these tips and tools for a brighter tomorrow.

START WITH SOME BASICS

- **CHOOSE THE BEST PLACE TO STASH YOUR CASH.** Locally owned and operated banks often have lower fees than regional or nationwide chain banks. Ask how you can qualify for an interest-bearing checking account, or for a break in fees if you use direct deposit or are an ATM-only customer. You might also try credit unions, which are usually nonprofit, so you get a higher savings rate and lower loan rates.

- **BEWARE OF HIDDEN BANK FEES.** There are over 225 different types of bank fees. They represent 90 percent of after-tax profits for banks. The one thing you do want is overdraft protection, even if your bank charges for it. Banks make money from bounced checks.

- **REMEMBER THE LATTE FACTOR.** We all waste $5 to $10 a day on little things, such as money for a designer cup of coffee, pastry, soda and candy bars. But a dollar here and there, if invested regularly through an automatic pay-yourself-first system, can make you financially secure for life. If you save and invest just $10 a day at 10 percent in a stock-based mutual fund (in general, the stock market has averaged over eleven percent for the past thirty years), you'll have a million dollars in 34 years.

- **GET ORGANIZED.** To keep track of how much you're spending through the year, buy a small filing cabinet and set up categories such as receipts, health (doctor/dentist/prescriptions), job/business expenses that may be tax deductible (gas/travel/cabs), purchases, ATM receipts, banking, credit cards and miscellaneous. When you get home each day, put receipts, credit card slips and other important documents in their proper place so you'll have the information when you need it. Organize your wallet, make files, transfer the information to a notebook and look at it regularly. Then you can start making sound financial decisions.

BOOST YOUR SAVINGS

- **INVEST $1 A DAY WITH AN ONLINE BROKERAGE ACCOUNT.** With sites such as sharebuilder.com and BUYandHOLD.com, you can take advantage of dollar-based investing. This means you can buy stocks or other investments by purchasing either fractions or whole shares, depending on the amount you invest. Unlike many online brokerage firms, which may require $2,000 or more to open an account, your initial deposit at BUYandHOLD.com can be as little as $20, plus a monthly fee. Both sites give you the option of opening a traditional or Roth IRA and having a set amount automatically deducted from your checking account or paycheck for savings or investments.

- **AVOID THE MIDDLEMAN.** You can buy stock directly from a company, eliminating the broker commission fees, by using a direct-purchase stock plan or Dividend Reinvestment Plans (known as DRIPS). Have a set amount automatically deposited to the account from your paycheck or checking account. Direct-purchase plans are a good way for folks to start investing small amounts of money on a regular basis.

- **GET PATRIOTIC AND SAVE.** Buy new Patriot Bonds (a Series EE U.S. savings bond) at half the face value—a $100 bond for $50, for instance. They mature in 17 years or less. You earn 3.40 percent interest at presstime (which accrues monthly and is compounded semi-annually), almost double what you would receive from a passbook savings account. Savings bonds are a safe and secure way to invest and save. Buy them at your bank or online at publicdebt.treas.gov. Or go to easysaver.gov and sign up for systematic online purchases.

- **TAKE ADVANTAGE OF FREE MONEY FROM YOUR EMPLOYER.** About 50 percent of employers who offer 401(k) retirement plans provide matching contributions. That's free money, so it's really silly to pass it up. Matching contributions usually start at 20 percent and can go as high as 100 percent. This means if you invest $1,000 of pretax income, your employer may contribute anywhere from $200 to $1,000.

- **DIVERSIFY, DIVERSIFY, DIVERSIFY.** After the Enron debacle, many employees learned this lesson the hard way. Diversification is key, especially with your 401(k). Many plans have at least ten investment choices, so pick four or five. You might invest in a money market, one or two stock funds, company stock and consider a bond fund, for example.

- **OR SET UP YOUR OWN RETIREMENT ACCOUNT.** If you don't have access to a company-sponsored program, such as a 401(k), then set up an individual retirement account (IRA) on your own. Go to any mutual fund provider or brokerage firm to start an IRA, and arrange for regular direct deposits from your checking account or savings. The key is to make sure a deposit is done automatically, otherwise you won't do it consistently. Self-employed people can set up a SEP (self-employed pension) IRA and sock away 25 percent of their gross income, up to $40,000.

- **GIVE YOURSELF A COOLING-OFF PERIOD.** Never spend more than $100 on anything without taking forty-eight hours to think it over. You'll give yourself a chance to decide if the purchase is really necessary.

- **TRIM EXPENSES WHERE YOU CAN.** You shouldn't shave everything to the bone; there has to be some pleasure. But something is not a treat if you do it every day. Cut costs by using public transportation and bringing your lunch to work. Even little things add up.

- **SET SHORT-TERM AND LONG-TERM FINANCIAL GOALS.** Ask yourself, "What do I want in the next year, the next three to five years, and ten or more years from now?" Write your goals down, divide them into three categories, and save or invest for each separately.

- **BUY THE CAR YOU NEED INSTEAD OF THE CAR YOU WANT.** Look at your car as transportation and think about what you use it for. Also consider the cost of insurance, maintenance, repair and gas. Find one that runs well, fits your lifestyle, is comfortable and safe. Check new car guides at your library or visit kbb.com and edmunds.com.

- **REALIZE SAVING TOGETHER IS NOT ALWAYS BETTER.** You and your husband are never going to agree on everything, so it's a good idea to open separate accounts for things that are important to you. After the primary bills are taken care of, agree to put a portion aside for common goals such as your children's education or your retirement. Then you can feel free to put the rest toward your individual goals.

CREDIT CARD DEBT BEGONE!

Know that one credit card is enough. Unless you travel a lot for business, one credit card is really all you need. This cuts down on the temptation to spend more, as well as annual usage fees that can average from $25 to $75. (Count on the higher range if it's an airline frequent-flier card.) To find low-interest and low-fee cards, go to bankrate.com. At the beginning of every week, put a self-stick note on your one card and jot down your charges as you go. If you are in credit card debt, you need to make a budget. The first step is to look at how much you are spending.

- **NEGOTIATE A BETTER DEAL.** If you think you have a credit card problem, you probably do. Leave your cards at home so you stop using them. Next, call credit card companies and find the one that will give the best rate—10 percent or lower—if you consolidate all your debt on one card. Ask what fee, if any, will be charged to transfer those other balances.

- **SAVE YOUR CREDIT CARD INTEREST.** Look at last year's credit card statements and you can see exactly what you paid in finance charges. This year, don't charge, don't owe, and put that money, say, $20 or $40 a month, in a savings account that you can ultimately use for investing. It may seem like a little bit of money, but it establishes a way of thinking about saving.

Start an Investment Club

- **Host a meeting.** Gather reliable friends, members of your church or coworkers interested in investing. None of you needs to be an expert.

- **Agree on a long-term goal.** Decide early on whether you want to invest in tried-and-true companies, up-and-comers or a mix. It's important to realize that making money from investments can take years of patience.

- **Decide on dues.** In most clubs, members give $20 to $50 a month to the group pool, which is used for stock purchases.

- **Assign responsibilities.** Nominate an organizer to set up meetings, a leader to keep them flowing and a recorder to keep track of transactions.

- **Select a broker.** Discount brokerage firms are the cheapest. Remember: They won't offer advice; they'll only place your orders.

- **Study companies.** This is the real work. Each member reads up on companies that interest her—software companies that sell popular video games, stores in the local mall, medical firms. Then she shares what she learns, and members vote on whether or not to invest in those particular stocks.

- **Invest every month.** And reinvest all dividends. With consistent investing, chances are good that you'll make an average 10 percent profit over the long term.

Advice from club members

"There's nothing about the stock market that is so mysterious that the average person can't succeed. Investment clubs are wonderful ways to amass wealth, and to learn that the stock market is not a gambling casino for the rich."

HELEN M., LAUREL PARK, NC

"I started a family investment club to teach our children how to invest. We keep monthly investments to $5 a person. Out-of-town relatives call or mail us their ideas. It's a great way to stay in touch and plan for the future."

ROSE K., CAMAS, WA

"Our investment club has no silent partners. Everyone contributes something at each meeting, whether it's a magazine article she read or her experience at a seminar. If a member wants to take a study break, she can be our hostess."

PEGGY S., BOWLING GREEN, OH

2. Kids and Saving

Ⓐ *What Kids Should Know Early On*

When Kathy C. gave her 8-year-old son a $10 bill to buy pizza for lunch, she expected some change. To her surprise, he had no money left at all when he came home from school. "Drew bought one slice of pizza for $2.50 and spent the rest on candy bars," she says. "He couldn't even tell me how many he purchased or how much they cost."

Kathy, a mother of three in Columbus, Ohio, says Drew never worries that he'll run out of money. "He just figures someone will give him more."

Children love to spend. The problem is that they often don't understand why the supply doesn't always keep up with their demands. That's why it pays to teach kids about money early on—before advertisers, retailers and credit-card companies do. You'll be equipping your children with financial skills that will last a lifetime.

Money Talks

Explaining the mechanics of money and banking is a good place to begin. Some kids think all their parents need to do is insert their ATM card into a cash machine, punch in a few numbers and the money will pop right out.

Children need to be taught that you have to earn money before you can spend it, and that you have to put money in a financial institution before you can take it out. Involving kids in the family finances shows them how we use money to operate our lives. Parents today are more open about sex and drugs but still hold back when it comes to money.

While kids don't need to know the exact amount of your income, they do need to know whether or not you're saving and how much you need to cover the bills. Sharing some of this information with them will bring you closer as a family.

Janet and Bill P. of Dayton, Ohio, took this step a bit further when they included their three older children, ages 10, 8 and 7, in a bill-paying session one evening. "We called it our 'Night at the Round Table,'" says Janet, who also has a 1-year-old. "We sat down together, wrote out the checks for bills, and the kids did the math, subtracting the amounts from our account balance. It was a fun family adventure and they learned that we can't afford to run out every time they want to buy something, that we work to pay the bills."

MAKING ALLOWANCES

Children learn the toughest lessons when they have hands-on experience. That's why many experts recommend putting kids on an allowance program. Teaching children how to manage money is an immeasurable gift. But the only way for kids to learn is if they receive some cash to work with on a regular basis.

Children as young as five can handle a small weekly sum. To come up with an appropriate allowance amount, consider your child's age, what you can afford and the going rate among other neighborhood youngsters. According to a survey by the Consumers Union, 9- and 10-year-olds receive $5-$8 each week on average; 11- and 12-year-olds receive $11-$13; and 13- and 14-year-olds between $13-$15.

Another popular strategy is to give a child $1 for every year that she has been in school (a seventh grader would receive $7 each week), or $1 for every year of her life.

Some parents gradually increase their children's allowance along with the expenses they are expected to cover. Ellen S. of New York City gives her 14-year-old son, Alex, between $20 and $25 every Sunday night. The cash is intended to cover school lunches, snacks, movies, bus fare, nonessential clothing and other extras. Plus, Alex is required to put $5 into a savings account each week. "This money has to last him until the next Sunday," says Ellen. "He's learning to function within a budget and that there's not an endless supply of money."

WORK FOR PAY?

Whether or not to tie a child's allowance to chores is an ongoing debate among family finance experts. Neale S. Godfrey, author of *A Penny Saved*, believes that children should be required to perform house and yard work to earn their bounty. "Money is not an entitlement. Paying for chores shows your child the relationship between work and money," Godfrey says. "Not only does your child have to work for it, but earning an allowance will underscore the fact that parents have to work hard for their money, too."

Peggy H., however, believes it's better to keep chores and allowance separate matters. "When you pay kids for every little thing they do, you run the risk of having them decide they don't need the money, so they refuse to help out." Instead, Peggy suggests this middle ground: Give children a modest weekly amount that they receive regardless of whether or not they've done their chores. Then post a list of extra jobs the kids can do to supplement their income.

Angie and Rick K. of Kent, Washington, don't give their 11-year-old daughter money for making her bed or loading the dishwasher. "She receives her allowance, $5 per week, because she is a member of the family," says Angie. If Ashley slacks off on her chores, her parents don't withhold her allowance—they take away television or playtime instead. She can earn more money by doing extra chores such as washing the car. "I think Ashley appreciates money more when she has to put out some energy to get it," her mother says.

Not all of a child's income needs to come from their parents. Earning money from shoveling snow from a neighbor's walk, mowing grass and babysitting helps build self-esteem, and teaches a youngster to be self-reliant.

To Market, To Market

Take advantage of teachable moments at the supermarket, video store or a restaurant. Explain what you're doing as you check prices, weigh your options and make good decisions. Your children will learn how to save thousands of dollars over their lifetime.

Jenise G. and her 6-year-old son, Kyle, set a budget and compared costs when they bought school supplies last fall. "You can spend tons of money on that stuff, and I wanted to show him that you have to make smart selections," says Jenise, of Antioch, California. When they looked at pencils, Mom pointed out that a large package of yellow ones was priced at 59¢, while a small package of fancy, psychedelic pencils ran 99¢.

"Kyle liked the idea that he could get five more pencils for less money if he bought the plain ones," Jenise recalls.

Children don't always appreciate the value of a dollar when they see their parents pay for purchases with plastic. That's why Catherine D. tries to operate on a cash basis when she's shopping with Lauren, 10, and 7-year-old Jonathan.

"When I pay for things with a check or a credit card, they don't always realize that money is changing hands," says Catherine. "It takes on more meaning when they see the bills and change going across the counter."

SAVING GRACE

Of course, money isn't always just for spending. Parents should have children earmark a portion of their allowance, gift money and earnings for saving. But don't just force kids to save with no real goal in mind. Having kids set aside money for a specific purpose, such as a new bike, skateboard or car, helps motivate them and puts them in control.

Patricia P.'s two girls, ages 5 and 2, are saving for a purebred puppy. They put any extra money in their "doggie bank." The family has also given up some cable channels to save more. "When I pay the bills, Claire and Meredith put the money that would have gone to the cable company into the doggie bank," says the Madison, Wisconsin, mom.

Jackie W., a mother of five in San Bernardino, California, gives Sherry, 8, a financial incentive to save while also teaching the power of compounding. "We pay her a percentage of what's in her piggy bank at the end of each month," she says. "Before my daughter's money earned interest, she always bought junk—ice cream, candy, gum. Now she has no desire to spend everything she gets. She wants to see her money grow!"

EASY MONEY

When your kids ask for an advance on their allowance, turn the transaction into a learning experience by charging interest and assigning a due date.

Paying interest and seeing how credit reduces the amount of real money available to spend later is a powerful lesson that needs to be taught early.

BIG SPENDERS

- Kids shell out lots of bucks on everything from ice cream to lip gloss to video games. According to a study by James McNeal, Ph.D., a marketing professor at Texas A&M University, 4- to 12-year-olds spend an average of nearly $10 each week of their own money—from allowance, gifts and neighborhood jobs.

- According to Teenage Research Unlimited in Northbrook, Illinois, children aged 12 to 19 spend even more—$44 per week of their own money!

MONEY STAGES

The concept of money is abstract, especially for very young children. It's important to gear money lessons to a youngster's developmental level. Here's a guide to help:

- **3 TO 5:** Preschoolers can begin to grasp the idea that money is valuable and one needs it to buy things. Help them learn to name coins and understand basic coin equivalents (four quarters equal one dollar).

- **6 TO 8:** School-age kids can begin handling their own transactions at a shop or fast-food restaurant. Teach them how to estimate the total of several items, count their money, figure in sales tax and check their change. Now's a good time to open a savings account in your child's name.

- **9 TO 12:** Preteens understand that when you make a purchase you are really making a tradeoff that involves not just money, but the time and effort you have to spend to earn it. Kids this age can budget for expenses such as toys, clothes and gifts.

Ⓑ *Put Stock in Your Kids' Future*

Since he was 10 years old, Scott Z., 18, of Lincoln, Rhode Island, has been investing in the stock market. Starting out, Scott didn't have much money to invest, but what he did have, his parents matched. Now that Scott is a college freshman, he owns stock worth $20,000, and he helped finance part of his tuition. Anyone can invest as long as he is willing to put the time into it.

The advantage of investing when you're young is that you get the long-term benefits of compound interest. Consider this: A person who invests $1,000 a year for the first 18-years of life will end up with the same amount of money as the person who invests $1,000 a year for the 46 years from age 19 to 65. The sooner you get your child interested in investing, the better his chances are for having a secure economic future. Get started today:

- **BANK SAVINGS ACCOUNT.** Kids as young as 4 or 5 can learn about saving by putting money in a bank account. Not all financial institutions offer children's accounts, however, so it may be necessary to shop around.

- **529 EDUCATION PLANS.** Although college savings programs are usually owned by parents, a child can be the owner, or at least a contributor. At the Ohio Tuition Trust Authority, the executive director says the program is structured to accept contributions as small as $15.

- **CERTIFICATES OF DEPOSIT.** CDs are a good way to begin if you want to avoid the ups and downs of the stock market. Try having your child put half her money in a CD and half in individual stocks, then track them to see which does better.

- **STOCK MARKET.** Young kids are so computer savvy. Following individual stocks online can be fun. Kids can invest as little as $10 a month. Consider your child's interests: If she likes to eat at Wendy's or shop at the Limited, those may be good stocks to research. Log on to jumpstart.org to get started.

- **MUTUAL FUNDS.** Mutual funds aren't as volatile as stocks, but it's harder for kids to relate to them. Kids interested in investing in many companies can log on to mfea.com for more information.

3. Make Extra Cash

 Boost Your Income

When the money runs out before the bills do, the first thing most people try is cutting expenses. But sometimes it's easier to balance the books by increasing your income. Today's economy offers a wide range of choices, from stopgap measures to long-term solutions.

- **TRY MOONLIGHTING.** With unemployment at the lowest level in decades, opportunities for part-time, seasonal and temporary work are better than ever. Working at a second job one evening a week, on your day off or during holidays and vacations can boost income significantly. Part-timers are sometimes paid more per hour than full-time staff because they don't receive health insurance, paid vacations and other costly benefits. Check the want ads, the Internet or a temporary employment service. You may even be able to work at home—especially if you get training as, for example, a notary public or a tax preparer.

- **ASK YOUR EMPLOYER FOR HELP.** Anyone who has been in the same job for a year should not hesitate to request a raise and/or a promotion. You may find, as I once did, that your boss is waiting for you to ask. One effective approach: Describe your duties and accomplishments, then say, "I think I've earned an increase; if you don't agree, please tell me where I need to improve so I can merit one soon."

  Whether you get a raise or not, don't stop there. Flexible hours, a four-day workweek, telecommuting or extra vacation time are all reasonable requests that make it easier to earn extra money elsewhere. Many firms also reimburse employees for the cost of job-related courses—and some give you time off to attend classes. Everything you learn can boost your earning power, so take advantage of all opportunities.

- **VOLUNTEER TO WORK OVERTIME.** Extra work could lead to a raise, promotion or bonus. Make your offer in a memo or at a meeting attended by executives who count—and devote your additional hours to special projects or new responsibilities, not the same old duties. Overtime work that's done grudgingly or so quietly that only the cleaning crew knows you're there is rarely rewarded.

- **RENT OUT UNUSED SPACE.** A spare room with a private bath can be a real gold mine in areas that draw numerous visitors. First, check local ordinances and register with a bed-and-breakfast service. It's possible to take in fees of $50 to $100 a night for a room and bath, plus a light meal in the morning.

  If you don't have a spare bedroom, examine your property for other possibilities: rent the unused half of your two-car garage or make your large city home available for small weddings and other events.

- **TURN YOUR CRAFTS INTO CASH.** Many creative women supplement their income by selling needlework, jewelry, pottery, baskets and other handiwork that began as a hobby.

- **MARKET YOUR EXPERTISE.** Almost anything you do well—from cake decorating or weaving to photography or yoga—might be taught at a community college or adult education program, or at schools, churches and community centers across the country.

- **SELL POSSESSIONS YOU DON'T USE.** Selling goods at a garage sale is a short-term solution, but it has long-term effects when the money is used to pay off high-interest debt. A motley collection of toys, appliances, tools and other household goods can bring in $500 or more. Joining forces with neighbors usually means less work and larger profits for everyone involved.

  Another idea: Take out an ad in a shopper's guide. If your castoffs include antiques, collectibles or jewelry, have them appraised before setting prices. Grandma's ugly brooch may be worth far more to a dealer than to bargain hunters at a tag sale. Damaged items can be valuable, too.

- **TRAIN FOR MORE LUCRATIVE WORK.** Expand your computer skills by taking courses at a community college or adult education center. Sales training is also valuable. One secretary doubled her income after a six-week course enabled her to switch to commission sales in the same firm.

- **PUT YOUR ASSETS TO WORK.** The average American pays nearly 18 percent interest on a credit card balance of $7,000. That adds up to $1,260 in annual interest that could go into your pocket instead. How? By using savings or investments earning less to pay off that debt. If, like millions of taxpayers, you usually receive a substantial tax refund, lower your withholding and use the extra income to reduce debt or increase savings. Anyone paying more than 8 percent on a home mortgage should also consider refinancing and investing the savings.

And make sure you're getting the maximum return on money not needed for current expenses. Why settle for a paltry 2 percent on a savings account when safe money market mutual funds pay around 5 percent? For long-term savings, growth stock mutual funds often yield 10 percent or more. If you lack the stomach for the ups and downs of the stock market, you can still earn 5 percent from certificates of deposit (CDs) in federally insured banks. The secret: Buy a series of CDs with staggered maturity dates. If you have $10,000, for example, buy ten $1,000 CDs—one for six months, another for one year, a third for 18 months, and so on. Known as "laddering," this gives you a CD coming due every six months. As each matures, you can reinvest at the highest rate without tying up all your money for long periods.

PLAYING IT SAFE

Laws and policies governing home-based enterprises vary with the community. Check with the local authorities about a business license and zoning requirements (most regulations apply to businesses with employees or customers on the premises). It's also important to ask your insurance agent about a rider to protect business equipment, as well as additional liability coverage against claims from business visitors. Spending a few dollars more on premiums could save you a fortune later on.

B *Have Fun, Make Money:*
Turn your Hobby into Easy Cash

You work all day, budget carefully and still wish you had a few thousand more to pay off your credit card bill or put in an emergency fund. Getting another job isn't really an option unless you want to work 24/7.

Still, you may be overlooking a source of income that's right under your nose—your hobby. Yes, it's possible to make a few bucks and not even feel like you're working. Don't believe it? These four women did it.

THE FLORAL DESIGNER

MOLLIE, age 25, married, San Francisco Bay Area, California
DAY JOB: Public relations

Mollie's love of flowers is practically genetic. Her grandmother was a part-time floral arranger in Minneapolis, and her mother's hobby was gardening. "I always loved helping my mom," says Mollie.

A year ago, a good friend asked Mollie to do the flowers for her wedding. The friend had seen arrangements Mollie had made for herself and loved them. "She offered to hire me, but I made it my wedding gift to her," says Mollie. Her friend was so ecstatic about the red rose-with-hypericum-berries bouquets that she suggested Mollie make floral arrangements for others. Mollie decided she was right. Her first step was to go to the florist shop Martha Stewart frequents. Told she needed a resale certificate if she planned to make and sell arrangements, she registered as a sole proprietor (for $120) with the county clerk in Brooklyn, where she was living at the time. Then she started marketing the old-fashioned way: she told everyone she knew about her designs. She also put business cards in every business and apartment building in her neighborhood.

She works at her "hobby" anywhere from 5 to 15 hours a week, but it never interferes with her day job. "I go to the flower market at 6 a.m., take the flowers back home and get into work by 9 a.m.," she says. "I do arranging after work and on weekends." Asked if it isn't stressful working all week, then going home and working some more, Mollie says: "When you're dealing with something beautiful, it's actually a stress reliever."

The payoff: Since March of 2006, Mollie has made $5,000, which she's earmarked for a down payment on a house. Her pricing secret: Florists tend to charge twice what they pay wholesale, but she charges only a third above wholesale.

Mollie refuses to take more orders than she can tackle comfortably, and she tries to limit far-away jobs to weekends, because she's also her own delivery person.

Mollie's advice: "If you're going to do flower arranging to make extra cash, be sure you research what others in your area are charging. And don't give up if it takes awhile. Once you do a good job for someone (maybe a friend), the word will spread."

What's It For?

It's easy to think of hobby income as "found" money, but it's better to think of it as special money, to be used in an extra-special way. Use it to:

- Pay off credit card debt.
- Save for retirement.
- Reinvest in your hobby.
- Set up an emergency fund.
- Start investing.

The award-winning cook

Joni, age 50, married, four kids, Sacramento, California
Day job: Running a cleaning products company

Fifteen years ago, when Joni and her family moved from California to Iowa, she used cooking as a way to connect to the community. "The Iowa Egg Board was sponsoring a cook-off contest at the local mall for creative egg recipes," she says, "and I thought it'd be a fun way to meet people." She came up with the Iowa Short Stack—several omelets layered with different fillings. She ended up winning second place ($100) and got her name in the newspaper. "I quickly became known," she says. And a hobby was born: entering cook-offs and recipe contests.

One thing Joni initially liked, and still does, about expanding on her hobby was that there are no big startup costs or daunting obstacles (such as finding clients). Her only expense is subscribing to a contest newsletter (cookingcontestcentral.com), which costs $25 a year. How does she decide which ones to enter? "If a contest is for a product I don't use," she says, "I don't bother with it." On the other hand, if it's something her family loves—say, chicken—she's game. "My husband and kids are my guinea pigs, so I never waste anything."

Over 15 years, Joni's won 70 contests, from the National Honey Board (Honey Crab Cakes with Mango Peanut Sauce) to the Contessa Food Products Convenience Meal Contest (Chicken Vegetable Chowder), winning prizes like trips to Hollywood, Disney World, New York City and France, as well as cash—anywhere from $100 for the Iowa Short Stack to $5,000 in the National Beef Cook-Off for Savory Beef and Cheese Roll-ups. She averages $2,000 to $3,000 a year in cash prizes, which has come in handy to help with college tuition and braces.

JONI'S ADVICE: Keep it fun. "If I felt I had to come up with creative recipes every day, I wouldn't enjoy this anymore," says Joni. Instead, she enters about one contest a week. "Winning cooking contests involves using simple ingredients in creative ways," she says. "Don't try to be a gourmet. Simply look for ease of preparation and interesting tastes that no one else has thought of."

THE COLLECTOR

CATHY, age 40, divorced mother of one, Springfield, Illinois
DAY JOB: Executive assistant

As a little girl, Cathy loved Marilyn Monroe. "I was nine when I saw *Gentlemen Prefer Blondes*," she says, "and I was blown away by how beautiful Marilyn was. I wanted to know everything about her." By the time Cathy was 21, she'd started collecting photos of Monroe, finding them at memorabilia shows in Chicago and St. Louis. She also joined the Marilyn Monroe Fan Club, which was how collectors bought and sold memorabilia in pre-Internet days. "Other collectors would send out lists of things they were selling—Marilyn salt and pepper shakers, Marilyn cookie jars—and whenever I had extra cash, I bought stuff." Within a few years, she had thousands of Marilyn collectibles.

In 2001, Cathy faced a $3,000 car repair that threatened to wreak havoc on her finances. "I didn't want to rack up credit card debt," she says. "I realized I had to look at my collection as an investment that was there to help me if I needed it." She then logged on to eBay and learned how to set up an account.

She posted photos of eight bottles of Marilyn Merlot, which sold in three days for a net sum of $3,000. Not bad for an initial investment of $19.95 a bottle. Her car repairs were paid for and her collection was not seriously diminished.

Because she's only sold when it was absolutely necessary, Cathy still looks at her hobby as just that. "I love looking at my things," she says. But the collection is also her safety net. "It's here for my enjoyment and for my financial security."

CATHY'S ADVICE: "Be passionate about what you collect and buy what you love," says Cathy. "If you have to sell to raise some money, go for items that will bring the largest sum in the least amount of time. You can't raise $3,000 quickly by selling $1 postcards."

THE SPIN INSTRUCTOR

LISA, age 33, married, Brookline, Massachusetts
DAY JOB: Marketing manager

Lisa has always been physically active; luckily, she's married to a guy who shares her passion. "Darren and I run, bike and go to the gym together," she says. In 2000, when the couple moved to California for her work, she signed up for a spin class at a local gym. "It was so bad," she says, "I told Darren that I could teach better than that." Two years later when they moved to Pennsylvania, again for her job, she made a decision: to get certified as a spin instructor. "I like doing it anyway," she says, "so why not help others, too?"

Lisa signed up for an instructors' course at a local gym. When the couple moved to Massachusetts a year later, she called a YMCA and applied to teach. The gym not only hired her for a few classes, but also paid for her CPR certification, which is required for all instructors.

As she gained experience, she applied to become a spin instructor at other gyms and eventually taught classes on Mondays, Wednesdays and Sundays.

She still keeps the same schedule. "I never tire of hearing students say that I've pushed them further than they ever thought they could go," she says.

Lisa makes $35 a class and can always teach extra classes if she wants more money. At this point, her only real hobby-related expense is buying CDs, to keep her music selection varied. What's her hobby money for? "I'm thinking about using it for a new dining room table or a piece of art."

"Teaching too many classes makes exercise feel like work," she says, "so I teach three days a week—with occasional sub jobs—as opposed to every day, and I always look forward to it."

LISA'S ADVICE: "The hardest part is getting that first teaching gig," Lisa says, "but be persistent. Offer to sub if someone's ill or out of town. That will get you in the door." And though the positive feedback is wonderful, she adds, there will also be people who come to your class once and never show up again. Don't take it personally!

HOBBIES AND THE IRS

Money made from a hobby is taxable only if you make a profit after deducting expenses. And there are a lot of expenses you can deduct. Even if you'd own a computer or CDs regardless of your hobby, you may be able to deduct them if they aid you in making cash. And don't forget magazine subscriptions that help you in your hobby (craft magazines, photography publications) and office supplies used to conduct your business.

A good accountant will be able to tell you if you can escape Social Security and Medicare taxes if profits are less than a certain amount of money. Bottom line: Keep track of all expenses related to your hobby and consult a professional tax advisor to see if you end up with a profit or loss.

Ⓒ Home Sweet Home: Boost Your Income Without Leaving Home

TELECOMMUTING

As a home-based tour sales representative for a company, Theresa J., 38, of Peoria, Arizona, earns a full-time salary with full benefits. Yet she has time to cook breakfast for her three children, greet them after school, and even see her husband before he leaves for his night-shift job. Plus, she's eliminated her 90-minute (each way!) commute.

"In a way, your salary increases because you save on gas and on paying for a babysitter," she says. "And my car insurance premiums have dropped since I stopped driving to work."

Today, major companies and even government agencies are hiring employees specifically to work from home. Telecommuters do the same jobs they would do in a corporate office, without the long commute or time spent hanging around the water cooler.

More than 11 million people now telecommute in the United States, up from only 3.4 million in 1990, according to FIND/SVP, a New York-based research firm. Here's how you can take advantage of this growing trend as well:

- **CONVINCE YOUR EMPLOYER.** If your boss thinks telecommuting is just a fancy word for goofing off, counter with these facts: Telecommuters save businesses money by reducing the need for office and parking space, permitting recruitment over a wider region, and eliminating office-related distractions. At the company where Theresa works, telecommuters are more productive, take fewer sick days and have less job turnover. The company is now considering allowing more sales agents to be home-based.

- **SHOW YOU'VE GOT WHAT IT TAKES.** Melissa D., an account representative for a phone company, is often in her home office at 6 a.m. and works some evening and weekend hours. "I tend to work more, but I don't mind because of the flexibility," she says. "If I worked downtown, I could never make my two teenagers' afternoon activities. Now I can."

- **LOOK FOR "TELECOMMUTING-FRIENDLY" COMPANIES.** For job leads, check the business section of your newspaper for articles or notices about telecommuting conferences. Also, some Chambers of Commerce hold seminars for companies on developing home-based workforces. Contact participating businesses.

- **FIND AT-HOME JOBS ONLINE.** The Telecommuting Jobs Page on the Internet (tjobs.com) lists openings at companies looking to hire home-based workers. Job categories include data entry, sales and desktop publishing. Before signing on with an unfamiliar company, check that it's listed in Dun & Bradstreet or another business directory.

- **BECOME AN INDEPENDENT CONTRACTOR.** Telecommute by working for legal and medical transcription services as an independent contractor rather than as an employee. Although Margo M. of Pennsauken, New Jersey, had never done medical transcription, she performed well on the practice tapes one service used as a test. For three years now, Margo, who gets paid by the line or by the page, has worked for the service from home.

- **KEEP YOUR CORPORATE LINK STRONG.** Out of sight sometimes means out of the loop for raises or promotions. Use e-mail and the telephone to stay in touch daily with your supervisors. Submit regular status reports and attend meetings in person whenever possible.

MOONLIGHTING

For Beverly A., 54, a management consultant in Evanston, Illinois, going to crafts workshops provided a great outlet for her creativity. Then she realized that some of her crafts projects could provide additional income as well.

Beverly now earns an extra $300 to $400 each month by making colorful lampshades and picture frames from unusual papers. She sells her products through a local store. "Create something you admire, then make cash moonlighting by producing it," she says. "If you like it, there's probably a market for it."

Most of us think of moonlighting as holding down a second job. But many women moonlight by working for themselves, starting home businesses in their spare evening or weekend hours. Some eventually quit their day jobs to work full-time for themselves. We recommend starting your home business slow and small, so moonlighting is a good idea. It's smart to test the waters before you let go of that job. Successful moonlighters suggest:

- **MOONLIGHT TO BUILD A CLIENTELE.** Laura C. was a special-education teacher when she started making beaded earrings, bracelets and pins. She sold them at home parties for $14 to $60. Laura's moonlighting goal was reached last year when she left teaching to run her jewelry business from her home.

- **USE MOONLIGHTING TO IMPROVE YOUR CURRENT JOB.** If you work in a general office, offer relief services to professionals such as accountants or lawyers. You'll learn the ropes in a new field, earn more cash, and maybe even find a better full-time, salaried position.

- **WORK TOWARD A SPECIFIC GOAL.** Want to build an education fund or pay off a debt? Put your moonlighting income into a separate account earmarked for that purpose. You'll reach your goal faster than if you add it to your general checking account.

- **EARN EXTRA CASH FROM WHAT YOU KNOW OR LOVE.** Use your work or hobby to teach classes in evening school. Or rent a meeting room and charge per person ($35 to $200) for a weekend session. Booklet publisher Paulette E. runs seminars by phone for $175 per person. To find facilities, check Teleconferencing Services in the Yellow Pages.

- **LET VOICE MAIL RUN YOUR BUSINESS.** While you're at your day job, voice mail can take and organize phone messages, as well as provide basic information. ("Press '1' to order a catalog; press '2' for our mailing address.") Retrieve and return messages in the evening.

- **TELL EVERYONE WHAT YOU DO.** Write a one-sentence description of your moonlighting business and use it in all introductions: "Hi, I'm (name). I provide in-home beauty care for seniors and the disabled." You'll be amazed at how many people ask for your business card.

HOME BUSINESS: BE YOUR OWN BOSS

Eight years ago, Michelle W., 43, left her position as a bank vice president to be at home with her two young daughters. She had always loved to bake and share her creations, so she decided to start a business. She was amazed to learn that setting up a commercial kitchen would cost thousands of dollars. "I couldn't justify investing that kind of money without having any real customers," the Dallas woman says.

Instead, Michelle subcontracted out the baking, while continuing to create recipes and market her business from home. Currently, 8 million women own businesses, and female ownership is growing faster than any other business sector, according to the Small Business Administration. Millions of these moneymaking enterprises began at someone's kitchen table or in a spare bedroom, and many remain home-based. Here's how to increase your earnings:

- **THINK CORPORATE.** Michelle W. first sold her liqueur-flavored cakes individually at holiday shows, but today she is targeting corporate accounts. Companies buy more of her desserts at a time, using them for gifts and premiums. "It helps make my business less seasonal," Michelle says.

- **SET ASIDE TIME EVERY WEEK TO MARKET YOUR BUSINESS.** Schedule time to call prospective clients, research new markets, or contact customers you haven't heard from recently.

- **FOCUS ON TARGETED ADVERTISING.** "Whenever I bought general advertising in the past, I regretted it," says Sheri D., a custom itinerary planner from Seattle. "Use your resources to find the people who are really interested." Sheri spent $400 to have a website designed to attract just those wanting to travel to the Pacific Northwest. Her site generates more than 20 percent of her business.

- **CONSIDER COOPERATIVE ADS.** If advertising is appropriate for your business but too expensive, get together with several related businesses and buy one ad together. The same strategy can work for printing costly brochures and mailers.

- **LET THE INTERNET WORK FOR YOU.** When writing e-mail, Venita G. of Montgomery, Alabama, recommends using a brief signature line to promote your business.

- **RAISE YOUR PRICE.** You'll boost income from current customers, and may also attract new ones looking for superior work. Offer regular customers a limited-time extension of the lower price. Of course, any price set by contract or written agreement must be honored.

- **VISIT CUSTOMERS.** In-person contact emphasizes your availability and allows you to discuss innovations or future plans. Send annual surveys (include a stamped return envelope) to ask for feedback on how well you've served customers and what new approaches they'd like to see.

- **LOOK FOR TIMESAVERS.** Sandy H. has had more billable time for working since she hired a teenager to do her typing. An after-school babysitter can help you squeeze in an extra profit-making hour or two. Hiring a messenger service may cost less than the time you sacrifice by delivering work or goods yourself.

- **COMPUTERIZE YOUR RECORDKEEPING.** Transcriptionist Linda A. says that by using bookkeeping software, "I could see what I was spending" and where to cut back. The program saves time and keeps her better informed about her finances.

KEEP MORE OF WHAT YOU EARN

To increase profits, start by cutting expenses

- **BARTER GOODS AND SERVICES.** Are you an office cleaner, caterer or secretary? Trade hours of your skill for printing services, computer advice or supplies. Like all business income or expenses, keep records of such barters for tax filing.

- **CONTROL BANK FEES.** Before opening a bank account for your business, compare costs. Business accounts are often charged extra for basic services. When Paulette E. of San Diego questioned a service charge of $191 included on her first statement, she discovered that her bank charged 12¢ every time she deposited a $3 check (the price of her product). She changed banks to find a better deal. If your business name is the same as your own name, try opening a second personal checking account to avoid high fees.

- **USE FREE SOFTWARE.** Sometimes all you need to do is ask. For instance, medical billing is a hot new field for the self-employed, with software costing hundreds of dollars or more. Medical billing specialist Sandy H. of Sharps Chapel, Tennessee, advises asking insurance companies directly for their billing programs, which are usually free of charge.

- **SAVE ON SUPPLIES.** Linda A. of Richmond, Virginia, spent $24 on each new ink cartridge for her printer. As a busy transcriptionist, Linda needed a fresh cartridge every two weeks. Then she discovered a $10 kit that enabled her to refill each cartridge twice. "Little things like that add up," Linda says.

- **LOCATE LOW-COST HELP.** At Alverno College in Milwaukee, students in the Business Enterprise Practicum provide marketing advice and other help for free. Similar programs exist in college business departments around the country. For inexpensive help with product assembly or shipping, contact nonprofit sheltered workshops.

- **KEEP INCOME AT HOME.** You can hire your spouse or teenagers as long as they're doing actual work. Paying wages to your kids cuts your income tax bill. Children aren't liable for taxes until they earn above the personal exemption limit.

- **PRINT YOUR OWN.** Computer software and color printers let you produce publicity material inexpensively and quickly. Diana W., who makes knitted and crocheted items, prints her own small catalog in her Porterville, California, home. Her three-page, double-sided guide costs about 10¢ per copy to produce.

GET YOUR NAME AROUND TOWN

- **START A SUPPORT GROUP.** Whether you moonlight, telecommute or have a home business, you can form an affinity group to discuss problems, refer customers or swap a variety of services.

- **WRITE A PRESS RELEASE CONTAINING A FREE OFFER.** Send it to local newspapers or publications aimed at your target audience. Write a tip sheet in your field and offer it for free in exchange for a self-addressed, stamped envelope. You'll gain a good list of prospects.

- **SEND A LETTER TO THE EDITOR.** When an issue or news event relates to your business, write about it for your local newspaper's opinion page. Most will mention your occupation and location, providing high-quality free publicity.

- **VOLUNTEER.** When people get to know you through charitable or civic efforts, they're more likely to buy from you. Judy C., an architect from Altoona, Pennsylvania, acquired several new customers while volunteering her help for historical exhibits and celebrations.

- **JOIN A LEADS CLUB.** These groups (more than 300 in the U.S. and Australia) promote member-to-member referrals for all types of businesses. Dues are $75 to join and $25 monthly. Call 800-783-3761 or write: Leads Club, P.O. Box 279, Carlsbad, CA 92018. You can also go online (leadsclub.com).

TRADE YOUR TRASH

Bartering won't put cash in your pocket, but it's a great way to banish clutter in return for something useful. A number of small online barter communities just for moms are springing up that offer good deals for little or no fee. Generally, items such as clothes, videos, crafts and home business products are posted in categories on the site, then members work out the trade details in private e-mails. Check out:

- Mommy Community (mommycommunity.com)
- MamaBarter (wearsthebaby.com/mamabarter.html)

Ⓓ *It's Easier Than Ever to Make Money at Home*

Opportunities are booming, and women are getting on board. If you've ever considered working at home, now may be the perfect time

Let's get one thing straight: Women have always been home-based businesspeople. The company they run is the family. In the past, some women also made a little cash from at-home efforts, but most who earned a living worked somewhere else—a classroom, an office or a factory floor.

Since the new millennium, however, home is suddenly where more and more women—and men—want to work. Nearly 27 million self-employed people run full- or part-time businesses from home, and that number increases annually, according to IDC/Link, a research organization. These days, about half of the entrepreneurs contacting the National Association of Home Based Businesses are women.

And just as work trends are changing, so are the types of enterprises women are starting. From filling out Medicare forms for seniors to cooking meals for harried families to marketing crafts on the Internet, the latest crop of businesses spawned at the dining room table or in that spare bedroom capitalize on hot new trends.

Ann N.'s new business, for example, is decidedly 21st century. After ten years as a 911 dispatcher, Ann, 30, began working from her home in Carmel Valley, California, designing informational and educational advertising sites on the internet. In previous decades, a woman with her background might have opened a telephone-answering service. Now, she earns $35 to $50 an hour doing something she loves.

Without a doubt, women are still making money in traditional ventures such as child care or sewing. But many more are turning the skills they developed in the workplace, through hobbies or education into successful businesses that meet new market needs and generate more income.

Women are very good at starting their own businesses because they're good at multitasking. When you're a home-based business owner, you're wearing a lot of hats. More than ever before, women are finding there is a way to merge home and work. You're not just making a living, you're designing your life.

Here, we've focused on the five hottest fields for home-based work. These areas will provide ever-increasing opportunities for women entrepreneurs.

From catering to career counseling, home health care to day care, there's a boom in service enterprises, businesses that save time and perform tasks that consumers used to do are growing rapidly.

There's good money to be made in helping people handle life's complications. Professional organizers, for instance, tackle clients' space and time problems. "People are inundated and overwhelmed with paper," says Julie M. For $65 to $150 per hour, she organizes closets, kitchens, offices and provides "efficiency coaching." "People in even the most remote areas turn to professional organizers for guidance," Julie says. "You can make a living anywhere."

Joan P. of Sebastopol, California, 53, sets up personal fitness programs for lapsed or non-exercisers of all shapes and sizes. She gets her clients moving with walks in the countryside and workouts in her home exercise room. "I work with them at getting over being afraid to try," says the aerobics instructor. Some clients need just one session; others work with Joan for several weeks or on an ongoing basis.

Addressing career needs is also a profitable growth area today. Beverly R., 30, from Tampa, aims her word-processing service at college students and job-seekers, instead of business clients. She types academic papers for $2.75 per double-spaced page. Her resumé service costs $50 and includes a one-hour consultation, ten originals and a free update. Her clients' schedules are flexible, so Beverly can work around the needs of her two young children.

By the year 2000, nearly 35 million Americans were 65 or over. More and more home-based businesses serve this expanding population.

"Our mailing list grows constantly," says 75-year-old Kay M., who runs motorcoach trips for older adults in Chappaqua, New York. Her Pied Piper Tours offers day trips ranging from $40 to $120 for museum excursions, dinner-and-theater packages and scenic rambles.

Helping seniors through piles of paperwork, Stacy D., 33, processes medical claims, a skill she learned while working for a physician. From her farmhouse in Paris, Missouri, Stacy also investigates and resubmits claims that have been denied. Often, she must sort through shoeboxes filled with her clients' medical bills. "Some of them are undergoing cancer treatment or dialysis," she says. "Especially when they feel so bad, this relieves some of the burdens they have."

Joan N. helps older adults with move planning, packing, unpacking and resettling in retirement communities or nursing homes. "It's not easy leaving a home after you've lived there 40 years," says Joan. Originally a home-based operation that handled two moves a month, the Centreville, Delaware, company now has three consignment shops and coordinates at least 40 moves every month.

As corporations cut staff, many "outsource," which means they hire independent providers to accomplish tasks once performed by employees. A large number of these providers are home-based businesspeople. Companies are looking to outsource office services, accounting, bookkeeping, even maintenance. Once a corporate meeting planner, Peggy H. was "downsized" and now runs PH & Associates meeting planners from her house in Amelia Island, Florida. "Working at home made sense because 99 percent of what I do is on the telephone," says Peggy. What she charges depends on the type of meeting and number of attendees. For corporations and associations, she arranges meetings worldwide, overseeing travel, accommodations and conference logistics, food, even recreation.

Elizabeth M. creates corporate logos and brochures. Her first customers came from a mailing she sent to newly registered businesses. "I got swamped with work," she says. Clients pay $50 an hour.

Milady L. began Business Overload Services while still holding a full-time office job. Milady charges $20 an hour for word processing and $25 hourly for desktop publishing, including producing brochures and overhead presentations. New technology allows entrepreneurs to work anywhere, for clients anywhere. Technology is the key tool that allows home-business owners to compete with businesses many times their size.

A computer program now "reads" court reporters' stenographic notes. Then, professionals, called scopists, translate, proofread and edit the notes. Katie L. of Clearwater, Florida, charges 85¢ a page and can scope about 200 pages a day. When Katie, 34, joined a computer online service, she connected with a group of court reporters. "It was an ideal place for me to market," she says of the clients she found.

Leslie K., who lives in Oxford, Connecticut, taught herself computer programming and then launched her custom software design company. Leslie charges $45 an hour to set up databases for several small businesses.

Selling popular products ranks high in home-based enterprises. Irene F. creates rubber stamps at home in Thousand Oaks, California, and sells to hobbyists at shows through a rubber-stamping magazine, and wholesales to shops. Although stamps retail for only $1.75 to $11.50 each, the demand is huge, so her business is thriving.

Photographer Deirdre F., 32, sells prints of her photographs of cats, America's favorite pet. Priced from $20 to $150, some are framed and hand-colored. Deirdre sells at juried art fairs, in home-furnishings shops and through mail order from her house in Hastings-on-Hudson, New York.

Mail order hasn't worked as well for soap-maker Debbie B. "The best way to sell my product is to let customers touch it, see it and smell it," she says. She sells her soaps and bath-soak sachets to stores, for $2 wholesale.

NOT JUST PIN MONEY ANYMORE

With more than 1 million start-ups each year, home-based businesses are no longer dismissed as low-paying, temporary alternatives to traditional work. The biggest trend is that home business has become legitimate.

Indeed, many at-home entrepreneurs are wrestling with the next stages of development: expansion, hiring employees, even possibly relocating to an office or store. Various Chambers of Commerce, once geared to traditional businesses, now present seminars to home-based workers. State cooperative extension services also provide guidance and networking opportunities.

As the phenomenon grows, new types of companies will join older, more established ones.

TRADITIONAL BUSINESS	WHAT'S HOT NOW
Housecleaning	Commercial cleaning of offices, stores and restaurants
Cookie and cake baking	Special-recipe salad dressings, salsas and barbecue sauces
Typing	Desktop publishing; medical billing or transcription
Errand services	Organizing; assisting the elderly
Childcare	Children's van services; arts and music programs
Toys sold by party or catalog	Books, CD-ROMs, other educational items, such as supplements to school or aimed at home-schooling families

COOKS FOR HIRE

HOT INDUSTRY: Personal Services
BUSINESS: in-home chefs
ENTREPRENEURS: Terry A. and Stephanie K.
LOCATION: Jacksonville, Florida

If you love to cook and want to profit from it, but your town won't allow cooking for resale from your home kitchen, consider starting a personal chef service. That's what Terry and Stephanie did after viewing a TV program on how to run such a business.

Most customers are working parents, so Terry and Stephanie go into clients' homes and cook eight entrées and four side dishes (enough for 10 or 12 meals), then package the food for refrigeration or freezing, clean up and leave reheating instructions. Cost: $285 for two people (which includes shopping for groceries), plus $25 for each additional person.

Helping Hands

Hot Industry: Services for Older Adults
Business: house chores and living assistance
Entrepreneur: Gayle Y.
Location: Kansas City, Missouri

"Find a need and fill it" is a time-honored rule for business success. Gayle could see a need all around her as relatives and neighbors aged, lost some physical abilities, but still wanted to live in their homes. Yet many could no longer tend a garden or replace a lightbulb. After becoming bonded and insured, Gayle left her career as a special education teacher. "I focus on making my customers more independent, more comfortable and more safe in their homes." Her clients are mostly women, in their mid-60s to mid-80s. For an average of $30 an hour, Gayle uses the skills she learned from her dad to caulk windows, change furnace filters and program VCRs. "Where else could you get a gardener and someone to order an adaptive toilet seat?"

Lasting Memories

Hot Industry: New Product Trends
Business: scrapbook supplies
Entrepreneur: Paula S.
Location: Canton, Connecticut

Preserving family memories in photo albums, journals and scrapbooks is both a popular current trend and a traditional pastime. Paula, who has made personalized albums since childhood, sells the products used in creating lasting memory scrapbooks—from acid-free papers to binders, markers and 30 different edging scissors. She buys supplies in bulk from wholesalers and sells them retail to those attending classes she holds in her home or at women's groups. The classes are free, with a $2.50 fee for supplies.

Through advice on computer online forums for craftspeople, Paula created a 22-page mail-order catalog for her company, Photographs and Memories. Mail orders now comprise about 50 percent of her sales.

Pitfalls To Avoid

- **Failure to research.** A great business idea is only the beginning of a successful venture. Do your homework. Who will buy your service or product? How will you reach them?

- **Ignoring zoning and other laws. Rules vary.** A few communities ban all home-based business. Others allow it, but not if clients visit. Check licensing and tax laws as well as insurance needs.

- **Buying general advertising.** The local newspaper may be a costly, ineffective way to promote your business. Word-of-mouth recommendations are best. Join groups such as the Chamber of Commerce and organizations aimed at your customers' interests.

- **Not hiring child care.** Mothers running home-based businesses find it hard to accomplish much when the kids are underfoot. With no child-care arrangements, count on working only when the children are asleep or in school.

- **Not designating a work space.** Many women fail to create boundaries for their home enterprise. If you don't have a separate office (with a door that closes!), use a screen or room divider.

Day Care: The Business For You?

Child care is in demand from consumers and an attractive business choice. But you'll need more than a high tolerance for runny noses to be a success.

- Not everyone is suited for the business. You have to love other people's children and not be a perfectionist about your house.

- If you are going into child care to spend more time with your own kids, think again.

- Find out state and local registration and licensing.

- Decide beforehand what ages you'll accept and how many hours you want to stay open a week.

E The $3,000 Challenge: Discover How to Make Extra Money

Is there anyone who couldn't use an extra $3,000 to ease the squeeze of the family budget? Probably not. But you may wonder if it's possible to generate that kind of money without getting a job. Surprisingly, the answer is yes! Discover how the following women found a way to use their talents, skills and a little elbow grease to bring in an extra $3,000 to $5,000 a year. With a little effort, you can do it, too.

CASH IN ON EBAY

Melissa M., 36, went to a three-day eBay conference near her home in Wesley Chapel, Florida, out of curiosity. On the third day, when she won a camera in a drawing, she took it as a sign.

She opened an eBay account to sell things she and her husband wanted to get rid of—books, records, costume jewelry, picture frames—before they moved. The items started selling almost immediately. "I got $9 for an Olympics pin that came out of a cereal box," she says. She also sold a clock for $57, as well as some audiotapes for $170. "I even sold motivational tapes I'd listened to only once," she says.

In Melissa's first year, she netted almost $4,000 after deducting expenses such as listing, selling and PayPal fees. Setting up an account is a cinch if you go to ebay.com and follow the easy directions. Melissa's only initial challenge was estimating postage correctly. "I'd estimate $4 and it would end up being $7," she says. "So at first I lost a little money." After that she wised up and bought a postal scale for $35 at an office supply store.

TEACH OUTSIDE OF CLASS

Two years ago, when Kelly M.'s daughter was 6 months old, the Phoenix mom quit teaching elementary school to stay home. To compensate for her loss of income, she started tutoring. She printed business cards on her computer and posted them at the YMCA and passed them out to former colleagues. Today her business is carried by word of mouth.

Kelly takes on nine students at a time and schedules them for one-hour appointments all on the same three days of the week. She helps students in any subject covered in kindergarten through sixth grade. She also supplies notebooks, folders and pencils, keeping costs low by buying during back-to-school sales. By tutoring at the local library, she can also borrow books.

Kelly meets students at the library to save time and gas. She asks her students' teachers to send an extra copy of any classroom text. Averaging about $150 a week (at $25 a hour), she gets to use her skills and bring in some extra dough.

Cash from Crafts

Little did 33-year-old Jill S. of Las Vegas know when she started scrapbooking her wedding four years ago that it would lead to a small business.

The inspiration came when she attended a scrapbooking convention and saw someone making notecards out of scrapbook supplies. "I bought supplies and immediately made Easter cards, which I sold at a crafts fair," she says. She continued marketing her notecards the old-fashioned way—by giving them to friends and family. Soon orders started coming in from recipients who also wanted to give them as gifts.

She works at night and on weekends since she has a day job.

Jill's biggest challenge was knowing what to charge. She researched prices of specialty cards at stationery shops. Her fee of $16 for eight hand-decorated cards is right in sync with the market. She's also gotten more efficient at using supplies, so there's no waste.

The Retail Deal

For the past 11 years Sheila C., 40, has brought in an extra $5,000 a year working eight to ten hours a week as a salesclerk at JCPenney. If that sounds too much like a job, she's quick to say it isn't. "I like being around people," says this Rochester, New York, mother of three. "It's fun for me." Unlike other jobs, when she leaves the store, she doesn't take work home with her. Penney's is particularly flexible with its part-timers, many of whom are women just like Sheila who want to make a little extra cash. Her weekly schedule involves one evening shift and one weekend shift. And if something comes up, she rarely has trouble switching with a coworker.

Just as important as the extra money she earns is the employee discount she gets on everything in the store. "We do all of our shopping here," she says. "Between my discount, sales and coupons, I can buy clothes for my boys, buy gifts at the holidays and get household items for a great price." She figures that what she saves on purchases would make her part-time pay the equivalent of full-time pay.

Don't be intimidated if you've never worked in retail; most major stores train their employees. The biggest issues for Sheila? The seduction of all that merchandise and making sure her work schedule coincides with her husband being at home.

It Pays to Shop

Imagine getting paid to go to a drugstore and ask an employee a question. You can get $10 for that 10-minute visit. That's how Lisa A., 36, a mom of two from Baltimore, made $3,000 working as a mystery shopper.

"I go apartment hunting, to drugstores, restaurants and specialty shops, and then I write up a report," she says. One of her most fun "shops" was going to see the movie *Win a Date with Tad Hamilton!* to record the audience reaction to the previews.

Lisa got into mystery shopping through a junk e-mail that caught her attention. After a little online legwork to find reputable companies, she was off and shopping. She puts in between 5 and 20 hours a week by regularly checking online for jobs in her area. She even checks for mystery shopping jobs at vacation destinations.

Just because you love to shop doesn't mean this is the job for you. "You have to be a pro at noticing details," Lisa says.

She records her experience on her phone's voice recorder and camera and keeps a notebook handy. She's also learned to "cluster" jobs. "I pay for my gas, so I take several jobs in an area in one day," she says.

Get More Cash

- **Fill out applications.** Did you once work at a job that involved processing applications? Consider offering your services on a freelance basis. Pay rate: up to $250 per application.

- **Focus groups.** Got opinions? Get paid for them. Contact consumer research firms in your area and check out volition.com for online groups. Don't join groups that charge you to sign up. Pay rate: $50–$150 for two hours of work.
- **Seasonal retail work.** Every retailer needs additional help during the holiday season. Pay rate: An hourly wage plus a discount.
- **Cooking for others.** Got a great recipe? See if a local restaurant wants to buy your goods. Pay rate: About $30 per cheesecake.
- **Elderly companion care.** Provide companionship, light housekeeping or run errands for the elderly. Pay rate: $10 to $20 an hour.

F *Show Me the Money! Four Ways to Make Extra Cash*

Substitute teach

Fill in for teachers and get paid by the day. Qualifications vary by state—some specify a college degree but not necessarily in education. (Visit sti.usu.edu for a state-by-state breakdown.) You usually receive a lesson plan and teaching materials, particularly in the younger grades. In addition, middle school and high school students are often left assignments to do on their own while you supervise, so you probably won't be put on the spot and asked to teach algebra!

Pros One of the best things about subbing is that it's very flexible. You can say yes when you want and no when you have something else planned. If you have children in the same district, you'll be on their schedule, so you don't have to worry about time conflicts. It's also very rewarding to know you've helped a child learn something.

Cons Since you're often called at the last minute, you generally don't know what your schedule will be from one day to the next. Also, the income is not always dependable because you don't have set days to work.

Get started Stop in the main office of the school where you want to sub and they'll be able to direct you. You usually apply through your town's

Board of Education or local education district. Most districts will require a background check and fingerprinting, which may cost you upwards of $25.

IT'S A GOOD JOB IF... you enjoy interacting with children. Subbing is also a great fit if you don't want to be tied down and like switching things up. You'll need a lot of patience and an assertive personality to keep order in a classroom.

SECRETS FOR SUCCESS

- For steadier work, apply to several districts in your area. It also helps to get friendly with school secretaries to find out if there are planned absences you can book ahead.

- Because of the last-minute nature of the job, you'll be less stressed if you always have an outfit ready and a dinner in the freezer.

- Always have a "bag of tricks" in case you have extra time to fill, such as a few good storybooks and word puzzles.

SELL STUFF FROM HOME

Consider direct sales for a company like Tupperware, Tastefully Simple, The Pampered Chef, FoundValue or Creative Memories. You sell products through home shows, catalogs or by appointment for a cut of 20 to 50 percent of the retail price.

PROS You're in charge of when you work and how many hours you clock. You work for yourself but not by yourself. You often have a wealth of educational and motivational resources available in the form of materials, products and meetings. Many companies also offer added perks such as contests and incentives such as money, merchandise or trips.

CONS The income can be erratic. The biggest challenge is keeping yourself motivated when things are slow.

GET STARTED Browse company websites, compare the policies of different home businesses and talk to people who have done this kind of work. You have to love the product to be able to sell it well. Think about how you envision your business. Do you want to build a customer base that comes to you regularly, or do you see yourself pumping out parties? Once you've made your choice, a company representative will tell you just how to begin. Usually there are startup costs ranging from $75 to $200 to buy an initial set of goods for demonstration or inventory. Ask if the company offers a buy-back or risk-free program so some of your investment can be returned if you decide this isn't the right career for you.

IT'S A GOOD JOB IF... you're a natural self-starter, an outgoing type and are able to read different kinds of people well.

SECRETS FOR SUCCESS

- In order to make the big bucks, you'll probably need to recruit others to be consultants. They'll work as part of your team and you'll get commission on what they sell on top of your own sales.

- Take advantage of all the training offered by the company to help get your business off the ground.

- To prevent procrastination, schedule specific times for work rather than just trying to fit it in.

WORK IN RETAIL

Get a job in a store as a sales associate or stock person. You'll be responsible for showing and selling merchandise and keeping displays attractive.

PROS You usually get a significant discount (20 to 25 percent), the hours are flexible, and you're the first to see new trends and styles. If you're craving some adult conversation, retail gets you into a lively environment.

CONS It's physically demanding, since you're on your feet most of the time. Also, retailers' busy times are often when you and your family are busiest: nights, weekends and holidays. If you have young children, you'll need a backup babysitting plan (the mall doesn't close just because school does).

GET STARTED Choose a retailer whose products you like. Bookworms could try Borders; lingerie lovers might opt for Victoria's Secret. A department store gives you the most options for maximizing your discount. Once you've settled on a store, fill out an application in person or online, then go for an interview if you're called. Once you're hired, the store should provide paid training on everything from running the register to security.

You may need a wardrobe update because many retailers require you to look professional and, if you sell clothing, you may have to wear their garments as extra advertising.

IT'S A GOOD JOB IF... you like shopping, dealing with people and can handle an environment that is sometimes extremely fast-paced. You need to be able to keep smiling despite tough customers, one-day sales and busy holiday seasons.

SECRETS FOR SUCCESS

- To boost your earning potential, go for a commissioned store or department such as fine jewelry, cosmetics or furniture.

- Have fruit or granola bars on hand. Keeping fueled with snacks and water is important because you don't always know when you'll get your next break.

- Treat your feet right and invest in a pair of very comfortable shoes.

GROW YOUR OWN BUSINESS

Start a business based on a talent or skill that fills a niche. How about organizing, custom cake baking or dog walking? Think about what you do best.

PROS You're your own boss, you're doing something you love and it can be a chance to fulfill a dream. You can charge by the hour, job or whatever makes sense, and the schedule is flexible. You push yourself to learn more about something you enjoy. Any investment you make comes back to you, not to someone else's company.

CONS You may miss the camaraderie of working with other people. It'll also probably take some time before you start making real income.

GET STARTED The amount of money it takes to get your idea off the ground varies, depending on the resources you need for the startup. Decide what you're going to sell or do and how much you'll charge. Then start spreading the word among friends and family. Look for low-cost ways to promote your new business, such as advertising in free papers or handing out flyers at community events.

WANT A LESS RISKY ENTRÉE? Get a job in the field you want to start your business in. Beth began working at a nursery on the weekends, where she learned about plants and handling customers before striking out on her own.

IT'S A GOOD JOB IF... you've discovered a unique product or service that you're passionate about. You also need to be resourceful and creative.

SECRETS FOR SUCCESS

- Donate your time or goods to a local raffle. This gets someone to try what you're offering and helps spread the word.

- Customer service is key. Returning calls and following up keeps patrons coming back.

- Hone your resiliency by acknowledging up front that you won't be able to please everyone. You'll feel less pressure and be more willing to take risks.

TAXING MATTERS

For a subbing or retail job, you'll receive a W-2 statement showing your earnings. If your work is steady, you can roughly calculate your income and add it to your current household income. Find out if it changes your tax bracket, which means you'll be taxed at a higher rate, by consulting an accountant or visiting irs.org.

You'll need to keep track of your earnings and expenses if you have a self-owned or home business. Expenses such as supplies, mileage and phone bills may be deductible, so save all bills and receipts. Try labeling file folders with each of your expenses (such as gas) to store receipts so they'll be easier to find when you need them. If you're working for a home-business company, they may send you a 1099 form, which shows miscellaneous income such as incentives or commissions. You'll need all of this information at tax time.

How to Turn Trash Into Cash

From old cell phones to broken bicycles, there's a market for almost everything. Take a fresh look at your clutter. Who knows—you might be sitting on some serious cash.

CRAMMED CLOSETS

Are your closets packed with stuff too good to toss? Once Valerie T., a writer in Cincinnati, started checking behind closed doors, she unearthed a cornucopia of clutter in good shape. "Our guest room and hallway closets were hiding items that were useless to me but not ready for the dump," says Valerie. She listed rugs, dishes, linens and more on donations site freecycle. org, and gave a computer and printer to a nonprofit organization. "I saved $200 on my taxes through the charity donation. I also saved the cost of placing ads and shipping, not to mention time answering e-mails and phone calls, to sell all of this stuff."

SOLUTION: Check out freecycle.org, a free online listing service that lets you give items to people in your community. Or try selling items at livedeal.com, which charges a variable fee scale, or ioffer.com, a trading community based on negotiation, which also charges sliding fees.

HEAVY METAL MONSTROSITIES

What about that rusty rubbish clogging the garage and backyard shed—from bicycles to broken lawn furniture? "People come in with truckloads of scrap metal that has accumulated over the years, and sometimes neighbors even pool resources," says Kathy Rongey, president of Louisiana Scrap Metal and Recycling in Port Allen, Louisiana. Even if you're only selling old aluminum pots and pans at 45¢ a pound, you save the fee at the dump.

SOLUTION: Look under "salvage" in the yellow pages and sell your junk by the pound. Prices, regulated by the American Metal Market, fluctuate.

CALL ON YOUR INNER ENTREPRENEUR

Mindy S., a stay-at-home mom in Concord, New Hampshire, is an expert at finding end-of-season bargains on children's shoes, sweaters and sundresses and selling them online when they're back in season the next year. "Lots of busy moms who don't want to drag their kids to the mall use me as a personal shopper," says Mindy, who has earned nearly $2,000 in less than a year. "My husband is in awe of my newfound entrepreneurial skills!"

SOLUTION: Scour end-of-season clearance racks and resell items for a profit online. Go to livedeal.com, ebay.com or ioffer.com, all of which have sliding fees.

ITEMS YOUR HOME HAS OUTGROWN

There's nothing too big, outdated or even broken that isn't valuable to someone else. Kate P., a pharmacy technician in Portland, Oregon, sold more than $1,000 worth of clutter on craigslist.org in 2004 alone. "I sold a gas washer and broken dryer for $75 to someone who picked them up in a truck. It would have cost me that much to have a garbage hauler take them away," says Kate. She also sold several bedroom sets her kids had outgrown, baby paraphernalia, her teens' gently used clothes and old video games.

SOLUTION: Place an ad for free at craigslist.org, a community-based site.

WEDDING ITEMS

Your wedding dress may have sentimental value, but even that depreciates with time. "I decided to pass along my gown to someone who will love it as much as I did, and wear it on her happy day," explains Hannah M., a financial services representative in Pittsburgh, who bought a used couture gown for her 2003 wedding and recently sold it on IndieBride.com for the same $300 she paid for it. "I'm using the proceeds to buy a special piece of jewelry—a wedding memento that doesn't take up so much closet space!"

SOLUTION: For tips on auctioning wedding items online, from decorations to ivory accessories, check out *Buying & Selling Your Way to a Fabulous Wedding with eBay*, by Leah Ingram. For bridal gowns, try IndieBride.com; there's no listing fee or commission.

OLD BOOKS

It's easy to turn bookshelves into a steady stream of cash. "Every few months I weed out the books I'm done with, as well as those my kids have outgrown," says Marcia Layton Turner, a journalist in Fairport, New York, who has earned $500 over the past three years through half.com. "It takes less than a minute to price and list a book. Then, every month that I make even one sale, I get a check—it can add up to a nice little surprise!"

SOLUTION: Sell books online at half.com, which charges no listing fee, but takes a commission off the selling price at the time of sale, or Amazon.com, which has many fee options you can choose from, including a 99¢ listing fee, plus a 15 percent commission.

LAST YEAR'S CELL PHONE

It may be worth anywhere from $5 to more than $100, depending on the make and model. Reselling old cell phones is good for the environment as well as your pocketbook. Recent studies by the University of Florida found that dangerous levels of lead and toxins could leach from the millions of old cell phones dumped into landfills.

SOLUTION: You can sell your cell phone at cellforcash.com, oldcellphone.com or trademyphone.com.

MISFIT CHINA AND SILVER

That old china or silver your great-aunt left you may be worth more than you think, even if it's not a complete set. Resellers will give you a phone or e-mail quote based on supply and demand for your pattern, and send you a check after you ship the goods and they pass inspection.

SOLUTION: Replacements Ltd., located in Greensboro, North Carolina, stocks more than 200,000 patterns of obsolete china, silver, crystal and collectibles. Call 800-REPLACE for a price quote, or visit replacements.com. Or go to eBay or snappyauctions.com.

PACK-RAT COLLECTIONS

Those collectibles, crammed in boxes under your bed, may be worth big bucks to someone else. Last year Sherry G., a stay-at-home mom in Hendersonville, Tennessee, cashed in on the Danbury Mint porcelain sports figurines she'd been collecting for a decade. "I thought I'd decorate my son's room in a baseball motif, and before I knew it he was into bugs," recalls

Sherry, who sold about 50 pieces through Snappy Auctions and made $2,716. "I bought a top-notch vacuum cleaner, paid for my son's school tuition and even had some fun money left over."

SOLUTION: Snappy Auctions, a nationwide chain of consignment stores, provides an easy way to use eBay. It handles the pricing, posting and shipping for a 15 to 35 percent commission. Also check out TIAS, an online collectors' newsletter (tias.com and click on the newsletter tab).

BECOME A JUNK CONNOISSEUR

When it comes to yard sales, the more stuff the better. Don Gabor and his wife, Eileen Cowell, have turned their spring and fall "stoop sale" into a way to meet their Brooklyn neighbors as well as subsidize their vacation expenses. "We started out really small 16 years ago, and now neighbors constantly ask when we're having a sale, and if they can add their junk and split the profits," says Gabor, author of *How to Start a Conversation and Make Friends*, who estimates his stoop sale profits at $300 annually.

SOLUTION: Have a neighborhood yard sale and charge a participation fee. Check out yardsalequeen.com or *Yard Sale!*, by Mitra Modarressi.

GET CRAFTY

With a little imagination, old buttons, fabrics and other clutter start taking on a whole new look, and are a new source of income. Kathy Peterson of Tequesta, Florida, has made a career out of creating beautiful recycled crafts. "I've always collected junk—glass, fabric, furniture, whatever catches my eye," says Peterson, host of the Town & Country Crafts with Kathy Peterson TV series. "One Christmas, I turned a few tattered beaded gowns into some lovely vintage-style angels and sold them at an upscale boutique. I invested about $3 a doll and they sold for more than $100 each—it blew me away!"

SOLUTION: Sell recycled crafts on consignment at local boutiques. Check out junkmarketonline.com or Clever Crafting with Flea Market Finds, edited by Leisure Arts.

ⓗ *Garage Sale: Get the Most Bucks for Your Castoffs*

Simplifying your life is more than liberating—it can also be profitable. How would you like to make a quick $1,000? That's how much the average family should be able to rake in at a yard sale. The trick is knowing all the tricks.

- **PURGE YOUR HOUSE.** As you scrutinize every cupboard and closet, ask yourself, "Do we really need this? When was the last time I used it?" If the answer is more than a year ago, sell it. Resist being overly sentimental. Think of that never-been-used wedding present as $10 that's just taking up space. Hot items: tools, exercise equipment, toys, baby gear, furniture, costume jewelry, '60s and '70s arcana (lavalamps, old posters) and collectibles like comic books, Christmas ornaments and '50s table linens. Do your homework on collectibles; make sure you know their value.

- **PLANNING THE SALE.** Call your city/town hall to see if you need a permit. Set the sale for Friday and either Saturday or Sunday (from around 9 a.m. to about 4 p.m.) so you'll get weekday and weekend traffic.

- **SCHEDULE IT SMART.** Saturday mornings are best, but avoid holiday weekends or Saturdays when major events might compete for shoppers' time.

- **ADVERTISE BIG.** Create an eye-catching ad announcing a multifamily sale. Highlight valuable or popular items and include directions. Place ads in your daily, community or neighborhood newspapers. Mention what you'll be selling (especially any large items), your address, and the date and time. On the evening before the sale, place signs at the corner of your block and at busy intersections near your home.

- **GO FOR THE CROWDS.** For anywhere from $10 to $50, you can secure a booth at a local outdoor flea market, placing you in the path of far more traffic than might pass by your garage or front yard.

- **MAKE IT FESTIVE.** Most tag sales flop because they fail to make visitors feel welcome. Let your kids earn, too, by selling lemonade or sodas. Or offer "free" coffee in 50¢ mugs you'd like to get rid of. Play background music and make sidewalk chalk available to shoppers' kids. The longer people stay, the more likely it is they'll buy something.

- **THINK LIKE A SHOPKEEPER.** Better to dress up your junk. Dust furniture, wash china, press and hang linens. Cover borrowed card tables, or planks propped by bricks, with tablecloths or pretty sheets to display wares at their best.

- **ORGANIZE YOUR GOODS.** Sales go up more than 50 percent if you make things easier for shoppers. Some people are too embarrassed to come up to you and ask a price or find a size they're looking for. Arrange like objects together and keep tabletops orderly. Make sure prices are visible. Use peel-off stickers; masking tape leaves a stain and writing directly on an object can lessen its value.

- **PRICE IT RIGHT.** Go enticingly low—25 to 40 percent of retail value is a good rule of thumb, depending on condition—but leave yourself a little room to dicker. (Everyone will want to.) Allow room to negotiate with bargain hunters by pricing items 10 to 15 percent above the lowest amount you'll take. If you're holding a multi-day sale, be firm on prices the first day but willing to slash later.

- **BUNDLE FOR BULK SALES.** A buyer may buy just one book for 50¢, but if they're three for a dollar, he'll take three because he likes the idea of a bargain. You net an extra half-dollar. Try this tactic for old magazines, records, CDs, baseball cards, silverware, even nails.

- **LURE 'EM IN.** Place items marked very low at the entrance of the sale outside the garage to warm up browsers. It's also smart to make intriguing items (old globes, furniture) visible from the street. String flags or balloons across your front yard to attract attention during the sale.

- **PLAN AHEAD.** Moneymaking sales-holders pack up what doesn't sell to try again next time. Throughout the year, earmark old stuff for an annual sale. Ask friends and family for items they don't want. The storage does take up a little space, but you'll wind up with more inventory, a larger selection—and more potential cash—than you ever imagined possible.

- **DISPLAYING YOUR WARES.** Rent or borrow tables, shelves and clothing racks so merchandise is easy to see. Group like items, such as shoes or toys, on blankets on the ground. Electrical items should be near a plug or extension cord. Clean, dust and polish everything so it's in the best possible shape.

- **DON'T BE SHY.** Junking is a social business. Greet visitors. If someone asks about an item or inspects it, engage him or her in a conversation about the object's history or merits. They'll be more apt to buy and you'll have a more enjoyable day.

- **PUMP UP THE GOODS.** A tag that describes an old table as solid oak, distinguishing it from veneer, makes it more enticing. If a knickknack is 20 years old, say so. On electrical equipment, say "It works" and describe features ("5-speed blender, comes with attachments"), or explain problems ("Needs minor repairs"). But always be honest.

- **BEWARE THE EARLY BIRDS.** Hardy hunters will begin to call on you an hour or two before your listed opening time. These are usually flea-market dealers or antique collectors looking to snare bargains. They buy a lot, but don't let them sweet-talk you into giving up something for nothing; if they really covet an item, they'll pay your asking fee or return later. Or ask for their number and offer to call them back if the item remains unsold at the end of the day.

- **DON'T OVERLOOK ANYTHING FOR POSSIBLE SALE.** Dismiss complaints from people who say they couldn't sell their clothes at their yard sales. Buy cheap clothing racks (separate ones for men, women and children) and clearly label the sizes and prices. Even objects that seem too silly to bother selling (chipped pottery, plastic tubs, kindling) will move if the price is right.

Editor's Note

Over the years, *Woman's Day* magazine has published a vast and impressive array of articles on the subject of women's finance. With all this material at hand, it seemed only natural to collect the best and most relevant pieces to create a well-rounded, comprehensive and invaluable book for the perfect one-stop resource on how to create financial health.

It's not surprising that over so many years of publication some of the subject matter overlaps from article to article. We feel that this only enhances the book, for who can hear "Stop enriching those credit card companies and enrich your savings account instead!" too many times? Each one of us can profit from a certain amount of, shall we say...emphasis (we don't like the word "nagging").

If the sheer quantity of information seems overwhelming, or even at times slightly contradictory, we believe that's okay, too. Each person has her different style, and no two women will go about cleaning up their financial house in quite the same way. Whatever works best for you will work best for your long-term strategy. We encourage you to keep reading until you find the techniques and pointers that are right for you to achieve the goals you set for yourself and best empower you to take control of your financial life—once and for all. No one else can do it for you, but we can certainly help!

Please note that despite our best efforts to provide the most timely information, some numbers (interest rates, prices, website addresses, etc.) may have changed from the time this book went to press.

Resources

While there are hundreds of websites for each of the categories listed below, following are the sites mentioned in the book for your easy reference.

Investing and Finances

FOR INFORMATION ON INVESTING AND WHERE TO BUY MUTUAL FUNDS

debtproofliving.com (Mary Hunt's website with information on many aspects of personal finance)

fool.com (Motley Fool; offers $10 online courses with downloadable workbooks)

mfea.com (Mutual Fund Investment Center)

morningstar.com (includes a retirement center and investing classroom)

mutuals.com (lists practically every mutual fund there is)

quicken.com (information on investing, banking, retirement, taxes and insurance) short-term savings, disaster-proofing your finances, investing, etc.)

HIGHLY RATED AND POPULAR MUTUAL FUNDS

domini.com (socially responsible funds)

fidelity.com

paxworld.com (ethical investing, socially responsible funds)

troweprice.com

vanguard.com

WOMEN'S FINANCES

finishrich.com (to find free Smart Women Finish Rich seminars in over 1,500 cities around the U.S. The site also has a section about kids and money)

wife.org (Women's Institute for Financial Education)

FINANCIAL PLANNING

fpanet.org/plannersearch

ONLINE BROKERAGE ACCOUNTS

buyandhold.com

sharebuilder.com

GOVERNMENT SAVINGS BONDS

bondhelp.com

easysaver.gov

publicdebt.treas.gov

CREDIT UNIONS/FREE BANKING SERVICES

bankrate.com (compare mortgage rates, home equity loans, CDS, credit cards, money market accounts)

cardtrak.com

creditunion.coop (Credit Union)

tnbonline.com (North Town Bank)

ing.com

hsbc.com

cardweb.com

Credit Bureaus (get your credit rating)
transunion.com
equifax.com
experian.com

Calculate credit card costs
cheapskatemonthly.com

Small business loans/ microloans
count-me-in.org (for not-for-profit provider of small business loans for women's economic Independence)
fieldus.org (Aspen Institute Microenterprise)
sba.gov (U.S. Small Business Administration)

Real estate valuations
zillow.com

Personal finance blogs
mdmproofing.com/iym/weblog
sharonhr.blogspot.com
womansday.com

Kids and money

Children and advertising
Many national organizations are supporting bills in Congress to limit advertising to children. Log on to commercialalert.org *or* commercialexploitation.org *to learn more*

Financial education for kids
www.jumpstart.org

Earn rebates toward college
upromise.com

Scholarships
fastweb.com

Shopping

Groceries/coupons/discount shopping
amazon.com/grocery
boodle.com
ciaro.com
clippermagazine.com
coolsavings.com
grocerygame.com
hotcoupons.com
jumpondeals.com
moneymailer.com
mothersnature.com/frugal/coupons
mygrocerydeals.com
smartdecorating.com
supercoups.com
thecouponclippers.com
thecouponmom.com
valpak.com
welcomwagon.com

Comparison shopping
mysimon.com
salescircular.com
shopper.cnet.com

Outlet stores
outletbound.com

Refurbished or almost new electronics
tigerdirect.com

New or used car pricing

caranddriver.com
edmunds.com
kbb.com
roadandtrack.com

Buying and Selling

Auctions (buy or sell almost anything)

craigslist.com
ebay.com
gsaauctions.gov
gov.gov/shopping/shopping.shtml
ioffer.com
i-soldit.com
junkmarketonline.com
livedeal.com
snappyauctions.com
yardsalequeen.com

Buy or sell used wedding gowns

indiebride.com

Sell your old cell phone

cellforcash.com
oldcellphone.com
trademyphone.com

Barter online

mommycommunity.com
wearsthebaby.com

Donate

freecycle.org

Travel/vacation/entertainment

Travel Sites (airline, car rentals, hotels)

bestfares.com
budgettravel.com
cheaptickets.com
completecruise.com
kayak.com
site59.com
smartertravel.com
travelocity.com
vacationkids.com

Hotels

quickbook.com
homewoodsuites.com (for families)
hoteldiscount.com

Homeswaps

homeexchange.com

Camping

nps.gov (National Park Service)

Transport/car sharing programs

zipcar.com (for automobiles)

Compare gasoline prices

gasbuddy.com
gaspricewatch.com

Discounts on entertainment

citypass.com
entertainment.com
ouraaa.com
playbill.com
themeparkinsider.com
vacationkids.com

Work, jobs

TELECOMMUTING JOBS
tjobs.com

Health care

DISCOUNT OR BULK DRUGS
AARP Pharmacy Service (membership
not required): 800-456-2277
drugplace.com: 877-599-8050
drugstore.com
smartchoicedrugstore.com

Miscellaneous

INFORMATION ON CONSUMER SCAMS OR TO REGISTER A COMPLAINT
consumer.gov
ftc.gov
A/PACT (Aging Parents and Adult
Children Together): 877-FTC-HELP
(to protect seniors)

PETS
banfield.net
discountpetmedicines.com
pedmeds.com

Donate

COMPUTERS, PRINTERS, FAX MACHINES AND OTHER OFFICE EQUIPMENT
NATIONAL CRISTINA FOUNDATION,
cristina.org. The organization will
hook you up with a charity in your
area that helps people with
disabilities, students at risk and those
who are economically disadvantaged.

WOMEN'S SUITS

DRESS FOR SUCCESS,
dressforsuccess.org. Each year over
46,000 women in more than 75 cities
wear these clothes on job interviews,
boosting their confidence and career.

EYEGLASSES
NEW EYES FOR THE NEEDY INC., 973-
376-4903. Goes to the visually
impaired in nearly 30 countries.

BICYCLES
PEDALS FOR PROGRESS, 908-638-4811
or p4p.org. Goes to partner charities
in countries worldwide where poor
people need cheap
non-polluting transportation.

WEDDING GOWNS, JEWELRY
MAKING MEMORIES BREAST CANCER
FOUNDATION, 503-252-3955 or
makingmemories.org. Donations are
sold via nationwide events and eBay
to raise money to grant wishes for
terminally ill breast cancer patients.

FORMAL DRESSES, SHOES AND ACCESSORIES FOR TEENS
THE GLASS SLIPPER PROJECT,
312-409-4139 or
glassslipperproject.org. Goes to
Chicago high school students unable
to afford prom attire.

Bibliography

Books

Applegarth, Virginia. *The Money Diet: Reaping the Rewards of Financial Fitness* (1996, Penguin)

Bach, David. *Smart Women Finish Rich: 9 Steps to Achieving Financial Security and Funding Your Dreams* (2002, Broadway)

Barbanel, Linda. *Piggy Bank to Credit Card: Teach Your Child the Financial Facts of Life* (1994, Three River Press)

Bowman, Linda. *Free Stuff & Good Deals for Your Kids* (2002, Santa Monica Press)

Briles, Judith. *Money Sense: What Every Woman Must Know to Be Financially Confident* (1995, Moody Pr)

Bullen, Martha, with Sanders, Darcie. *Turn Your Talents into Profits* (1998, Pocket)

Camp, Jim. *Start with NO...The Negotiating Tools that the Pros Don't Want You to Know* (2002, Crown Business)

Carlson, Chris and Kristal. *Disney on a Dime: Money-Saving Secrets for Your Walt Disney World Vacation* (2005, The Intrepid Traveler)

Causey, Kimberly. *Furniture Factory Outlet Guide* (2006, Home Decor Press)

Chatzky, Jean. *Pay It Down: From Debt to Wealth on $10 a Day* (2006, Amazon Bargains)

Doble, Richard. *Savvy Discounts: The Best Money-Saving Advice from America's #1 Cost-Conscious Consumer* (2003, Perigee Trade)

Eisenson, Marc. *A Banker's Secret: The Booklet That Can Save You Thousands of Dollars on Your Home Mortgage* (1984, A Banker's Secret)

Eliot, Eve. *Attention Shoppers!: The Woman's Guide to Enlightenment Through Shopping* (2003, HCI)

Farr, Kendall. *The Pocket Stylist: Behind-the-Scenes Expertise from a Fashion Pro on Creating Your Own Unique Look* (2004, Gotham)

Food and Nutrition Services. *Team Nutrition's Food, Family and Fun: A Seasonal Guide for Healthy Eating, Commemorating 50 Years of School Lunch* (1996, US Government Printing Office)

Freebies Magazine. *The Official Freebies for Kids: Something for Nothing or Next to Nothing* (Lowell House Juvenile, 1998)

Gabor, Don. *How to Start a Conversation and Make Friends* (2001, Fireside)

Gabriel, Rennie. *Wealth on Any Income: 12 Steps to Freedom* (2000, Gabriel Publications)

Gallagher, Patricia C. *Start Your Own At-home Child Care Business* (1995, Mosby)

Gershman, Suzy. *Born to Shop* series (Frommers)

Glink, Ilyce. *50 Simple Things You Can Do to Improve Your Personal Finances: How to Spend Less, Save More, and Make the Most of What You Have* (2001, Three River Press)

Godfrey, Neale S. with Richards, Tad. *Penny Saved: Taking Your Work Skills Home* (1996, Fireside)

Holzer, Bambi. *Retire Rich: The Baby Boomer's Guide to a Secure Future* (1999, Wiley)

Horowitz, Shel. *The Penny-Pinching Hedonist: How to Live Like Royalty With a Peasant's Pocketbook* (1995, Accurate Writing & More)

Hauser, Peggy, with Bradley, Hassell. *How to Teach Children About Money: A Step-By-Step Adult Guide to Help Children Learn About Earning, Saving, Spending and Investing Their Money* (1997, Western Freelance Writing Services)

Howard, Clark, with Melzer, Mark. *Clark's Big Book of Bargains: Clark Howard Teaches You How to Get the Best Deals* (2003, Amazon)

Hunt, Mary. *Debt-Proof Your Holidays* (1997, St. Martin's Press)

Inlander, Charles, with Weiner, Ed. *Take This Book to the Hospital With You: A Consumer Guide to Surviving Your Hospital Stay* (1997, St. Martin's Press)

Jackson, Carole. *Color Me Beautiful* (1987, Ballantine)

Johnson, Stacy. *Life or Debt: A One-Week Plan for a Lifetime of Financial Freedom* (2005, Ballantine)

Kay, Ellie. *A Woman's Guide to Family Finances: Finding Real Money in an Unreal Economy* (2004, Bethany House)

Kincaid, Shelley. *Garage Sale Decorator's Bible: How to Find Treasures, Fix Them & Furnish Your Home* (1997, Feline Books)

King, Trisha, with Newmark, Deborah. *Buying Retail Is Stupid!: US: The National Discount Guide to Buying Everything at Up to 80% Off Retail* (2000, McGraw-Hill)

Knuckey, Deborah. *Conscious Spending for Couples: Seven Skills for Financial Harmony* (2002, Wiley)

Knuckey, Deborah. *The Ms. Spent Money Guide: Get More of What You Want with What You Earn* (2002, Wiley)

Kerber, Lisa. *Countdown to a Thousand Dollars* (1987, Winker Productions)

Kristof, Kathy. *Investing 101* (2000, Bloomberg Press)

Lawrence, Judy. *The Budget Kit: The Common Cents Money Management Workbook* (2004, Kaplan Business)

Lewis, Allyson. *The Million Dollar Car and $250,000 Pizza* (2000, Kaplan Business)

Linfield, Leslie E. *Budget! It's Not a 4-Letter Word* (2005, Fla Publishing)

Linn, Susan. *Consuming Kids: The Hostile Takeover of Childhood* (2004, New Press)

Lonier, Terri. *Working Solo: The Real Guide to Freedom & Financial Success with Your Own Business* (1998, Wiley)

Lonier, Terri. *The Frugal Entrepreneur: Creative Ways to Save Time, Energy & Money in Your Business* (1996, Portico Press)

Luhrs, Janet. *The Simple Living Guide* (1997, Broadway Books)

Martin, Charles L. *Owning and Operating a Service Business* (2003, Crisp Learning)

McCoy, Jonni. *Miserly Moms: Living on One Income in a Two-Income Economy* (2001, Bethany House)

Mellan, Olivia. *Money Harmony: Resolving Money Conflicts in Your Life and Relationships* (1994, Walker & Co.)

Mellan, Olivia. *Overcoming Overspending: A Winning Plan for Spenders and Their Partners* (1997, Walker & Co.)

Miller, Mark. *The Complete Idiot's Guide to Being a Cheapskate* (1999, Alpha)

Morris, Virginia. *A Woman's Guide to Personal Finance* (2005, McGraw-Hill)

Ogintz, Eileen. *The Kid's Guide to New York City* (2004, Globe Pequot)

O'Neill, Barbara. *Investing on a Shoestring: Finding the Money to Invest Making Up for Lost Time Identifying Inexpensive* (1999, Dearborn Trade)

Palder, Edward L. *The Catalog of Catalogs: The Complete Mail-Order Directory* (1999, Woodbine House)

Parlapiano, Ellen H., with Cobe, Patricia. *Mompreneurs: A Mother's Practical Step-by-*

Paris, James, *Absolutely Amazing Ways to Save Money on Everything* (2002, Perigee Trade)

Pederson, Daniel. *Savings Bonds: When to Hold, When to Fold and Everything in Between* (1999, TSBI Publishing)

Pedigo, Cathy. *How to Have Big Money Garage Sales* (2002, Winning Edge Publications)

Perle, Liz. *Money, A Memoir: Women, Emotions and Cash* (2006, Picador)

Price, Joan. *Joan Price Says, Yes You CAN Get in Shape!: Make Exercise a Treat, Not a Treatment* (1996, Pacifica Press)

Pybrum, Steven. *Money and Marriage: Making It Work Together: A Guide to Smart Money Management and Harmonious Communications* (1996, Abundance Publishing)

Robin, Vicki, with Dominguez, Joe. *Your Money or Your Life: Transforming Your Relationship with Money and Achieving Financial Independence* (1999, Penguin)

Robinson, Joe. *Work to Live* (2003, Perigee Trade)

Roth, Larry. *The Best of Living Cheap News: Practical Advice on Saving Money and Living Well* (1996, McGraw-Hill)

Schor, Juliet B. *Born to Buy: The Commercialized Child and the New Consumer Culture* (2005, Scribner)

Stern, Linda. *Money-Smart Secrets for the Self-Employed* (1997, Random House Reference)

Strong, Howard. *What Every Credit Card Holder Needs To Know: How To Protect*

Yourself and Your Money (1999, Owl Books)

Swartout, Kristy, *Encyclopedia of Associations: National Organizations of The U.S.* (2006, Thomson Gale)

Tyson, Eric. *Personal Finance For Dummies, 5th edition* (2006, Wiley)

Walker, Christine K., *The Smart Mom's Guide to Staying Home*

Willdorf, Nina. *City Chic: An Urban Girl's Guide to Livin' Large on Less* (2003, Sourcebooks)

Zalewski, Angie. *Cheap Talk with the Frugal Friends: Over 600 Tips, Tricks, and Creative Ideas for Saving Money* (2001, Starbust Publichers)

NEWSLETTERS

Hunt, Mary, *Budget Proof Living*

Pagliarini, Robert, *SixStepsOrLess.com*

Williams, Laura, *Frugal Living Newsletter*

Acknowledgments

We would like to extend a special thanks to the many people who contributed valuable information to the articles reprinted in this book. Although for editorial reasons the names were not included in the articles, their knowledge, experience and expertise is greatly appreciated:

Susan Anderson, Janet Bodnar, Pat Boudrot, Bob Bulmash, Jacqueline Byers, Jonathan Clements, Catherine Cooke, Theresa Corcoran, Nancy Coutu, Sharon Danes, Jacqueline Dzierzak, Teri Gault, Susan Grant, Eileen Harrington, Douglas Haskell, Celia Hayhoe, Lisa Hone, Angela Hresan, David Laurion, Sharlea M. Leatherwood, April Lewis-Parks, Stacie McAnuff, Michael McAuliffe, Katharine McGee, Robert Niles, Marjorie Norton, Suzanne O'Connor, Robert O'Hara, Kathy McNally, Charles L. Parker, Chris Pullig, Steve Rhode, David T. Roen, Kathy Rongey, Sharon Seiling, Jeff Sheets, Timothy Silk, Martin Sloane, Bridget Small, Ruth Susswein, Jim Tehan, Ginita Wall, John Waskin, Ellen Welner, Jacqueline Williams, Laura Williams, Lois Wright Morton, Dayana Yochim.